MEASURED EXCESS

# MEASURED EXCESS

Status, Gender, and Consumer Nationalism
in South Korea

*Laura C. Nelson*

COLUMBIA UNIVERSITY PRESS ▰ NEW YORK

Columbia University Press

*Publishers Since 1893*

New York    Chichester, West Sussex

Copyright © 2000 Columbia University Press

Library of Congress Cataloging-in-Publication Data

Nelson, Laura C.

Measured excess : status, gender, and consumer nationalism in South Korea /
Laura C. Nelson.

p.    cm.

Includes bibliographical references and index.

ISBN 978-0-231-11616-9 (cloth) – 978-0-231-11617-6 (pbk.)

1. Consumption (Economics) — Korea (South) 2. Women consumers—
Korea (South) 3. Korea (South) — Economic policy. I. Title.

HC470.C6 N45 2000

339.4'7'095195—dc21                                     00-021051

Casebound editions of Columbia University Press books are printed on
permanent and durable acid-free paper.

Printed in the United States of America

# CONTENTS

I went to South Korea for the first time in 1985 as an English teacher, responding almost on a whim to a small employment ad in the Sunday edition of the *New York Times*. At that time, in my imagined geography of Asia, the Korean peninsula hung somewhere close to Vietnam—two nations severed by the violence of the global ideologies of capitalism and communism, both wrenched apart by the same horizontal north-south divides in postcolonial civil wars, both battlefields where Asian and U.S. soldiers (among others) had tried to hold (or move) "the Line." But I believe that if someone like me—someone as ignorant as I was at that time—were now, in 1999, idly flipping through the classifieds and encountered that particular listing, that person's imaginary map would place South Korea near Japan. The fact that this image corresponds more to geographical reality than my original misconception has more to do with changes in Americans' ways of portraying and perceiving that part of the world than it does with a more geographically sophisticated American society. In the years that have passed since I sent my résumé to Sogang University in Seoul for a job teaching English, the Republic of Korea, along with Taiwan, Hong Kong, and Singapore and more recently Malaysia, Thailand, and Vietnam, has joined the group of nations first acclaimed in the media as "Asian Tigers" following the Japanese lead to trade-based economic prowess and now pitied and feared for their weakened condition in the wake of the "Asian flu." Even the People's Republic of China is mentioned in the popular American press first and foremost as an economic behemoth, secondarily as a human rights problem, and then, generally only as an afterthought, as a military threat. As memories of old wars cool, new trade antagonisms are remapping international space, in both reality and imagination.

World geography is constantly remade, not only by grand historical events shifting political borders or environmental forces eroding shores but also by individuals assimilating new impressions and knowledge acquired over time. The changes in my own understanding of the world coincided with an utter transformation in the image many South Koreans have of their nation and its place in the international system. In fact, both processes were in part responses to the same global changes. In the 1980s increasing trade tensions between the United States and South Korea fertilized a budding popular disenchantment with the United States' role as a benevolent "older brother" to the South Korean nation. During this same period, in the context of an apparent waning of American industrial hegemony and growing Asian power in global trade, many ambitious South Koreans turned away from a U.S. model and toward a new vision of South Korea as a vanguard nation in an Asian renaissance.

In this book I attempt to capture a slice of this transformation, and its ambivalent effects, by focusing on one of the most direct and material connections people in one place make with those elsewhere: consumption. Decisions about what to buy and what not to buy; the emotions generated by the contemplation of purchase and, later, the condition of ownership; the social significance of taste, affluence, and generosity; the sense of distant connection that can come from international currents of production, distribution, sales, and styles—all these are significant elements in the experience of self and community throughout most of the world today. In South Korea I had the opportunity to observe a period during which consumer opportunities expanded dramatically and South Koreans scrambled to make sense of their new circumstances of material plenty.

My first year in Seoul forced me to turn my attention to how local people experienced the economic and social transformations that were being touted—both abroad and in South Korea itself—as the "Miracle on the Han." Seoul's sleek subway system had opened a year earlier, and all over the city massive construction sites were sprouting new apartment complexes, office buildings, and highways. My own apartment tower in the Shinbanp'o neighborhood was just a few years old and was still within a short walk of undeveloped fields. There were few cars on the streets, and many of those were brand-new. Yet much of the city consisted of ramshackle single-story homes on crooked, narrow concrete lanes.

My job was to teach English to employees of the Samsung corporation. In my classes the students—engineers and managers and all men, employees of one of the most prestigious corporations in South Korea—exerted themselves to help me see South Korea from their perspectives. Class discussions frequently wandered toward nervous criticism of the repressive policies of then-President Chun Doo-Hwan, who, it was rumored, had recently forced another corporation (the Kukje group) into bankruptcy as an act of political vengeance. The men were keenly interested in international trade issues; most were in the training program to improve their abilities to negotiate with foreign buyers or to communicate with foreign engineers. U.S. trade policies, and particularly U.S. accusations that South Korea was guilty of "dumping" and other unfair trade practices, drew their ire. Many of the men also seemed at once uncomfortable with and proud of their newfound affluence; several told me in clumsy English childhood memories of shoeless winters and hungry days and months. Through these English lessons I gained a sense of the shallow and uneven social foundation on which South Korean economic development rested. The few young South Korean friends I made outside of the training center revealed to me even more about the tenuous hold many people had on the benefits of the economic "miracle": they were nearly all migrants to Seoul from the provinces, several lacked a permanent place to sleep, few owned more than three or four changes of clothing.

After a sojourn back in the United States I returned to Seoul to attend a Korean language program in the summer of 1989. In the intervening years popular uprisings had forced an end to the military dictatorship of President Chun and had brought about democratic elections in 1987. South Korea had hosted the 1988 Seoul Olympics. The cultural and economic center of gravity in Seoul had definitively shifted from the old town core to the new neighborhoods south of the Han River. What had been pockets of wealth seemed to have spread widely through the city: the streets were thick with cars, restaurants were full, stores were stocked. And yet the country was not in a celebratory mood. Real estate prices had climbed so high that the newspapers carried stories of suicides in despair over rent increases. Industrial workers were engaged in protracted, bitter strikes, and people were apprehensive about the effect of rising wages on the international competitiveness of the national economy. The U.S. recession boded ill for South Korean exports. The general unease was not only related to this sense of vulnerability; many people openly worried that the Korean soul had been lost in the pursuit of material comfort, and still others, glad for the comforts gained, criticized the inequitable distribution of wealth.

This book explores some of the ambivalence with which people in Seoul have greeted the changes they experienced over the past two generations. Some people revel in new freedoms and new amenities, while others are concerned about lost traditions; some have not yet had the good fortune to experience many of these benefits themselves. Nearly everyone takes some pride in the national accomplishments of the past four decades, and yet many worry that these achievements will transform the nation into something hardly recognizable as "Korean." What is clear is that people actively, explicitly, and continually try to make sense of these dynamic circumstances by defining and redefining a Korean nation in an international context. One of the principal themes through which they attempt to understand the meaning of these transformations is by considering the material changes in South Korean daily life. Mundane material culture and simple consumer practices are focal points of a widespread, active public and private discussion of what it means to be (South) Korean today.

Writing an ethnography is an anxious process these days. The field of anthropology is fraught with debates about representation, evidence, and drawing conclusions, and it is hard to shrug off the criticism that people travel from rich countries to poor places to extract information for personal and professional gain. My task was complicated by the fact that while many of the people I encountered in Seoul were happy to help me understand their lives, many others told me specifically that they did not wish to be subjects of my research.[1] For some, the topic itself—their consumer practices and desires—was too intimate or too inflammatory; for others, the idea of becoming an object of analysis in a social science research project was repugnant. I have tried to respect the explicit requests these people voiced not to be written about. But many of the other people I spoke with or observed, while they may not have told me *directly* that they were uncomfortable appearing as anecdotes in my obscure academic composition, indicated as much with obfuscation, the stubborn obtuseness with which they avoided understanding my more annoying questions, or even with the dwindling number of invitations I received from some of them to come along, join in, or just watch as they lived their lives. Unlike classic anthropologists, though, I lacked the motivation and the spirit to push people to reveal much more than they were comfortable in telling me, and this was even more the case when I came to know them better (cf. Evans-Pritchard 1969:12).[2] Rather, their strategies of avoidance reshaped my own research strategy, pushing me further toward analyses of public discourses and observable practices, toward watching and listening to what people volunteered to reveal, and away from prying questions and controlled interviews.

Most of my fieldwork research was conducted in the most casual environment as I built up my sense of understanding (as well as my awareness of my own ignorance) in unstructured conversations in a variety of contexts. I taped almost nothing. I found that taping my initial interviews generally inhibited the kind of personal detail I was hoping to hear. I was also often frustrated when, at the end of an interview, the person whose statements had so closely echoed the opinions of the daily newspaper would, while walking me to the bus, let slip a detail or insert an ironic comment that undermined and illuminated the entire preceding exchange—as though the act of leave taking liberated them from the constraint of a formal voice. So I soon gave up bringing my tape recorder with me to interview appointments. I point this out because many ethnographies contain long quotations that give the impression of verbatim accuracy, despite the fact that the conversation quoted appears to have occurred in a bar, on a train, in a potato field, or in some other place where it is hard to believe the anthropologist had a recorder going. Moreover, several senior researchers who *do* tape-record their interviews have admitted to me that the most interesting comments are uttered just after the tape recorder is switched off. In writing this book, however, I realized that I could not convey a sense of life without offering characters for the reader to imagine and that I could not portray people without in some way representing their personal voices. In the interest of academic honesty, I wish to make it clear at this early point, therefore, that almost all the conversational quotations included here are reconstructions from notes I wrote down immediately *following* a conversation—not at the time the words were spoken. (I always took notes during formal interviews, but rarely during casual conversations.) Although I was occasionally able to remember a few important phrases in their entirety, most of the quotations convey the speaker's meaning and tone (and generally the order in which thoughts were offered) rather than the actual words. I trust that readers will be able to allow this rhetorical device to give them a more vivid picture of Seoul while at the same time maintaining a certain incredulity toward the "reality" depicted—this tactic should, in fact, help readers keep in mind the particularity of my perspective and memory. To distinguish constructed quotations from word-for-word quotations, I will mark the former with quotation marks and asterisks ("*Like this*") while I will treat true quotations in the usual manner.[3] Lengthy constructed quotations, set as extracts, will be marked with asterisks alone.

I carried out all my research in Seoul itself. I spoke with almost anyone who was willing to talk to me about the issues that are the focus of this book. Eventually I found two neighborhoods where the residents were willing to allow me a certain amount of access, and as each of these places suited aspects of my interest in urban planning policies and local involvement in urban changes, I consider myself lucky. I lived in Yoido, a mostly upper-middle-income district, for nearly half a year as a guest of a family wishing to study English. My association with Talgoljjagi,[4] a mostly low-income neighborhood, was mediated by the organizers of a nonprofit *kongbubang* ("study room"), which offered literacy programs to adult women as well as a variety of classes and activities for school-age children. I never lived in Talgoljjagi, but for several months I tried to spend two or three days a week there. I spent most of my time at the *kongbubang*, but I also wandered the streets, chatted with elderly men and women who were often tending their grandchildren during the day, and exchanged English lessons for hand acupuncture instruction with the local progressive minister.

To learn about social change, national identity, and consumption I created two formal interview formats: a short version for encounters on the street and for hesitant participants, and a longer version for people willing to be generous with their time. Both were intended only for first encounters (some people spoke with me only once; others agreed to several rather formal meetings). While the information I obtained through these interviews helped me to identify fruitful topics for further investigation, I make no claims to statistical significance. I conducted nearly one hundred interviews of this sort.

In addition to interviews, I experimented with a few exercises to prompt other kinds of information and responses: after taking thirty photographs of people on the street (in various locations in Seoul), I showed the photos to people and asked them to tell me what information they could gather from these pictures. I also asked about twenty-five people to identify five places of personal importance to them on a schematic map of Seoul. Finally, I gathered information on the previous day's personal itinerary from about the same number of individuals. I discuss these exercises in the text.

In view of the material interests of my research, I also paid careful attention to the objects people owned: their homes and furnishings, clothing, cars, books, cameras, and so on. A few individuals allowed me to catalog some of their possessions, but generally my observations were perforce surreptitious. Often people would show me selected items, but grew uneasy if I pressed them in order to learn more about objects to which they did not themselves draw my attention. In particular, people frequently expressed discomfort when I jotted down the brand names of consumer appliances (Sony television, Goldstar rice cooker, Westinghouse refrigerator, and so on).

The focal moment of my research is the period between August 1991 and October 1992, when I was in Seoul conducting my fieldwork for my doctoral dissertation. I draw on documents and memories from earlier years, including secondary sources for comparative and historical background and for information about more recent events. However, in part because of the inherent limitations of a fieldwork project and in part, as I will argue, because the late 1980s and early 1990s were a significant period in the reformation of national, gender, and class identities in South Korea, this text is essentially about a brief interval. Others have critiqued the misleading sense of enduring stasis that the ethnographic present tense evokes (e.g., Fabian 1983:33; Clifford 1986:11). I have elected to write in the past tense, despite the fact that this often gives the impression of too sharp a separation between the very recent past of observation from the present of writing. I must again rely on the reader to encounter this ethnography not as a depiction of a finished period, but as a study of particular processes that can *be delimited* both temporally and spatially but that also defy those limits.

I attempt (as we all do in this profession) to protect the privacy of the people I learned from by renaming people and places. Of course, anyone who knows me or who knows Seoul will probably not find it difficult to guess the neighborhoods where I conducted my research, and those who live in those neighborhoods may even be able to guess the individuals themselves. In order to make the guessing more difficult, I have in many cases created character composites, mixing some family histories, apartment sizes, and educational records in ways I believe do not undermine the essential human, personal groundedness of the stories. While we all know that these are sheltering gestures and not actual fortifications against snooping neighbors, I wanted to write what I had learned, and these were the only tools I knew for the protection of my sources.

Writing this text, I have mulled over the old issues of representation and the question of "For whom is this text written?" Because so many South Koreans read English, I am aware that whatever I write is vulnerable to the critical perspectives of not only the "native" scholarly community but also the very informants who are rather transparently disguised by the conventions of anthropological anonymity. When I report a certain housewife's enthusiasm for Japanese plastic laundry pins, I worry that this woman, as well as her neighbors, will not only believe they recognize the individual but will take personal offense on her behalf at my wry tone. The work of anthropology is often accomplished through attending to local gossip, but we rarely acknowledge that the act of writing is, in large part, the evaluating and passing on of stories told behind turned backs—however much the point of the composition is synthetic or analytical. If any of the generous people who welcomed me into their homes and who offered me carefully peeled and sliced pears along with their memories feel that I have abused their hospitality, I can only apologize here. I personally believe we are *all* made a little foolish by the objects through which we attempt to express ourselves, but no more so in Seoul than in San Francisco.

But as to the question "For whom?"—the honest answer is that I am not writing "for" my informants nor even for Korea specialists. My intention is to write about issues of particular salience in South Korea—the renegotiation of status and class in the swirl of economic expansion and the implications this has for national identity and gendered social configurations—in part as a contribution to a general understanding of contemporary South Korea and also as a way to enter into the scholarly conversation about how identities, subjectivity, and the material and cultural context of economy and politics impinge upon and motivate each other. Fortunately, there are a great number of texts and films available now, produced by people of varied backgrounds that represent aspects of South Korea. This is just one more, and I can only present the perspective of one particular anthropologist. My awareness of the modest place of this book has helped me determine my goals and scope.

## TRANSLATION, TRANSLITERATION, AND KOREAN NAMES

Throughout the book, all translations from Korean originals (oral or written) into English are mine, unless otherwise noted. I believe it is important to admit here that I never felt at ease with the Korean language. Although I conducted most of my research in Korean, even at the end I had difficulties following group conversations or understanding subtle references. My analysis was constrained and reshaped by my linguistic shortcomings.

Transliterations are according to the McCune-Reischauer system, except in those cases where common usage differs, or where someone has selected another transliteration of his or her own personal name.

Please note in general I have followed the Korean practice for Korean names, that is, the family name precedes the given name. I have made a few exceptions for Koreans or Korean-Americans who themselves are known by names written in the western style of given name first, family name second. In a few instances in the reference list authors who write in both English and Korean are listed with the transliteration used in their English publications and with a cross-reference to a McCune-Reischauer transliteration of their names.

# ACKNOWLEDGMENTS

Anthropology is impossible without a great deal of help and cooperation. My research was funded by grants from both the International Cultural Society of Korea and the Fulbright Commission. I owe my greatest thanks to the people in South Korea who have worked with me and given me advice and assistance over the years. Several South Korean scholars have helped me from time to time; in particular, Dr. Cho Hyŏng and the faculty and staff of Ewha Womans University, Korean Women's Institute, as well as Dr. Cho Hae-jŏng of Yonsei University, have taught me a great deal about the conditions of life for South Korean women and provided new visions and new analyses of social processes. Dr. Yoo Jae-hyŭn helped me understand the importance (from a theoretical and an activist standpoint) of the Seoul real estate market to the distribution of wealth. The women I interviewed in Yoido, in Talgoljjagi, and in various homes across Seoul shared stories, interpretations, and secrets with me out of kindness and an abstract value they placed on helping me to understand their lives. I hope I haven't misconstrued their words too egregiously. I am especially grateful to my host family in Yoido: the boys were always fun; Uk-i's father was generous, and I learned more from my hours with Chi-wŏn than I could ever repay in English lessons. Special thanks also go to the women who run the *kongbubang* in Talgoljjagi. Yu Young-nan was my guardian angel in Seoul: even though she demands the highest effort of herself and everyone around her, she tolerated my bad *han'gungmal*. Her older daughter, Kim Chi-Young, provided essential research assistance during the final phase of my revisions. David Kosofsky and Shin Song-min are my most valued second family in Seoul (and they are invaluable friends *wherever* I encounter them), with good food, a clean *yo*, and challenging conversation always on offer.

In the United States, my gratitude goes to my graduate advisers during my years at Stanford: Sylvia Yanagisako's keen eye and sharp mind, Akhil Gupta's broad, committed vision, Nancy Abelmann's warmth, wisdom, and appreciation for the particularities of working in South Korea, and Tom Rohlen's humane manner and useful warnings against vague postmodernist gibberish and conspiracy theories. I am grateful to Yunshik Chang of the University of British Columbia for inviting me to two very interesting gatherings of Korea-focused scholars. Thanks also to Ted Bestor for helping me find anthropology to begin with.

Most of the greatest pleasures and lessons of scholarship come from the companionship of colleagues; I wouldn't know nearly as much as I do about how cultural critique works in real life if I had not been guided by Deb Amory and Jared Braiterman. Amy Borovoy gave me useful feedback and support during the revising process.

I've appreciated the long years of fun and support from a gaggle of irreplaceable and patient friends: Betty Cho; Eli Coppola; the Fulbright 1991–1992 crowd: Andre Schmid, Charles Armstrong, Denise Lett, Diana Lee, Jordan Rief, Garbo the cat, Katharine Moon, Victor Cha, and, of course, Fred Carrier; Kristin Harrington and Eugene Yim; Brad Hartfield; my Hunger Relief Fund for North Korea co-founder, Grace Lee, and our colleagues Annette Kim, Nan Kim, David Malinowski and Tim Savage; Kim Soon-yi; Leslie Kramer; Lori Magistrado; Frieda Molina; Rich Pekelney; Sarah Reilly and Jim Gardner; Lisa Harries Schumann; Helen Song; and Karie Youngdahl and Seth Magalaner.

Last but not least, I'm grateful to my family: my sister Margo, who inspires me with her stubborn creativity; my father, who sets high standards for research, analysis, and good humor; and my mother, who has always had time to be warmly interested in what I'm doing even in the midst of her own exciting scholarly endeavors. I dedicate this project to my grandmother, who passed away in 1998 two years shy of a century of living. She was an example of life-long curiosity about why people do the strange things they do in many places around the globe (and even at home).

MEASURED EXCESS

# CHAPTER I

## CONSUMER NATIONALISM

*The task of ethnography now becomes the unraveling of a conundrum: what is the nature of locality, as a lived experience, in a globalized, deterritorialized world?*

Arjun Appadurai, "Global Ethnoscapes: Notes and Queries for a Transnational Anthropology."

In 1997 the economies of eastern Asia stumbled. Even before the summer devaluation of the Thai baht, industrialists, international financiers, and global money traders were signaling their shaken faith in what had seemed to be the world's most vigorous economic region. As investors pulled out of Asia, currencies and stock markets from Thailand to Seoul tumbled toward disaster. By the end of the year, the South Korean government was forced to admit that the nation had insufficient foreign currency reserves to make upcoming payments on its external debts. The International Monetary Fund proposed a "rescue package" of U.S.$57 billion in loans, tied to a number of financial and commercial reforms, to save the nation from bankruptcy.

Yet only a few months before the "Asian Crisis," the western side of the Pacific Rim had been touted as the world's growth engine. Japan held a long-standing position as an industrial leader, but the economies of South Korea, Hong Kong, Taiwan, and Singapore were themselves now considered substantial players, and close behind them was a flock of new "Tigers": Thailand, Malaysia, Indonesia, and the Philippines, along with the enormous looming economic potential of China. These countries shared a set of development characteristics—high rates of savings, impressive investment in human capital, investment in production capacity—that policy makers had viewed as the miracle prescription for other struggling nations in Africa, Latin America, and the former Soviet Union. Indeed, what made the Asian financial crisis particularly unsettling for many analysts was that the Asian model of development had appeared to rest on solid, strategic economic foundations.

The causes of the Asian economic collapse are complex and beyond the scope of this book; the prospects for the Pacific Rim and for South Korea, in particular, are still unclear. Yet in their efforts to rebuild their economy the

South Korean government and South Korean people are drawing strength from many of the same themes that motivated the work of industrialization in preceding decades. The key role of economic policies often obscures the subtle importance of cultural factors in the process of economic development, and the selection of an export-focus for the domestic economy—the strategy shared by all the Pacific Rim nations—creates identifiable stresses on the local population. In this book I examine how South Koreans' sense of national identity motivated much of the hard work of development beginning in the 1960s and continuing through the early 1990s and how intersections between international economic processes, the flow of time, and the mundane experience of life shape and strain the sense of national mission.

Within a week of landing in Seoul to conduct research into South Korean consumer practices, I set about equipping myself as an urban anthropologist. Among the items I purchased was a clipboard to provide a stiff backing for the paper I would hold on my knees as I recorded my observations. Although I had brought along from the United States an old, battered, particleboard clipboard, I decided to replace it: not only did I feel, in situ, that it gave off a jarring "impoverished student" impression, but the A-4-sized paper most common in South Korea hung raggedly over the bottom of the American-made product. I went to Dong-Bang Plaza, a rather small but sleek marble-faced department store owned by the Samsung Corporation and built next to Samsung's headquarters in the center of town. I chose a dusky lavender-colored plastic clipboard designed with a handy penholder at the top right corner and a ruler marked on the right side.

When I made my selection, I considered several factors: aesthetics (the color appealed to me), efficiency (I appreciated the penholder as well as a ledge along the left to keep my pages straight), the apparent durability (satisfactory), and the price (although it seemed a little high, it was not outrageous). I wanted to buy a useful object that would please me and communicate a feminine professionalism to the women I would be interviewing.

During my fourteen months in Seoul, I received a score of compliments on this clipboard. Women admired, with me, the color and the design. Several inquired where I had purchased the clipboard. Every one of them asked me whether it was made in Japan or (South)[1] Korea.

The reader may be surprised to learn that although I had come to Seoul to study consumer practice and nationalism, when I selected this clipboard I had not considered its country of origin. This was a fortunate oversight, as

I almost certainly would have chosen a product made in South Korea to as-sert my solidarity with the women I would interview, and I would thereby have missed the following encounters:

The first woman who asked me about the clipboard was a contact at the South Korean governmental organization that had granted me my initial re-search stipend. When she asked me where the clipboard was manufactured, I turned it over and together we discovered the "MADE IN JAPAN" mark, in English, on the back. "*It's very nice,*" she said (we were speaking in Eng-lish), "*but I would never buy it. There must be ones almost exactly like it made in Korea.*" This provided a nice segue to her reminiscences of her col-lege days (which, like those of many young South Koreans, included among other activities participation in a study group examining South Korea's con-temporary relations with Japan and the United States through a neocolonial analysis), but although her demeanor remained friendly I felt a little like I had been caught by the hostess of a party flirting with her lover.

The next time I was asked about the clipboard, I was chastened and afraid of giving offense. I told the woman, who lived in the upper-middle-class neighborhood where I conducted much of my research, that the clip-board was made in Japan but that I hadn't known this at the time I'd pur-chased it. The tone of apology in my voice didn't register with her. "*Things made in Japan are so much cuter than the ones made in Korea, and they're better quality, too,*" she responded. She then got up and took me to her laun-dry room, where the maid had left some clothes hanging to dry. "*Look at the difference between these clothes pins. These,*" she said, taking some small pink clips from the rack, "*were made in Korea and these—*" she took a few more from another rung of the rack "*—were made in Japan. The color is nicer, and the Japanese ones are stronger.*"

These and similar scenes replayed themselves throughout the year.[2] My clipboard was not the only object to elicit such commentary. My shoulder bag, shoes, pens, cosmetics, clothing, and short-wave radio (an item banned in South Korea) were all noticed and often admired. I was always asked, "*Where is it from?*"

Seoul in the early 1990s was a sophisticated city rich in consumer goods, but nevertheless my foreign-made belongings generated significant curiosi-ty. Although the consumer market in South Korea had expanded greatly dur-ing the previous decade, the array of products still lacked diversity. Manu-facturing and selling were highly concentrated in the South Korean economy: the South Korean economy was notoriously oligopolistic. In the early 1990s the thirty largest industrial corporations (known as the *chaebŏl*) accounted for 28 percent of the nation's total manufacturing capacity (U.S. Department of State 1994). South Korea's industrial concentration was in part a matter of the extent to which the *chaebŏl* were diversified (and so commanded within each corporate group a share of the economy spread across a range of sectors) and was in part a matter of the dominance of a small number of these firms in any single sector of the economy. In the early 1990s the three[3] domestic automobile makers—Hyundai, Daewoo, and Kia—for example, shared almost the entire personal car market, with only a dozen or so models between them. Most major appliances were manufactured by Samsung, Lucky-Goldstar, Daewoo, or Hyundai. Blanc-Noir, Esquire, Renoir, and one or two other brands of shoe dominated the brand-name market, so that one encountered the same pair of shoes over and over again on the feet of women passing by. In her study of the structure of South Korean industrial successes, economist Alice Amsden concluded, "*Korea has acquired one of the world's most concentrated economies*" (italics in original; Amsden 1989:121).

Amplifying this effect of market dominance, even small-scale competitors often chose to imitate each other rather than to innovate. When fresh-brewed-coffee shops suddenly sprouted everywhere in the early 1990s, the successful chains (Jardin, Doutor, Waltz, for example) had nearly identical interior design themes (sparse and clean, decorated in primary colors with wood trim) and charged the same prices for the same selection of coffee drinks; in a short span of time many new, independently owned cafés emulated the established players, and ultimately the new style cafés shouldered aside older, homelier coffee and tea houses (*tabang*). Similarly, the success of the gleaming 7-Eleven and Circle-K convenience stores that opened in the wake of the Seoul Olympics prompted more than a few mom-and-pop corner shops to transform their cluttered, dingy aisles of wares into orderly product displays. The stores' names mimicked their models: my bus to town passed by a 9-Ten shop every morning. In the fashion sector, the popular Tomboy and Village clothing boutiques for young consumers were nearly indistinguishable, and they were closely shadowed by a herd of other, smaller fashion shops with outfits of the same cut and color.

This imitative tendency generated a precarious seesaw between novelty and uniformity. The underlying sameness offered a stark background for contrast, and innovations, fads, and fashions stimulated curiosity, desire, and criticism as well as imitation. Novelties appeared and proliferated so fast that they soon became ordinary; while I was there this was true of the cafés and convenience stores as well as of the new "traditional" style tea houses, the Belgian waffle stands, and the *p'ansori* craze.[4] While the youth market was the most visible market segment for many fashions (a phenomenon that consistently drew critical commentary from the media), mature members of the middle and upper classes often followed fads as well: for example, when the South Korean version of the Japanese karaoke club (*noraebang*) swept through Seoul social life in the early 1990s, many leisure-class housewives carefully polished their renditions of popular songs to enliven their evenings out.

Even the architecture of the city exhibited this pattern. Apartment complexes erected by Hyundai, Samik, or Woosung were assemblages of nearly indistinguishable blond concrete blocks, each building rising a dozen stories or so, punctuated by three or four entryways and by verandas displaying racks of drying laundry, children's bicycles, and brown pottery jars for staple condiments and kimchi. Bars, restaurants, and small grocery stores not only offered similar items and looked alike in almost any neighborhood in Seoul, but despite their different functions, they were very similar in design: they had the same aluminum-frame sliding windows looking on the street (and often the same blue plastic coating to cut the heat of the sun), aluminum swinging entry doors, bare concrete floors, low ceilings, and dark walls. Snaking through the alleyways in different neighborhoods, I was likely to encounter in each a bakery named for one of the ancient dynasties ("Koryo" or "Shilla"), a cramped real estate office with two or three men lounging inside, and more than one small church, each marked with a red neon cross. Women and old men wandered the streets or rested in the shade in the daytime. In almost every neighborhood I passed by old women (*halmŏni*s, literally "grandmothers") wearing colorful loose, printed trousers or a skirt and a loose, printed short-sleeved shirt, both of slick, artificial fiber.

This is not to say that neighborhoods were identical. There were major distinctions: between mostly commercial and mostly residential districts, between the apartment block neighborhoods and the neighborhoods composed of smaller-scale residences (single-family houses, duplexes and triplexes, and three- or four-story "villa" apartments), between rich neighborhoods and poor ones. And within these categories people themselves marked and learned the textural distinctiveness of their communities. Much less were homes, or *halmŏni*s, or neighborhood restaurants (with special recipes and familiar hosts), indistinguishable. Nevertheless, the material culture created an underlying impression of reiteration and familiarity. And, as I shall argue later, overall this similarity helped to reinforce the constructed image of South Korean social coherence and homogeneity.

But this material backdrop was more than the stage setting of everyday life in South Korea. Since the early 1960s the South Korean population had participated in a national project to forge out of their poverty, through industrial development, a nation that could claim international respect on account of its economic strength. During the period of my fieldwork, the proliferation of products and the improvements in the material environment were visible signs of national success in achieving this goal. They were also, paradoxically, a cause of widespread public anxiety.

## MAKING A NATIONAL ECONOMY: AN OVERVIEW

It is impossible to appreciate the significance of consumption in the creation of discourses of South Korean national identity without some familiarity with the outlines of South Korea's dramatic economic development. At the beginning of the 1960s South Korea was ranked among the world's poorest nations, with an average annual per capita income estimated at less than $125 (United Nations 1962). This group included such countries as Burma, Congo, India, and Kenya and was below a group of better-off developing countries: El Salvador, Ecuador, the Philippines, and Rhodesia, for example. In 1991, a generation later, the average urban household head earned about $1,700 (829,350 wŏn) in *monthly* wages alone[5]—South Korean incomes had reached parity with those of many European countries. The story of the South Korean economic "miracle" has been told and retold many times in a search for lessons other nations can take from South Korea's success (for example, Mason et al. 1980; Amsden 1989; Haggard et al. 1994; Chung H. Lee 1995), and it has also been examined from more critical perspectives (e.g., Hart-Landsberg 1993; Clifford 1994; Lie 1998). It bears telling again here, at least in brief,[6] to provide a frame of reference for understanding the individual and collective actions and outlook of contemporary people in South Korea.

Well into the nineteenth century, Korea retained the political structures and cultural practices that characterized the period generally known as the "Chosŏn era," five centuries (1392–1910) of continuous rule by kings of a single lineage. Neo-Confucian philosophy guided government and literature; the economy was based on feudal relations of peasant cultivators and a landlord class of scholar-bureaucrats known as the *yangban*. Unlike neighboring China and Japan, Korea failed to develop much in the way of urban culture or merchant and artisan society. The royal court generated little commercial demand, and the countryside was characterized by a subsistence-level economy. Most Koreans were farmers. Korea shunned most foreign intercourse: the Korean court had a tributary relationship with the emperor of China, and many of the court's luxury goods were Chinese imports, but aside from that Korea engaged in only a small amount of occasional, regulated trade with Japan (and in some unauthorized exchanges at the Chinese border). In the last quarter of the nineteenth century, however, Korea, known to many Westerners as the "Hermit Kingdom" because of its resistance to foreign religious, trade, diplomatic—and military—emissaries, was suddenly brought into the maelstrom of competing colonial and imperial plans. The new Meiji government in Japan saw the neighboring peninsula as a market for Japanese goods and a testing ground for imperialist energies focused, ultimately, on Manchuria and China. Russian eastward expansion included designs on Manchuria as well, and Japanese and Russian interests clashed over influence in Korea. China wished to protect its suzerainty in Korea as well as its authority elsewhere from Japanese encroachments. These three powers competed (as did, to a lesser extent, the United States, Germany, France, and Britain) in Korea, marshaling diplomatic skills and military might and appealing to different elements at the Korean court.

Weaknesses internal to Korea had left the country vulnerable to the predatory interests of foreign powers (Palais 1975). The Korean court in the second half of the nineteenth century was crippled by factional antagonisms: between orthodox Neo-Confucian scholars and students of Western culture ("enlightenment"), between those who were open to foreign influence and the isolationists, and between family-based power groups, in particular between the queen's family (the Yŏhŭng Min), the regent (the Taewŏngun), and King Kojong. Alliances and power shifted among these camps. The government was also confronted by domestic unrest: an armed peasant movement known as *Tonghak* ("Eastern Learning") swept across the countryside in 1894. At root *Tonghak* was a spiritual movement, which blended elements of Buddhist, Confucianist, Taoist, and Catholic beliefs with indigenous shamanism and proclaimed the essential equality of all people. At the same time, *Tonghak* inspired violent rebellion; the aggression of the *Tonghak* peasant army was fed by the prosaic facts of destitution and desperation in the Korean countryside. By mid-century, increasing rents and growing tax levies pressed hard on Korean peasants; after the country was opened to international trade in 1876, rising taxes, along with exports of rice to Japan and the encroachment of Japanese fishers in Korean coastal waters further impoverished Korean farmers and fishermen. Armed *Tonghak* bands rose up across the nation (mostly in the southern half), demanding a purge of venal officials from government, an end to slavery and caste oppression, alleviation of the tax burden, and the expulsion of foreigners from the country. Ultimately, the king, unable to put down the revolt with Korean troops alone, requested assistance from China and thus provided the Japanese with an excuse for the Sino-Japanese war.

The Sino-Japanese War (1894–1895) was ostensibly fought over which of those two foreign powers had the right to supervise the Korean government. The Chinese army was humiliated in this brief war, and in victory Japan gained its first new territory (Taiwan) as well as a greatly improved position in Korea. The Russo-Japanese War (1904–1905) was the culmination of Japanese and Russian rivalry over Manchuria, northern China, and Korea; as Japan prepared for war with Russia (which it initiated with a surprise attack on Russian installations at Port Arthur, at the tip of the Liaotung peninsula west of northern Korea), Japan sent troops into Seoul and forced the Korean government to sign a protocol authorizing any measures the Japanese considered necessary to protect the Korean king from domestic or foreign threat. With the Treaty of Portsmouth ending the Russo-Japanese War, Japan was recognized by the international community as the paramount power in Korea. Five years later, Japan formally annexed the Korean nation.

The period of Japanese colonial rule on the Korean peninsula, from 1910 until the end of the Second World War, was a time of almost continual economic exploitation and cultural oppression. By 1945 three and a half decades of colonial rule had transformed Korea from an isolated peasant-centered society into a nation participating fully, albeit deeply subjugated, in the world of trade, industry, and warfare. In the countryside, tenancy increased from 41.7 percent of farming households in 1913 to 69.1 percent in 1945 (Eckert et al. 1990:307). Destitution in the countryside pushed many people to the cities and mines in Korea and Japan as well as to Manchuria and beyond. Near the end of the colonial period, close to 12 percent of all Koreans had left the peninsula for work elsewhere. Employment as well as residence patterns were dramatically altered: the number of factory employees rose from 12,088 to 212,924 between 1912 and 1940 (Mason et al. 1980:78), and while wage earners made up only 7.3 percent of the labor force by 1940 (Koo 1990:671), this was nevertheless an enormous change from the beginning of the century. Overall, the Japanese economy dominated that of Korea (in 1934, for example, 95 percent of Korean exports were sent to Japan [Eckert et al. 1990:311]), and the Korean economy was structured to provide a smooth link in Japan's East Asian Co-Prosperity Sphere. Korean farms sent rice to Japan while Koreans ate millet imported from farms in Manchuria. Korean railroad lines facilitated the transport of goods and people from Japan's foothold on the continent, Pusan, through China or Russia and on to Europe. While some scholars (Kohl 1994; Haggard et al. 1997) have pointed to the positive economic legacies of the period of Japanese rule (infrastructure, education, initial efforts at industrialization), even the most pious American economists allow that "Korean economic growth in the colonial period was carried out by Japanese and was intended to serve the economic needs of Japan, not Korea" (Mason et al. 1980:76).

Many Koreans actively resisted colonial domination throughout the period not only in Korea but wherever Koreans encountered the Japanese. Resistance took a variety of guises: violent, religious, linguistic, artistic, cultural, economic. The development of Korean industrial capacity was seen by some as a patriotic act (see Eckert 1991). Both before the actual annexation and later, in the 1920s, Koreans launched nationwide campaigns to protect—or regain—national independence through directed savings or consumption practices. (I will discuss these in chapter 4.) Just as there were many forms of resistance, there were many visions of the best path to national liberation. Some sought international support, some advocated for a gradualist approach, some fostered a spirit of revolution. Two of the strongest institutional frameworks for resistance were the Christian churches and the Communist Party. These variations in ideology and approach left fissures in the population that outlasted the colonial period. It is also true that many Koreans ultimately embraced the colonial structure and found an active role in it. Over time, the seeds of class division, too, were fertilized by the benefits that accrued during the colonial period to a few entrepreneurs and landowners.[8]

By all rights, Japan's surrender at the end of the Second World War should have freed Korea from foreign occupation. Upon liberation in August 1945, however, the peninsula was sliced in two, stranding halves of the economic whole: the most fertile rice paddies were in the south, the energy generation plants and richest mineral resources were in the north.[9] The U.S. occupied the south and shaped its political evolution in ways that have had long-lasting repercussions. Anticommunism and ignorance about Korea coincided in U.S. policies; local political committees were undermined, and instead the Americans shored up the power of former collaborators and anticommunists. The U.S. Military Government during this period took command of, among other things, the identification and management of critical industries and the distribution of essential consumer goods to the populace. The humble circumstances of southern Korea at this time are reflected in the reports these occupying forces published listing, item by item, distribution of soap (laundry and toilet), matches, tires and tubes, rubber and leather shoes, underwear, cotton socks, and bolts of fabric (U.S. Army Forces in Korea 1948).

The 1948 establishment of two Korean states, the Democratic People's Republic of Korea in the north and the Republic of Korea in the south, fixed this separation and condemned each part to a process of constructing the economic pieces missing from a functional national economy. Furthermore, the war (1950–1953) crippled South Korea's economy;[10] much of South Korea's urban housing and manufacturing capacity was damaged or destroyed. In Seoul alone, more than 40 percent of the housing was destroyed, and over one thousand factories were damaged (Seoul Metropolitan Government 1992:124). In the war's aftermath, throughout the 1950s, South Korea remained heavily dependent upon foreign aid (from the United Nations and the United States, primarily), and the economy stagnated under the corrupt administration of President Syngman Rhee. United Nations reports classified South Korea among the world's poorest countries, with alarmingly low rates of savings and investment and little to inspire optimism about the nation's future (United Nations 1962). Rhee was finally tossed out of office in 1960 as a result of nationwide protests led by students and college professors (the proximate cause was a rigged presidential election), but the brief one-year-long experiment with democracy that followed was ineffectual and unstable. At that point, impatient with the incompetence of earlier leaders and convinced that South Korean national security would, in the long run, rest on economic strength, a small group of army and marine officers led by Park Chung-Hee took control of the South Korean government in a coup d'état.

When Park took power in 1961, he inaugurated a period of rule by military leaders that lasted until 1993, five years past the restoration of democracy. Park himself held power until he was assassinated in 1979; he personally set many of the priorities for South Korean economic development strategies throughout his years as head of government. Park anchored his administration's legitimacy to an improved national economy. One of Park's first actions was to publicly humiliate and punish the businessmen who had profited during the Rhee regime, mostly off the income from scarce import licenses (all the more valuable in the context of a stunted national industry). Shortly thereafter, however, in consultation with essentially the same group of businessmen, Park established a new course for the nation: South Korean industrialization strategies since that time have depended upon balancing exports and imports in a way that would stimulate industrial expansion. By the mid-1960s, President Park had determined that increasing South Korean exports would be necessary to keep afloat a national economy that was dependent upon imports of most raw materials. With a national population of 25 million and per capita annual income averaging less than U.S.$150, most South Korean families were exclusively concerned with the problem of staving off hunger and had little left over to spend even on basic consumer goods such as clothing or furnishings. Clearly, the South Korean domestic market was not strong enough by itself to lift the national economy out of the doldrums. With a firm push from the state, exports became "a compulsion rather than a choice for the private sector" (Amsden 1989:69).

Park's emphasis on national economic well-being was motivated by a variety of factors. With only a few exceptions, South Koreans both in the countryside and in the cities lived in harsh poverty, and a straightforward desire to alleviate their suffering is easy to imagine. At the same time, South Korea's political circumstances pointed particularly to the objective of prosperity, framed by North Korean communism on the one hand and the presence of thousands of relatively affluent American soldiers on the other. For the next three decades, South Korean material improvements were viewed as anticommunist victories, and consumer opulence distinguished South Korea from the North. Into the 1970s, North Korea's economy was expanding as fast as that of the South, which exacerbated the sense of political competition through a comparison of industrial growth. The U.S. soldiers stationed in South Korea added a further edge to the linking of national pride to prosperity: the contrast between the well-fed comfort of the foreign soldiers and the humble circumstances of many South Koreans generated in many a sense of national humiliation that lingers in memories and stories into the 1990s.

Park took a personal role in designing industrial strategies and establishing export targets throughout the period of his administration. Through both the formal structures of five-year plans and the informal structures of weekly and monthly meetings with key industrialists, the Park administration set strategic export priorities for the national economy: light industrial development in the 1960s, heavy and chemical industry in the 1970s, and (after Park's death), electronics and consumer goods in the 1980s. The strong role the South Korean state has played in shaping industrial development in South Korea—in determining what sectors to focus upon, in deciding which corporations will be allowed to enter into promising sectors, in tolerating a bifurcated finance market (separating the formal from the informal "curb market") to cross-subsidize industrialization, in setting tariff structures and import laws, and in a myriad of other ways—has been the subject of several in-depth studies (see, for example, Luedde-Neurath 1986; Amsden 1989; Woo 1991; Haggard et al. 1994). South Korea's success has been fostered by state policies that distorted key prices to stimulate economic activity. To encourage the development of export-oriented industry, the South Korean government created an assortment of positive and negative incentives for private firms and protections from lower-priced or better-quality foreign goods. Richard Luedde-Neurath has documented the complexities of domestic incentives and controls set on trade in South Korea. In the early 1960s, he writes,

> Korea transformed itself . . . into a country which had struck a balance between export orientation on the one hand, and a closed domestic market on the other. Exports were vigorously promoted, through incentives, a devaluation, preferential credit allocation and through a liberal import policy toward export inputs. The domestic market, on the other hand, was subject to different rules: only traders who satisfied specific export obligations were allowed to import. What is more, only essential types of (non-export) production were encouraged and allocated foreign exchange to import their raw materials and related requirements. *All other types of production and consumption were discouraged at this stage, partly through import controls, partly through taxation, and partly through the withholding of credit.*
>
> (Luedde-Neurath 1986:68; emphasis mine)

Although the particulars of the government's tactics in this area did not remain static (for example, Luedde-Neurath charts a general trend in which tariff structures play an increasingly more important role in discouraging imports compared to nontariff restrictions, such as difficulties in obtaining import licenses or controls on foreign exchange), the government consistently pursued the general goal of stimulating export-oriented industrial development through protectionist policies and the allocation of credit, trade and production rights, and foreign exchange (Luedde-Neurath 1986). Moreover, even though different ministries within the government may not have agreed on policy (Luedde-Neurath notes that the Ministry of Finance tended to take a more liberal attitude toward trade, while the Ministry of Commerce and Industry, not surprisingly, favored protecting domestic producers), often these differences resulted in a stalemate in which the liberalization of trade in a certain sector would be announced, but the means of implementation did not follow. Ultimately, Luedde-Neurath concludes, the trade controls established by the South Korean government were not just a means of shielding South Korean domestic producers from competition before they were ready; the structure of these controls allowed cross-subsidization of export sales by allowing producers to charge higher prices in the domestic market.

> The practice of granting industry-specific import rights in relation to export earnings acted both as an incentive to exports, given the high rate of profits associated with such import rights . . . and as a means of allowing domestic firms to protect their market share. Domestic producers as sole importers of products related to their own output are likely to price imported goods in such a way that their [own] market portion is not seriously threatened.
>
> (Luedde-Neurath 1986:73)

As later chapters will show, this particular tactic was just one of the elements of the strategy for national economic growth that ultimately depended upon South Korean consumers to bear the costs of export expansion.

The South Korean government had another principal tool to shape domestic industrial policy besides the import/export strictures: the allocation of finance. Political economist Jung-en Woo has examined the ways in which the South Korean state, over a period of decades, strategically "deployed financial resources at home and abroad to accumulate power unto itself, in order to force a rapid industrialization and to create—out of a historical vacuum caused by colonialism and war—a new class of entrepreneurs" (Woo 1991:x). Woo shows that the success of the "big push" of the 1970s—President Park's scheme to transform the South Korean economy into one based not on light industry (such as textiles) but on heavy industry and chemicals—was engineered by the strategic deployment of capital to producers in targeted industries. South Korea's security position helped to draw large sums of capital from American banks; as Woo explains, "there are some countries whose strategic importance to the United States makes them practically undefaultable . . . , and some banks so huge that they can only go belly-up at great risk to the home economy. . . . For such borrowers and lenders, America is the lender of last resort, and bankers do well by lending big, and to countries that are American-supported through and through" (Woo 1991:155).[11] The state then directed this capital to the heavy industrialization program on preferential terms.

Throughout the 1970s, all banks in South Korea were state controlled. This enabled the South Korean government to direct formal lending to those borrowers it deemed appropriate, and it was able to allocate funds at artificially low rates. Woo calculates that "the average real cost of bank loan[s] for 1974–1980 came to minus 6.7 percent" (1991:159). In other words, there was money to be made simply by borrowing. Banks were required by the state to make loans (known as "policy loans") to support exports; in effect, these loans supported *chaebŏl* expansions because the state selected *chaebŏl* as the agents of export industrialization. According to Woo, by 1983, "The extraordinary concentration of domestic credit *in* the *chaebŏl* might be gleaned from the following: 400 large firms belonging to 137 different *chaebŏl* claimed . . . 69.6 percent of total bank and 47.6 percent of total financial institution loans outstanding. . . . The share of the 50 largest *chaebŏl* in total domestic credit came to 26.5 percent, and the combined share of the three largest (Hyundai, Daewoo, and Samsung) was over 10 percent of the total" (Woo 1991:170).

In sum, from the 1960s until the early 1980s, the state fostered a particular kind of economic development: export-oriented industrialization dominated by a few enormous corporations. Measured on the scale of economic growth, the success of this strategy was remarkable. South Korea's gross national product increased at an annualized average of over 8 percent between 1965 and 1985 (Amsden 1989:56); the growth rate of the gross domestic product during the same period was close to 10 percent per year (Janelli 1993:56). The course was not always smooth. The South Korean economy was battered by international shock waves (such as the oil price increases in 1974 and again in 1979–1980, climbing world interest rates in the early 1980s, and the appreciation of the dollar during the early Reagan years) as well as by domestic troubles, including a significant harvest shortfall in 1980, a year already fraught with political and economic difficulties. Nevertheless, throughout this period, the South Korean government successfully focused public attention on the project of industrial development. Economic growth and national security (the threat from the north) were the best arguments for the maintenance of a strong state. As Woo put it:

> Legitimacy is . . . a matter of creating and reinforcing politically expedient myths. For economic growth to substitute for legitimacy, it has to be transmogrified into a symbol that appeals to some collective primordial sentiment—such as, for instance, nationalism. That symbol in Korea was a number: a talismanic double-digit GNP growth figure that was the Korean score in the race to catch up with Japan and also to surpass the DPRK's [Democratic People's Republic of Korea] economic performance.
>
> (Woo 1991:98)

While the South Korean state had several ways of pulling the puppet strings of the institutions of industrialization (the *chaebŏl*), Woo's statement points to a vulnerability in this strategy for South Korean development: securing the cooperation of the general populace.

In addition to the establishment of financial subsidies and protection from foreign competition for the *chaebŏl*, South Korea's industrialization strategy depended upon the cooperation of the South Korean people as workers and as citizens. The trick was to make the industrialization process appear to be a national project with benefits that would accrue not just to the *chaebŏl* and wealthy individuals, but to the nation as a whole. In fact, throughout this period student uprisings and labor unrest were continual, violent testimonials to the fragility with which the state retained its position of legitimacy.[12] Political stability was crucial to economic expansion, but as long as the government and the *chaebŏl* were seen as partners, popular dissatisfaction with working conditions or limits on political freedom threatened the entire compact.

And the South Korean people had grounds for protest. For one thing, South Korea's international competitive advantage was achieved in large part by keeping labor costs low. The state played a strong role in suppressing wages, outlawing autonomous labor unions and not merely turning a blind eye to industry's use of private thugs as a violent response to labor action but indeed supporting private force against worker protests with assistance from the police and the (South) Korean Central Intelligence Agency

(Ogle 1990; Amsden 1989:324; Lie 1992:287). In the early years of President Park's administration, real wages rose at a greater rate than did productivity, but by 1971, while wages continued to rise, they dropped behind productivity increases. In 1980 wages actually *decreased*, and in 1983 the state froze wages (Irwan 1987:387); in that year, the Federation of Korean Trade Unions was forced to admit that average industrial monthly salaries amounted to only 52 percent of the minimum living expenses for a family of five (Irwan 1987:401). Moreover, South Korean workers labored long hours for their pay: average work hours in South Korea topped the International Labor Organization charts in the 1980s (Lie 1992).

The citizenry bore other economic costs as well. During the same period for which Woo calculates real bank loan rates as negative (1974–1980), rates for borrowing on the curb market (the only source of loans for most individuals) averaged about 18.5 percent (Woo 1991:160). Between 1972 and 1986 she notes a spread between returns on curb investments and bank deposit rates ranging from a low of 13.5 percent in 1985 to a high of 20.9 percent in 1975, with an average spread of 18 percent (Woo 1991:197). The discrepancy between the curb and the banks had two effects on households and small businesses: they were highly unlikely to make deposits into the banking system, and individuals (and small businesses) were much more inclined to invest in assets or to play the curb market themselves. Woo reports that a survey of urban households in 1980 shows that more than 70 percent of their savings were deposited in the curb market (Woo 1991:161). But while the curb offered high rates of return, it was also insecure and, officially, illegal; the state could, at will, shake down the curb for funds when formal finances ran thin— and it did so in August 1971. At the same time, households and small businesses were essentially denied access to the favorable bank loans; government-mandated ceilings on the loan portfolios of banks and specific directions as to the type of loans banks could make left individuals and small and medium-sized businesses out in the cold. Small borrowers were forced to borrow on the curb market at high rates of interest, short loan terms, and high risk.

One important aspect of this bifurcation of the finance market was that until the late 1980s there was no formal home mortgage system to speak of in South Korea. In general, households purchased property for cash. The difficulty of accumulating sufficient savings to purchase a home and the skyrocketing real estate prices in South Korea from the late 1970s throughout the 1980s had a significant effect on consumer practices. To a much greater extent than in places where mortgage arrangements spread the cost of home purchase over time into the future, resources that might have been deployed for consumer purchases in the present needed to be saved in the hope of eventual home ownership.

Moreover, the very *chaebŏl* that had benefited from favorable loan terms and the bifurcated finance market exacerbated the process that disadvantaged individuals and small businesses seeking financing. Many of the *chaebŏl* invested their borrowed funds not in the intended productive activities, but in speculating in the curb market itself (taking advantage of the wide spread between the two rates of interest) and in real estate. Real estate prices rose sharply in the late 1970s, driven up in part by the money flowing in from wages and profits gained in the Middle East construction boom in which South Korean firms had participated (and also by the petrodollar-fueled, easy-borrowing atmosphere of the time). Between 1963 and 1980 the average annual increase in land prices in the major cities exceeded 30 percent (Cho 1989); although there was a lull during 1985–1986 (when land prices increased "only" by around 7 percent per year), between 1983 and 1990 the average annual increase was 16.3 percent, peaking in 1988 with a 27.5 percent year-on-year price increase (Korea Housing Bank 1990). The increase in real estate prices during this period was consistently much higher than that in the consumer price index and in wages. Real estate prices have slowed only in recent years, and *chaebŏl* speculation in real estate was widely blamed for fueling the upward spiral, thrusting housing prices beyond the reach of many households—and helping others to grow rich with the real estate boom.

In addition to poor working conditions and distorted economic opportunities, South Koreans were governed by a series of authoritarian, undemocratic administrations. Although Park took power in a coup, he legitimized his position by winning two subsequent national elections (in 1963 and 1967), but in between he had declared martial law to quell demonstrations against the normalization of relations with Japan. By 1970, however, with an unstable business atmosphere and the popularity of the political opposition on the rise, Park turned increasingly to the exercise of brute power, culminating in 1972 with the Yushin constitution, which gave Park lifelong rule and granted him broad discretionary power over personal rights and over the legislative process. After Park's assassination in 1979, General Chun Doo Hwan attained power by declaring martial law and dissolving the legislature, and his respect for civil liberties was no greater than his predecessor's. In 1987 large numbers of the middle class joined student protesters in the streets in what were often violent clashes with riot police; Chun was forced to accede to demands for democratic elections for the nation's next president. Democracy did not bring an immediate end to the rule of the military; the first elections confirmed Chun's handpicked successor, Rho Tae-woo, himself a general, as the next president of South Korea.

In sum, during the course of South Korea's transition to industrial and commercial success, the people were asked to make great sacrifices, to work long hours for poor pay for unelected governments that offered rich rewards to large corporations owned by a small number of opulently wealthy families, and to expect little for themselves. How, one might ask, did the nation endure?

Certainly, direct state violence and the threat of violence was a palpable part of the relationship between the state, the *chaebŏl*, and the South Korean population during this period. In this respect, sociologist Anthony Giddens's discussion of the nation-state as "a set of institutional forms . . . its rule being sanctioned by law and direct control of the means of internal and external violence" (Giddens 1987:171) is instructive. Although in a sense South Korea still shared control over its army's movements outside—and even inside—its national boundaries, we should note that the United States played a complex supporting role in the persistence of these relationships. The confidence of foreign buyers and potential investors as well as that of South Korea's military partners depended upon the ability of the South Korean government to quell riots and maintain a level of domestic calm. Giddens also argues, however (following Michel Foucault), that the widespread control necessary for capitalism to function is achieved largely not through violent display and explicit threat, but through "the disciplinary power of surveillance" (ibid.:176), and in South Korea there existed both a well-articulated structure of surveillance and more subtle forms of Foucauldian discipline.

Nevertheless, it would be misleading to argue that the many millions of hours of labor that lifted the South Korean economy to its position of prominence and comfort were motivated by fear alone, even propped up by an industrial habitus. I will argue that in fact in large part the accomplishments of this period were motivated by a potent elixir of nationalism and hope that was widely held throughout the population.

## NATIONALISM IN CONTEMPORARY SOUTH KOREA

Nationalism in South Korea is a more complicated matter than it might at first appear, particularly when one is confronted with the variety of crude nationalistic slogans that make up not just government campaigns but ordinary advertisements and the substance of everyday conversation. My own work is part of the stream of thought that has evolved in recent years from examination of how national identities, rather than being natural outcomes of a primordial sentiment of social and political unity, are continually constructed in particular contexts, in various modes, and often in a process consciously led by interested parties (see, for example, Hobsbawm and Ranger 1983; Chatterjee 1993; Williams 1989; Anderson 1983). South Korean nationalism clearly shares many of the forms and themes of nationalism found elsewhere: a focus on language, history, tradition, culture, and ethnic homogeneity. Yet South Korean popular nationalism faces a troublesome ground for the formation of a national identity. Certain aspects of Korean history—the recurrent theme of foreign invasion,[13] ambivalence regarding the legacy of the long Chosŏn era, the shame of Japanese colonial domination, and the brief period of U.S. occupation as well as the legacy of South Korean authoritarian leadership—diminished the power of history to generate positive national feeling. More important, the "nation" was divided into two states, and the national people were officially at war. Moreover, the narration (Bhabha 1990) of "Korean history" itself gives voice to problems of national division, since the populations on each side of the truce line take equal pride in their shared past, and telling the full story of that past implies a critique of the current separation. Cultural critic Homi Bhabha writes that "appeals to the national past must also be seen as the anterior space of signification that 'singularizes' the nation's cultural totality" (1990:317), but whereas in many other places and among other people the construction of a shared national story has come to be seen as a critical foundation of national unity, the Korean national past of the twentieth century divides the present nation of "Koreans" as a people north and south of the border between their two states.

On the other hand, by imagining Korean reunification South Koreans can envision the achievement of that most elegant national configuration, a pure national identity where history and language are coterminous with land. Partly for this reason, South Korean nationalism makes frequent reference to an imagined national—unified—future. In his examination of South Korean discourses of division and unification, anthropologist Roy Richard Grinker explores the theme of "the unified nation as an idealized past and future" (1998:ix). Grinker's analysis focuses in part on the reasons why South Koreans "want to maintain the dream of unification even more than they want to achieve an actual unification" (1998:xiii): by keeping unification as an ideal rather than working to achieve it, South Koreans are able to imagine that the "real" Korea is socially and economically homogeneous without confronting evidence to the contrary. In this way the fact of division facilitates the formation of a sense of unity among South Koreans (and with imagined North Koreans) as long as the focus is on the future rather than on history.

While unification is a powerful image, it is not the only element of the idealized national future. Indeed, the goal of a socially and economically equitable national future has been a key element of the industrialization discourse at least since the early years of President Park's administration. Historically, Korean society was divided into rigid status groups. (Slaves were not finally liberated until the nineteenth century.) Yet the economic ravages of Japanese colonial rule and the Korean war had a leveling effect on South Korean society. Sociologist John Lie has observed that "The devastation of the Korean War only accentuated the pervasive sense of egalitarian origins, assiduously fostered by nationalism that stressed homogeneity (and hence equality) of South Koreans. An egalitarian sentiment became a noted characteristic of South Korea" (1998:40). This egalitarianism was counterbalanced by a highly developed status-consciousness, particularly among the descendants of well-known *yangban* families (Lett 1998); yet an egalitarian ideal formed one of the principal rallying points motivating the hard work of development. In the first years of his administration, Park himself wrote: "The economic, social, and political goals we set after the revolution are: promotion of the public welfare, freedom from exploitation, and the fair distribution of an income among the people. It is obvious that these goals cannot be reached overnight. They are, nonetheless, the fundamental aims of the economic order towards which we must move" (quoted in Amsden 1989:49). As the South Korean economy grew, however, the grand goals remained a part of the image of the future. Sacrifices made for the initial phase of industrialization were multiplied, not alleviated, by the efforts demanded of workers in the "big push" era. Throughout this period, the carrot of a better, more equitable, wealthier, democratic (and unified) Korea was dangled before the population by the government and its media and institutions. From the government's perspective, compared to the past as a unifying (but passive) discourse, the future had the galvanizing advantage of being a vision that must be *achieved* through leadership (the government) and public action (the citizens).

This orientation toward the future was linked with other aspects of personal purpose. The hope that their children would live to see a prosperous, unified Korea was a complex and powerful motivation for many South Koreans to endure hard labor and rough circumstances. Anthropologist Cho Hae-jŏng has written about how Korean mothers, often deprived of domains of personal agency, invest themselves in their children's future and develop prodigious patience (1986). And indeed, during the period of rapid industrialization South Korean mothers as well as fathers demonstrated this patience. The passage of time alone, however, eventually gave the lie to this element of the promise. By the middle of the 1980s, the generation that had been young in Park's early years was beginning to measure the personal returns on their own sacrifices as their children reached adulthood. Many were sorely disappointed—this coming of age of their children coincided with the flowering of South Korean consumer society, and it quickly became clear that not every family was still waiting for the attainment of an ideal nation.

With nationalism as the fuel for South Korean industrialization, the emphasis on an imagined future as the site of the "real" nation helped to defer judgment on the success and fairness of economic and political policies. Ironically, the achievements of the national economy themselves contributed to the waning persuasive power of the discourse of the future nation.

## CONSUMPTION AND CONSUMER NATIONALISM

In 1990, with 42 million people and per capita annual income estimated at over $5,000, South Korea's domestic market was no longer a trivial part of the economy. Yet, as we have seen, until the early 1980s South Korean economic development was based upon a low-wage, labor-intensive organization of production, with strong state leadership in strategic decisions and with state-directed deployment of capital. The domestic market was not at that time the focus of national economic policy. In the early 1980s, however, the South Korean economy began a process of change that has shaken some of the foundations of the South Korean economic, political, and social nexus.

First, the South Korean state came under increasing international pressure throughout the 1980s to change economic laws so that South Korean trade and commerce would conform to "free-market principles." During the 1960s and 1970s, South Korea benefited from relatively open world trade and from a felicitous coincidence between its own export push and rising consumer demand in the industrialized nations; moreover, there was relatively little foreign competition for the targeted export markets.[14] But the worldwide recession of 1979–1980 signaled the beginning of an extended period of international trade anxiety, and from the early 1980s on South Korea was forced to respond to almost constant pressure from its trading partners to alter its production support policies at home and to open its markets to foreign competition. Woo notes that between 1981 and 1982 alone, "Korea's exports subject to import restrictions in industrialized countries . . . increased from 32.3 percent . . . to 42.9 percent" (Woo 1991:188). South Korea's success in international trade, in fact, contributed to this pressure: by 1988, South Korea was the twelfth largest trading nation. Many countries (both those more *and* those less successful) demanded it give up the privileges accorded developing countries, such as the Generalized System of Preferences benefits, and assume a responsible, mature position in the international trade community. Opinions differ as to the degree to which South Korea *has* liberalized trade; Amsden quotes both the World Bank's statement that "Korea's liberalization program is very much on track" (World Bank 1987, in Amsden 1989:134) and the United States embassy's nearly simultaneous contrary evaluation that "use of the word 'liberalization' in reference to Korea's shifting items off its restricted list is somewhat misleading. . . . Generally, other NTB's [nontariff barriers] (e.g., the rule that only Korean cosmetics manufacturers can import cosmetics) remained in place" (U.S. Embassy 1986, quoted in Amsden 1989:134). Nevertheless, from the perspective of South Korean consumers it would be hard to deny that, following the Olympics, local markets offered a greatly increased supply of imported consumer goods. These imports entered into the material and imaginative lives of people in Seoul. Imported goods linked South Koreans to the rest of the world and expanded their knowledge of the lifestyles of other people, but imported goods were simultaneously seen as a potentially dangerous infiltration into South Korean space, posing a threat to South Korean businesses.

At the same time, South Korea was also pressured to open its financial markets. South Korean commercial banks were "denationalized" between 1981 and 1983, and although to a certain extent the *chaebŏl* were able to evade the regulations intended to prevent the banks from coming under *chaebŏl* control, banks also began to better serve the needs of private households and small businesses. Foreign banks gained access, and while many of the foreign banks acted mostly in the realm of business finance, some altered local banking practices by offering new banking services to households, such as home mortgages. In 1989 Citibank advertisements in Seoul subways publicized some of the first substantial long-term home mortgages available in the South Korean market. The state began to relax some of its demands on domestic banks to provide loans at special rates to priority industries. Banks also began to offer credit cards and other consumer credit services to individuals, facilitating the new practice of buying on time.

In addition to the foreign pressures on South Korea to open its finance market, the state had another set of reasons for making these changes: after the assassination of Park Chung Hee in 1979, General Chun Doo Hwan had a difficult time consolidating his position as chief of state. Violent uprisings (including most infamously the rebellion in Kwangju,[15] the provincial capital of the southwestern province of South Chŏlla) and popular distrust and dissatisfaction (in part a result of spiraling inflation and stagnant wages in the wake of the second oil shock and a poor harvest) combined with a sense that those huge engines of growth fostered by the Park administration, the *chaebŏl*, had grown too powerful. Some of the financial reforms can be seen as the state's attempt to reconfigure the relations of authority.[16] By criticizing the *chaebŏl*, the Chun administration made a bid for popular sympathy; the state had also been placed in a high-risk position by the huge debt-equity ratios carried by the *chaebŏl* in the late 1970s, and financial privatization was seen as one way to help reduce that risk.

In addition, in the 1980s South Korean companies were greatly expanding the range and volume of products for sale to the domestic market. New appliances, new services, new furniture for all the new apartments were advertised on ubiquitous billboards and on commercials shown on the quickly proliferating televisions, which by 1985 could be found in 99 percent of South Korean households. Just ten years earlier, less than one-third of South Korean families had owned a TV. This diversity and amplification of consumer opportunity had contradictory effects on South Korean national sentiments. On the one hand, there was genuine excitement both about this newly visible domestic opulence and about the export successes that were the driving force behind it. Yet at the same time, the expansion of the domestic market created a palpable distinction between the people who had benefited from economic growth and those who had not.

Of course, the rich in South Korea had always been easy to identify. Their lifestyle was distinctive: they lived in particular neighborhoods; they were chauffeured from place to place. They were among the fortunate few who were given permission to travel abroad. Despite feelings of envy, most

South Koreans saw little point in comparing their own circumstances to those of the elite. As long as the domestic consumer market remained stunted, however, economic differences between poor and middle-income individuals (or households) did not reveal themselves as much in ordinary material possessions. Visible differences seemed more like points along a narrow continuum: the ability to afford to ride in a bus with air-conditioning rather than one without—both would be crowded—or to eat pure rice rather than rice with barley. A vigorous campaign of protests and labor disputes was carried out without the formation of a widespread working-class consciousness (Lee 1997). While it would be wrong to say poor South Koreans felt no envy for the households supported by white-collar work, nevertheless, with few brand names and a limited range of products, most people felt they *shared* a sense of deprivation. With the growth of the consumer market came a new source of dissatisfaction and social division.

Beyond the most basic level of satisfaction of needs, consumption is a system of human communication. While few economists share this perspective (cf. Scitovsky 1992), it is common among anthropologists and historians. The economists' doctrine of consumer sovereignty holds that the individual consumer makes choices independently of all others, but an anthropologist would argue that no individual has a process for rational choice that is divorced from culture or from the dynamic social world that frames and alters values. Thorstein Veblen (admittedly an economist) long ago sketched out a cultural system of conspicuous consumption intended to demonstrate honor and decency (1994 [1899]); for Veblen, however, there was one standard of honor and one system of consumer practices by which honor was made conspicuous. Pierre Bourdieu's research into French variations in taste provides evidence that there may be multiple interrelated systems of taste and that not all consumer choices are emulations of the practices of the elite (1984). As Mary Douglas and Baron Isherwood put it, "Man is a social being. . . . Man needs goods for communicating with others and for making sense of what is going on around him. . . . His overriding objective as a consumer, put at its most general, is a concern for information about the changing cultural scene" (1979:67).

The South Korean domestic market did not grow unimpeded by government interference, however. Though South Koreans attained a moderate level of personal income by the middle of the 1970s, the domestic market was retarded by government policies until the 1980s. Thus, people were deprived of a key source of information and of materials for communication.

Then quite suddenly, with the development of the domestic consumer market in the 1980s, novel opportunities for expression proliferated.

Status assertion was indeed a large part of what consumers communicated with their purchases (Lett 1998), but even this was not a simple project. The wealthiest consumers discussed, negotiated, and even generated structures of meaning to help distinguish whether a Hyundai Grandeur automobile or a Mercury Sable was a higher status possession, or whether an apartment in the Hyundai Apartments in Apkujŏngdong or a house in Yŏnhuidong was more exclusive. At the same time, there were other factors to consider. Criticism of the nouveaux riches was rampant, so a certain restraint was key to the correct demonstration of elite status. This value also resonated with the popular historical image of modest *yangban* scholars. For members of the less wealthy strata as well, the market offered an opportunity to demonstrate personal character and achievements. A large part of public discussion of the new consumer market focused on whether consumption on this scale was in itself a corrupt Western influence. Moreover, it was through consumption of foreign products, people feared, that "Korean" culture would fall victim to Japanese or Western infiltration.

What is striking about the South Korean situation is the phenomenon I call "consumer nationalism." Although there was a widespread public movement to buy products made in South Korea and avoid imports, consumer nationalism went beyond this crude formulation. Rather, as South Korean consumers encountered an increasingly complex market, they brought to this context their sense of identification with the nation. At a deeper level, consumers set themselves the larger task of making consumer choices that were in the best interests of the nation—choices that were most "Korean." At various moments and for different people, this decision might, for example, rest on a sense of what the Korean tradition is with respect to material possessions or on a concern about the effects of conspicuous consumption on the feeling of national unity or on quandaries about whether by buying foreign-made products one might actually be helping South Korea to participate in the cosmopolitan world. That is, in making purchasing decisions, people weighed how best to protect the South Korean economy or whether, as a woman, by considering one's family's needs and desires first, one isn't doing one's best for the nation.

Looking at the consumer side of the South Korean economy exposes hidden material and cultural elements of national industrial development. The export-focused strategy did not merely ignore the domestic market—it used and shaped the domestic market in particular ways toward particular ends. The South Korean state/*chaebŏl* nexus fostered a national culture of patience that helped to defer consumer demand. Later, when it served their interests, the *chaebŏl* encouraged domestic consumers to buy their experimental products, to subsidize their export sales, and to absorb their excess inventory. South Korean consumers responded to dramatic changes in this environment with skill, curiosity, and eagerness but also, at times, with anxiety and resentment.

This book rests on research into how several women in Seoul discuss and enact national identity in their consumption choices. I conducted my fieldwork from August 1991 through October 1992, with a return visit of one month in October 1993. I chose to work most intensively in two neighborhoods, one an upper-middle-class apartment complex in Yoido ("the Manhattan of Seoul"), the other a working-class hillside community center I call "Talgoljjagi" located just to the north and east of the city. In addition to extended fieldwork in these neighborhoods, I spoke with a variety of individuals across the city. In essence, I was interested in understanding how the development of the consumer market in South Korea had affected the sense of national community that had been fundamental to the stability and effectiveness of South Korean economic development strategies during the preceding decades. During the 1980s, class differences were increasingly demarcated in space and by possessions, and I attempt to understand and describe how people experienced this phenomenon.

The study of "classes" in South Korea is a complex and delicate arena. I have not elected to take an analytical approach to class categories (I do not, for example, distinguish classes by their relations to the means of production), although this has clearly been of use to other scholars in understanding certain structural aspects of South Korea's political economy (see, for example, Choi 1993). My use of the word "class" refers to status and income groupings, but is not intended to represent statistically identifiable categories (such as income quartiles) or communities. This approach reflects common perceptions of similarity and affiliation, and opens "class" to the relations of consumption as well as those of production (see Bourdieu 1984). One of my main concerns is to trace some of the ways national and gender identities come to differ when "class" as a local social category takes on greater salience, as it has in South Korea in the past decade and a half. To explore this issue, I have focused on how people respond to changes in consumer culture in Seoul; consumer culture (*sobi saenghwal*) is not merely a discursive focus for statements about propriety, equity, success, excess, and the position of South Korea in the world, it also shapes perceptions through its continuing practice.

Change has been a disorienting constant for Koreans for a century; the changes of the past decade and a half are neither more extensive than those of earlier periods nor are they disjointed from earlier transformations. I do, however, believe that the 1980s and 1990s have made visible both current changes as they occurred and earlier changes that had been obscured through new consumer choices and practices. The explosion of the consumer society in the 1980s *materialized* changes that were already well underway during the Park administration.

Among other transformations, the nature of work has changed. In 1960 more than two-thirds of the working population was engaged in the primary sector (agriculture, mining, forestry, and fishing), and as late as 1974 nearly half of South Korean workers were farmers, fishermen, or foresters. By 1980, however, the primary sector accounted for only 34 percent of the labor force, and it had shrunk further to less than 20 percent by 1990. Growth in jobs in manufacturing and services, of course, took up the slack. Then there has been massive movement of people; in 1960, 72 percent of all South Koreans lived in the countryside, but by 1980, 57 percent were in cities. In 1988 more than one in four South Koreans lived within the city limits of Seoul, and nearly half the nation's population lived within commuting distance of the capital. Moreover, the composition of households has changed. In 1985 the balance shifted from two- or three-generation households to one or two generations living together, and since 1985 there have been more single-generation households than three-generation households. Increases in average income have brought South Korea from destitution to prosperity. In 1975 the average per person annual income was less than U.S.$500; by 1989 it had reached nearly U.S.$4,000. Furthermore, these benefits have been shared widely (National Bureau of Statistics 1990); South Korea has won praise from the World Bank (and many others) for its relatively equitable distribution of income (as opposed to wealth; see, for example, Leipziger et al. 1992). Nuclear households, urban dwellers, service and manufacturing workers, growing prosperity, along with the consumer goods output of growing *chaebŏl* and the inflow of products and images from abroad combine with the shifts in historical memory as the colonial generation is aging and a youthful generation, in which few have experienced real deprivation, comes to maturity: this is the foundation for the growth in consumer culture in South Korea in the 1980s.

Baek Uk-in, a South Korean sociologist, remembers that in the 1960s and 1970s, "for ramen, toothpaste, clothes, and such things, names or brand labels had not yet become a problem. If it was ramen, it was ramen; if it was toothpaste, you understood it was toothpaste. Even though we were at the center of mass production-mass consumption, because of chronic low wages and shortages of goods, the brand names of things could not play such an important role. But now," Baek continues, "even for just toothpaste there are more than about ten brands to buy, and even a variety of imported toothpastes are openly exhibited" (Baek 1993:35).

In focusing on consumer practice and the discourse about consumption in South Korea, I will explore the nexus of nationalism, new configurations of gender and class, and changes in the international economy. My interest in consumption is rooted not just in the important role material culture plays in making and illustrating differences and allegiances but also in the special significance consumption tends to have in the reinforcement of gendered identities. In South Korea women are the primary agents of material consumer practice. Of course, this broad statement obscures differences between women (according to age, income, experience, personal predilection, and style) in their engagement with consumption, and it ignores the way men benefit from the consumption carried out for them by women (wives, mothers, secretaries, daughters, and daughters-in-law) as well as the ways they personally spend money (on objects, but more importantly on services: in bars and restaurants and the sex-for-sale world with colleagues and friends [E. Kim 1998]). All these subtleties and distinctions are important parts of this analysis, but the complications should not overshadow the ways in which new consumer practices implicate gender and class in new configurations of South Korean nationalism.

In the next chapter I focus on the city of Seoul as a context and also a factor in the formation of national, class, and gendered identities. People's experience of Seoul as a place to live, and the effects of the real estate market on people's lives, were important orienting points for consumer practices. In the third chapter I look in more detail at the interrelations between South Korea's export-focused national economic development strategies and local consumer patterns, drawing out the particularities of how consumers have been *formed* and how certain forms of consumption itself make the nation. In the fourth chapter I examine the discursive reaction, *kwasobi ch'ubang* ("eliminate overconsumption"), to these social and material changes, looking at how popular themes and government slogans intersect. In the fifth chapter I focus on the ways in which gender and patriotism have become intertwined in the South Korean focus on consumer practices and examine how women themselves struggle to make appropriate consumer choices. I point to the variety of threats consumption poses to the sense of South Korean national unity and the analyses South Korean women arrive at of the relationships between their social roles, consumption practices, and patriotism. Finally, in the last chapter, I revisit these issues in light of the "Asian Crisis" that began in 1997.

The material for this book is drawn from discourse and practice: I look at the frameworks within which people define themselves. In different places at various times, particular aspects of living become central to imagining and enacting identities. In South Korea in the early 1990s, consumption held this position. I opened this chapter with a vignette involving an object as mundane as a clipboard; I hope to show that every act of consumption from the mundane to the grandiose, every purchase, every admiring glance or dismissive judgment, each calculation of cost and value, all the moments of quiet satisfaction in ownership or nagging irritation with an inadequate acquisition implicates and shifts just slightly the sense of who people are in Seoul.

# FIRST VIGNETTE: 1992

Seoul in the early 1990s was not an easy city to navigate. People would often give first-time visitors directions not to their ultimate destination but rather to some major intersection or distinctive building near the goal, and suggest the visitors call from there so they could be met and led personally the rest of the way. In the older parts of town, avenues gave way to twisted, unnamed alleyways with few landmarks more significant than the neighborhood video store or *dong* (administrative neighborhood) office. In the newer districts and in those parts of the older neighborhoods that had undergone redevelopment, mammoth boulevards carried eight lanes of aggressive traffic, and long block after long block was fronted with sleek, faddish, nearly indistinguishable constructions. Old buildings and neighborhoods were being demolished, and new ones were appearing at such a dizzying pace one could not count on landmarks to linger; they were like the breadcrumbs in the fairy tale of Hansel and Gretel.

When Seoul's new subway system opened in 1985, in several stations the subway authority had helpfully placed at the foot of exit stairwells, looking up toward the light of the outdoors, huge photographs depicting the ground-level view from that egress. In the tangled undergrowth of subway station exits, these photos helped disoriented travelers choose the right pathway out. By 1991, however, just six years later, where they had not been removed, these placards served as ad hoc local history exhibits: at the Pangbae station in Kangnam, for example, the empty lots, ramshackle houses, and homey grocery stores in the pictures had been replaced by Dunkin' Donuts, apartment complexes, and rows of granite-faced, four-story office buildings.

I took some pride, therefore, in my own knowledge of the routes from here to there across the city. I have an ingrained sense of orientation and place, and I enjoy finding my way around urban spaces anywhere. My fieldwork took me to many different neighborhoods, and I carried a detailed Seoul map with me so that I could walk from one appointment to the next, or at least to a new subway stop, in order see as much street life as I could find. I could recite the subway stations, in order, on several of the lines, and I knew which bus lines would carry me fastest from Apkujŏngdong to Yoido, from Namdaemun to Taenung, from Taehangno to Insadong, from Tongdaemun to Talgoljjagi. I knew the quickest footpaths (above or below ground)[1] to reach the major landmarks (historical, commercial, and public) in the center of town. I enjoyed dispensing this knowledge to my friends: tourists, expatriates, and Koreans alike.

I was more than ready, then, with the answer one day when a stooped *halmŏni* (old woman), after turning her head to look twice all around her, sought my advice. "*Haksaeng (student),*" she began, still glancing around in a distracted effort to find some orienting memory, "*which way is Kwang-hwamun?*" This was an easy question: we were just three blocks down along Chongno, a main thoroughfare, from Kwanghwamun, the gate to Kyŏngbok Palace. I gestured toward the west, and replied, "*It's that way—*"

I could hear the woman's intake of breath, and she peered at me sharply. I am short for an American, which means I am about average height for a South Korean woman of my age, and my eyes and hair are dark brown. Apparently, the *halmŏni*'s weak eyes had tricked her, and she had mistaken me at first for a native, but my linguistic awkwardness alerted her to the fact that she was not dealing with *uri han'guk saram* (literally, "our Korean people"). She began to wave her hand back and forth urgently, fingers spread upward and palm facing me, to indicate "no," and she said, out loud to herself, "*Oh! A foreigner!*" She looked at me an instant longer and turned to find someone else to help her.

I persisted. "*Halmŏni, Kwanghwamun is not far. It's this way.*" I am not proud of my command of the Korean language, but I speak it quite well enough to offer directions. The old woman, however, did not understand me—in fact, she was no longer even listening. With a face revealing something between embarrassment, horror, and the discomfort of her own disorientation, she responded as she turned away, speaking English words she may have learned during the war or in some working experience or perhaps in the time just before the Olympic games, when simple English phrases were taught over the radio: "*Excuse me. Excuse me. Excuse me.*"

The feeling of being in place or out of place is an intimate emotion. It is an essential element of national identity in many cultures, expressed as a sense of rootedness, of being one with the soil and the landscape. As in many nations, in South Korea schoolchildren were taught to name and love the natural monuments of the Korean peninsula: from the beauty of Mt. Halla in Cheju Island off the southern coastline to the grandeur of the inaccessible Paektu Mountain at the furthest northern tip of what is now North Korea. The sense of possession of the national land, the sense that Koreans are *of* the land, was reinforced in the context of a history of foreign invasion and occupation and in the current, painful division of Korea into two political entities, all factors that marked foreigners as violent trespassers. The making of a collective space, the act of navigating around it, the cognitive command of its topography, these have all been a part of the creation of (South) Korean identity.

# CHAPTER 2

# "SEOUL TO THE WORLD, THE WORLD TO SEOUL"

*Sŏurŭn Segyero—Segyenŭn Sŏullo*
Official billboard for the 1988 Seoul Olympics

In the early 1990s about one of every four South Koreans lived in Seoul. Nearly one-half the population lived within commuting distance of the capital. Seoul is simultaneously unique—it is unlike other cities in South Korea—and representative—whereas a generation ago South Koreans imagined their nation as a nation of farmers, now Seoul stands for the nation to the outside world and to South Koreans themselves. The city has played an important role both in the material establishment—literally, the construction—of South Korea's modernity as well as in its image making. The story of the development of Seoul as a cosmopolitan urban space brings together the flows of international finance, the visions of government functionaries, the profit motives of industrialists, and the dreams and daily experiences of ordinary South Koreans.

## MODERNIZING SEOUL

In 1964 the Tourist Section of the Seoul Metropolitan Government published an English-language guidebook with this charming description of the South Korean capital:

> Seoul is an old city with lots for you to see to attest to its age. However, Seoul is also a modern city and is being transformed at breakneck speed. The scars of the recent war are all but gone. The result of all this change is a curious blend of East and West, old and new. Old palaces in an excellent state of preservation vie with modern office buildings for attention. Single-story buildings in Korea's unique and aesthetically pleasing architecture, especially the upturned tile roofs, stand side-by-side with

multi-storied buildings of all shapes and sizes. Oxcarts and bicycles compete with the latest trams, buses, and taxis for their own right of way.

(Seoul Metropolitan Government 1964)

At the time this was published, some three-and-a-half million people resided in Seoul. The administrative bounds of the city had been expanded outward in the previous year, roughly doubling the city's area from 270 to 594 square kilometers. South Korea, with Seoul as its capital, was then at the threshold of the long, intense push of Park Chung Hee's industrialization initiative. A generation later, when I arrived to conduct my fieldwork in 1991, Seoul's population had tripled.[1] The more than ten-and-a-half million people living in Seoul in the early 1990s saw not oxcarts but personal automobiles jostling with buses on the roadways. Many of the single-story homes "in Korea's unique and aesthetically pleasing architecture" had been torn down in redevelopment projects to make way for "modern" apartments or simply to remove from view what had come to be seen as an embarrassing symbol of backwardness.[2]

During this period, the space and form of the city has been the object of a persistent contest over resources and meaning. Large-scale plans for changes in the city's layout not only provide evidence of how the city has been envisioned by planners and bureaucrats over time but also show—in the very incompleteness of their execution—the limits of the planners' power to overcome the inventiveness of social forces (such as the undeterrable influx of people to Seoul) as well as the resistance of other powerful players (other government institutions, private investors, or corporate interests) to certain aspects of the plans. The modernizing intentions of professional urban planners were forced time and again to accommodate less orderly, less orchestrated processes of change. The result is a cosmopolitan city— the world's tenth most populous—almost unrecognizable from the quaint description of just three decades earlier.

The official perception of the city has altered with these physical changes: shortly after the Olympics, the Seoul Metropolitan Government expressed this very different viewpoint:

Five years from now Seoul reaches its 600th anniversary as the capital of Korea. Yet Seoul is a young metropolis still in the making. More than half of the city's ten million inhabitants live and work in districts that used to be paddy fields and orchards only a generation ago. Even older districts have gone through an extensive rebuilding process. Seoul's history is not readily recognizable in its everyday cityscape. Only a few remaining isolated monuments such as palaces and gates hint at the city's long history, and the general impression of the city is one of brashness, dynamism, and the formlessness of a booming city. Even the people themselves are new: a majority of Seoulites are newcomers drawn to the city during the last two decades of rapid economic growth and urban expansion and thus possess little emotional attachment to the city and little memory of its past.

(Seoul Metropolitan Government 1989:18)

The transformation of the city's perspective is clear: in 1964 Seoul was "an old city with lots for you to see to attest to its age," while in 1989 "Seoul's history is not readily recognizable in its everyday cityscape." In the later document, the happy mingling of past and present was replaced by a less positive "brashness, dynamism, and . . . formlessness." In the same volume[3] the authors put the point even more sharply: "The present Seoul manifests Korean society's collective determination to overcome the historical vicissitudes that have plagued the modern history of Korea" (ibid.:10). The city that was the Korean national capital for 600 years was officially portrayed as a *new* city. Although this newness was recognized as the manifestation of social processes, it was also presented as evidence of the success of planning and policies that made Seoul into a cosmopolitan, modern metropolis.

Throughout the twentieth century Seoul has grown at a record-setting pace.[4] Seoul had been established as the capital of the new Chosŏn dynasty in 1394; it was primarily an administrative (rather than a commercial) city, and its population never grew to much more than 200,000 people until Korea's "opening" to foreign trade and envoys in the last quarter of the nineteenth century initiated a dramatic change in the capital. At the time of the Japanese annexation in 1910 there were approximately 236,000 residents in Seoul (known then as *Kyŏngsŏng*); by 1945, at the end of the colonial period, there were four times that many people. People had come to Seoul during the Japanese occupation as farming grew increasingly untenable and as the city became more of an economic and cultural center. Upon "liberation," unmoored masses returning from Japan, Manchuria, and more distant points ended up in Seoul if there was no land for them to farm in their hometown or if they had grown accustomed to city life abroad or if they were themselves essentially foreigners, born abroad with no sense of home

other than the nation itself. Several hundred thousand Koreans fled to the
south after national division and made new lives in Seoul.[5] The dislocations
during the war between the two new Korean states brought more immigrants, and after the truce people continued to come, from villages, towns,
and smaller cities until the capital was gorged on people and the government began, in the 1960s, to bulldoze neighborhoods and cart the people
away. Even so, people still came: the city swelled beyond its boundaries,
consuming farmland and flood fields and pear orchards in Kyŏnggi-do, the
province surrounding the city. The national government considered policies to curb the immigration; for example, new industrial complexes were
built far from Seoul; an extensive farmers' support program was established
to stem the rural exodus; a greenbelt where new construction was forbidden
encircled the city to halt the physical spread; plans were drawn up to move
the public capital functions to Taejŏn, a site two hours south—and yet
Seoul grew in magnitude and significance (see table 2.1). By the beginning
of the 1990s, Seoul's official population stood at ten million, but the greater
Seoul metropolitan area was home to over twenty million people—more
than one-third of the entire population of South Korea.[6] All this movement
of people (the displacement of the [South] Korean population) was closely
tied to (South) Korea's commercial activities as well as its position in international politics.

TABLE 2.1    Seoul Population (1910–1990)

| YEAR | SEOUL POPULATION | NATIONAL POPULATION* | SEOUL AS A % OF NATIONAL POP. |
|------|------|------|------|
| 1910 | 233,590 | | |
| 1944 | 988,537 | 25,900,000 | 3.8% |
| 1949 | 1,446,000 | 20,190,000 | 7.2% |
| 1951 | 648,432 | | |
| 1953/1955 | 1,010,416 | 21,526,000 | 4.5% |
| 1960 | 2,445,402 | 24,989,000 | 9.8% |
| 1970 | 5,433,198 | 31,466,000 | 17.3% |
| 1980 | 8,364,379 | 37,436,000 | 22.3% |
| 1990 | 10,627,790 | 42,793,000 | 24.8% |

*Korean population through 1945; South Korean population thereafter.
Sources: Seoul Metropolitan Government; National Bureau of Statistics.

Since the early 1960s, both the Seoul metropolitan government and the South Korean national government have seen the growth of the city as a problem in need of public management, and initial plans called for the distribution of the city's functions to other areas of the nation. There were several reasons for concern. First, Seoul lies just 25 miles south of the Demilitarized Zone (DMZ), the armed truce line separating the Republic of Korea from the Democratic People's Republic of Korea to the north. In 1950 it took only three days for northern troops to overwhelm the city (Seoul was twice occupied by the DPRK's Korean People's Army during the war), and Seoul lies within a few minutes' flight for missiles or rockets the DPRK might choose to launch in any future war. Although the South Korean government has at times manipulated the Seoul population's sense of vulnerability to attack, the threat of armed conflict in Korea cannot simply be dismissed as merely a phobia constructed by the ruling regime.[7] There were recurrent plans (from the late 1960s until the early 1980s) to move many of the government functions further to the south; these were inspired by a sense of security priorities in one of the world's most heavily armed border regions. Most (although not all) of the large-scale new developments in the Seoul region have been erected to the east, south, and west of the city for security and for market reasons, which in turn are affected by security concerns. The geography of defense is on the minds of Seoul citizens just as it is on those of the planners: in the early 1990s, when thousands of apartments became available in Ilsan, a new satellite city to the northwest of the city, they sold much more slowly than those in Ilsan's sibling development, Pundang, another suburb to the south of Seoul.[8]

The disproportionate share of the nation's population, economic and cultural resources, and dynamism represented in Seoul was a source of concern itself. At what point, planners wondered, would the agglomeration economies of Seoul's size and scale be outweighed by the inefficiencies of urban congestion and sprawl?[9] Most of the functions of the capital were concentrated in the center, within and around the old city walls, exacerbating the problems of congestion. In their projections of population growth, Seoul's planners worried that unless Seoul's growth were managed, the city would eventually become a drag on the economy, rather than a source of its vitality (Simmons 1979). For this reason, officials drew up plans to disperse Seoul's commercial and industrial functions and encourage economic growth in other regions.

Purely political considerations, of course, were also important. Government documents from this period repeatedly promise to distribute development and infrastructure investment beyond the capital and the line between Pusan and Seoul in part to placate voters in the peripheral provinces.[10] As the Chŏlla economy lagged relative to Kyŏngsan, Seoul attracted a stream of migrants from Chŏlla looking for work, establishing a strong base for opposition politics in the capital.[11] In the presidential elections of 1971, the opposition party candidate, Kim Dae Jung—who was finally elected to that post in 1997—carried nearly 60 percent of the Seoul vote. The Park administration also contended with other communities of dissent in Seoul. Home to more than half the nation's postsecondary educational institutions, Seoul also became the center of student activism. In the mid-1970s the prestigious Seoul National University was removed from the city center to what was then a fairly remote location in the hills south of the Han River and west of the main planned Kangnam development area. While the new campus provided the university with plenty of room to grow, new buildings and facilities, and a peaceful landscape within the bounds of the capital, it is widely believed that the university was moved to reduce the visibility of student protests against the government. Thus, while Seoul worked as an administrative center and performed well as a national economic engine, for the Park administration the urban populace was something of a political liability. Plans to improve rural conditions (to keep the farmers at home) and to disperse industry and the working-class population (as well as students) outside Seoul's city center must be interpreted as in part efforts to defuse one of the strongholds of the political opposition.

But for all this, public plans to limit the growth of Seoul faced an internal bureaucratic obstacle: Seoul's attractiveness to the government and public employees themselves. Government officials and employees were reluctant to exile themselves from the national center of power and culture. The most prestigious schools and universities were in Seoul, and most of the best housing and entertainment was also concentrated in the capital, along with the headquarters of the major corporations. For the government, Seoul was a goose laying golden eggs. Not only did the capital city generate a disproportionate share of the tax revenues collected by the national government, but the very centralization of government and business functions ensured that both leading partners (i.e., the national government and the *chaebŏl*) in South Korea's economic development initiative had easy access to one another, smoothing policy coordination and financing (legitimate and illegitimate). Despite increasing investment of energies in the planning of a new capital city during the 1970s (see Kim and Hwang 1979; Meier 1979), the grand scheme was never realized. Instead, beginning in the 1980s several government functions were moved to the *immedi-ate* periphery of Seoul itself, to Kwach'ŏn (Ra 1986).

These competing interests and concerns left their mark on urban policies for South Korea in general and the capital city in particular. The earlier goal of distributing primary commercial, industrial, and public functions more equitably across the *national* space was scaled down to plans for dispersing Seoul's functions over a wider *metropolitan* region. National development was transformed into Seoul-focused development, and the image of the nation shifted inexorably from the provinces to the capital. Earlier visionary policies for shaping the urban structure and redirecting growth away from Seoul were generally reduced to plans for ensuring the city remained an efficient element in the growing national economy.

To accommodate this economic expansion, new districts were created, leaving Seoul's historical center behind. In the 1970s and 1980s urban development policies focused on the development of diversionary, secondary nodes (Yoido, Yŏngdŭngp'o, Chamsil, and Yŏngdong—all south of the nucleus) within the city limits to reduce the radial flow of traffic, people, and investment to and from the old city center. This was supported with plans to develop satellite cities, bedroom towns, and industrial estates outside the city but within its orbit. To achieve this goal, the associated infrastructure plans included the construction of new bridges across the Han River (in 1966, Seoul had only three road bridges across the Han, but by 1980 there were twelve), three tunnels through Namsan (a small mountain blocking the city center from the southeastern neighborhoods), the widening of major trunk roads and the construction of a citywide subway system. In a sense, as the plans shifted from diffusing development throughout the nation to managing Seoul as the nation's development leader, the city was transformed from a legacy of history to a space of modernity. The improvement of Seoul itself was made into a symbol of the nation's future.

Utilizing a novel approach to fund urban redevelopment,[12] in the 1970s and early 1980s the state-owned Korean Land Development Corporation (KLDC, formerly known as the Korean Land Bank) redesigned and constructed an area of Seoul almost equal in size to the preexisting city. This region, known generally as Kangnam (literally, "south of the [Han] river"), carved out of fields and small towns and suburbs, has been settled by the wealthier strata of Seoulites. The development of Kangnam spawned the neologism "Kangbuk" to refer to those parts of the city *north* of the Han river. The division is seen as a metaphor for history and society. In the catalog accompanying Seoul's official exhibition at the XVIIth Milano Trienniale Exhibition, "World Cities and the Future of the Metropoles," the Seoul metropolitan government offered this image:

> These two districts contrast with each other in many respects and represent extremely different faces of Seoul. In terms of their place in the history of Seoul's urban development, Munan [the area inside the old city walls, the heart of Kangbuk] is the starting point and Kangnam the destination. Conceptually, Munan is the eternal root of Korea and a guarantor of her historical continuity while Kangnam is a symbol of modernization, a new world expressing the desire to be free from historical captivity. . . . If Kangbuk . . . is the thesis, then Kangnam constitute[s] the antithesis.
>
> (Seoul Metropolitan Government 1989:22)

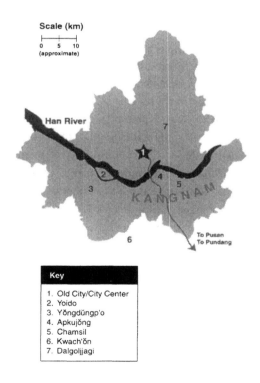

FIGURE 2.1    Seoul: Administrative Boundaries and Selected Neighborhoods

The experience of this construction has had profound effects on both the material and imaginative lives of Seoul residents.

## MAKING MODERN SPACES

Before the new construction began, Seoul was already a proud capital city. The old walls encompassed most of the important political, cultural, and commercial functions. Within a short walk of Seoul's city hall were the National Assembly Building, the U.S., British, and Japanese embassies, the Korean Broadcasting Company, the most important hotels, South Korea's three grand department stores—Lotte, Shinsegye, and Midopa—as well as *Namdaemun sijang*, the bustling, sprawling South Gate Market, and Myŏng-dong, a lively entertainment district. This district was known as Chung-gu, the center point of Seoul. The area drew people from all parts of the city and even from the provinces in search of objects and experiences they could find nowhere else in the country. Yet for all its glamour, Chung-gu was an old district, with tight, winding alleyways, old tile-roofed buildings, and the atmosphere of history underlying the bustling activity.

The task of dispersing essential city functions was undertaken in stages. Before Kangnam, the first major Seoul neighborhood construction project was carried out on the muddy island of Yoido.[13] Yoido was, in a sense, a grand trial run at planning and constructing huge new districts in Seoul. Historically, Yoido had served as a pasture for cows, horses, and sheep. The island was situated near the southern banks of the Han River, about five kilometers southwest of the walls of the old capital. Subject to flooding and offering only sandy soil, it had never been more than sparsely populated. During the Japanese colonial period, the island was made into the city's airstrip, and it continued to be used as Seoul's airport into the 1960s. Not until February of 1971 was the old Yoido airstrip finally closed down. By that time, massive transformations were well underway.

In 1968 Yoido was chosen as the site for the construction of the new National Assembly Building, to replace the center-city government building dating from the Japanese colonial era and considered by many to be "unfit" (Seoul Special City 1985:62) because of its colonial origin.[14] It was also thought to be too old-fashioned a structure for a forward-looking nation; an official city history notes: "It was decided to draw up plans for a National Assembly Building which would eliminate international inferiority" (ibid.:62). Plans were drawn up for the "largest National Assembly Building in Asia";

construction was begun on July 17, 1969, and the Assembly Building was opened in 1975.

The construction of a new, modern seat of government free of the symbolism of colonial heritage was the principal motivation for the construction on Yoido, but the scope of the Yoido master plan was grand, including other government buildings, modern offices, a vast public plaza (asserted to be the largest in East Asia) capable of holding 550,000 people, cultural facilities, and apartments for nearly 9,000 families in high-rise buildings. The construction efforts were gargantuan, and the entire nation was called upon to provide both tangible and intangible support. The establishment of new embankments required the mobilization of heavy construction equipment and trucks from across the country, and operators worked around the clock in three shifts to complete the work before the rainy season started. Yoido's high ground was leveled and the dirt was used to elevate the entire island as a bulwark against the annual flooding. Two new bridges were built; the first opened in spring 1970 and connected Yoido with the northern bank of the Han River and finally provided a direct avenue from the southern factory district of Yŏngdŭngp'o to the city center. Yoido also benefited from new technologies. In contrast to the tangled mess of wires that had only recently brought electricity and telephone service to many buildings in the rest of the city, in Yoido electricity and telephone wires were installed underground to keep the district's sky free of utility poles and lines. One of the earliest residents of the new Yoido remembers what it was like then:

*When I started college, my parents bought one of the first apartments in Yoido. It seems a little silly now, but I remember I thought it was very modern, really special to live in Yoido. You know, at that time they were building the new National Assembly Building, and it seemed as though the whole island was under construction. There was no place like it in Seoul, or anywhere else in Korea. The tall apartments, the wide roads. . . . It was so modern.*

Savvy businesses understood the advantage of locating near by the seat of political power. In addition to the National Assembly Building, Yoido attracted the headquarters of the major broadcasting networks, MBC and KBS (and, in the early 1990s, the new SBS), and many other organizations with interests in keeping a close connection to the government have located there: the Federation of Korean Industries and the Federation of Korean Trade

Unions, for example. The Full Gospel Church, which boasts the largest congregation in the world (500,000 parishioners—10,000 can pray at one time in the chapel [Kim Hyŏng-kuk 1989:107])—is in Yoido. Well into the 1980s Yoido continued to draw major businesses: the Korean Stock Exchange is near the island's center; South Korea's tallest building (for a while it was said to be the tallest in Asia), the Daelim Life Insurance building, a sixty-three-story tower sheathed in copper-mirrored glass, was completed in 1985; and Lucky-Goldstar (now LG) built its chic, new corporate headquarters in Yoido in the late 1980s.

Yoido was portrayed to the nation's people as the modern city center, an alternative to the old center north of the Han River; tourist literature referred to it as "the Manhattan of Korea." For more than a decade, Yoido was the ultimate example both of the accomplishments possible in the present and of the future awaiting the nation. Because the entire island had been erected afresh, there was no lingering sign of colonial oppression or the poverty of farm life or the urban working class. In this transitional period between the old city and the modern metropolis, a few selected symbols were placed in Yoido to recall the nation's history: the Korean War Museum displayed airplanes dating from the Korean War in open air lots across the road from the plaza.

Yoido was still a center of political power in the 1990s, but Yoido's period of broader social preeminence was short-lived. Yoido never displaced the center of the city (particularly Myŏngdong and Chongno) as a mecca for social encounters and shopping. The grand plaza was crowded with families in the summertime, but the unrelieved expanse of asphalt was anything but cheerful. By the time of my fieldwork, Yoido had come to be seen as a rather conservative neighborhood, with aging apartment buildings and few fashionable entertainment spots. In the meantime, the project of making the modern city had moved on to new ground.

After Yoido, Seoul had gone on to direct the construction, in the 1970s and 1980s, of newer districts south of the Han River. These new districts would ultimately nearly equal the size of the previously populated city space. Of the four secondary nodes identified for development in the late 1960s, Yoido and Yŏngdŭngp'o (the latter is perhaps best known for its factories) are on an axis running southwest from the city center; Yŏngdong and Chamsil are on a southeastern axis in the area known as Kangnam.[15] Over time, this southeastern part of southern Seoul acquired a cachet—and a notoriety—unmatched by other neighborhoods. By the 1990s, Kangnam had become the thriving, second Seoul, the New Seoul, the international face of a cosmopolitan South Korea. It was this area that the Seoul metropolitan government described as "a symbol of modernization, a new world expressing the desire to be free from historical captivity" (Seoul Metropolitan Government 1989:22).

Work had begun on developing the land in Yŏngdong and Chamsil between 1968 and 1970, but these projects had proceeded more slowly than Yoido. In contrast to Yoido's political role, these areas were from the beginning targeted for residential and commercial development. Only after 1981, when South Korea won the privilege of hosting both the 1986 Asian Games and the 1988 Olympics, did Kangnam development accelerate. Chamsil was chosen as the site of the Olympic Stadium and the Athlete's Olympic Village, and architects of international renown were hired to design the housing and public spaces for the Olympics. Postmodern architecture made its earliest public appearance in these districts, where large expanses of land were cleared for planned development on a massive scale. Government policies encouraged members of the South Korean upper classes to move to Kangnam: the most prestigious boys' and girls' high schools were moved from central Seoul to Kangnam and high school selection was based on residence in a neighborhood, rather than on an examination. Since high school alumni networks remained important in political and commercial circles, many families moved to Kangnam in order to establish residence in the "right" school district.

Soon new, luxuriously appointed department stores appeared in Kangnam: Hyundai, New Core, a second Lotte, and the Grand, making the department stores in the central city redundant. (In response, Midopa, Lotte, and Shinsegye all underwent renovations to defend their position.) There were more exclusive and wealthier parts of Seoul (Pyŏngch'ang-dong or Yŏnhŭi-dong, for example) but Kangnam, and in particular the neighborhood Apkujŏngdong, quickly became the focal point for aspirations and experiments in affluence. The Hyundai apartments in Apkujŏngdong became the symbol of modern residential luxury. Foreign designer boutiques and foreign-style restaurants, along with the most exclusive South Korean brand names and many of the most famous personalities, clustered together in one unique district. Whereas Yoido lay under the shadow of the National Assembly and was enmeshed in political networks of power, Kangnam was a district built for comfort, entertainment, and consumer pleasure. It was frequently used as the setting for movies, television shows, advertisements, and stories and even nonfiction reports focused disproportionately on the Kang-nam area. Ultimately, while Yoido's existence had had little impact on Chung-gu's preeminence, the development of Kangnam in a real sense displaced the old center of Seoul.

The development of Kangnam transformed the Seoul real estate market as well as the social landscape of the city. According to the 1970s census, the total population in those areas was about 86,000. By 1990 there were 1,524,000 people living in what had become the administrative areas Kangnam-gu, Sŏch'o-gu, and Songp'a-gu.[16] The original landowners were well paid for the sale of their land,[17] and as property prices appreciated, real estate transactions generated increasing profits in the Kangnam area. The district was tainted with a reputation as the home of the nouveaux riches, people who had come into wealth either through various illicit activities or through the sale of land. The latter group were doubly despised, as both beneficiaries of unearned income ( *pullo sodŭk* ) and as unsophisticated farmers.

Kangnam's wealth and distinction attracted admiration as well as envy and criticism. Middle- and upper-income women I interviewed expressed ambivalence about Kangnam, especially Apkujŏngdong. "*Many of my friends live in Apkujŏngdong,*" said one Yoido housewife, "*and my son goes to his after-school program there. The shopping is good, the eighth-district schools are the best, there are some restaurants I like. I like to go there with my husband and our friends to sing at a *noraebang* [the South Korean equivalent of a karaoke room]. But, well, on television I saw a story about the drinking and wild lifestyles of young people there, and I know the atmosphere is perhaps not the best for children. . . . There are so many bars.*" A few women referred to recent stories they had seen in the newspapers about the extramarital affairs of Apkujŏngdong women and about brutal attacks on women in Apkujŏngdong shopping centers.[18] Several Yoido women explained that Apkujŏngdong was attractive, but that they preferred the quiet domesticity of their island neighborhood. Other women mentioned that *other* South Koreans thought Apkujŏngdong was too Westernized and that Kangnam culture encouraged a selfish individualism. When I asked which Seoul neighborhoods were the best and the worst to live in, excluding references to the neighborhoods in which the respondents *currently* lived, Apkujŏngdong topped *both* lists. A few women even included Apkujŏng-dong in both of their *own* lists, and they themselves laughed at the contradiction. Clearly, Apkujŏngdong evoked strong and ambivalent feelings.

In 1992 several writers, cultural observers, and professors collaborated on a project that examined (and, incidentally, fed) the national obsession with Kangnam and Apkujŏngdong in a volume entitled: *Apkujŏngdong: Utopia Dystopia*. The book includes photographs, collage works, interviews with Apkujŏngdong residents, and essays on the importance of Apkujŏngdong as a contemporary symbol. Kang Nae-hŭ, an English professor, wrote:

> What is this "Apkujŏngdong" to us? What is the meaning of "Apkujŏngdong"? Why is our interest so concentrated on "Apkujŏngdong" lately? If we ask these questions, "Apkujŏngdong" the object of study breaks out of that dimension and now surfaces as a phenomenon. . . . Isn't this composition itself proof of this? (Kang 1992:13)

Later in the same volume, anthropology professor Cho Hae-jŏng quotes a college student's sardonic protest:

> In English the word is "scapegoat." In our language it would be translated "sacrificial lamb." Why is it that reports are written as though the degenerate youth who have bathed in the waters of corruption swarm to Apkujŏngdong? Isn't this like a conspiracy to separate Apkujŏngdong from Seoul and, more broadly, from Korea? (Cho 1992:41)

Apkujŏngdong (and Kangnam more generally) brings into focus two of the conflicts inherent in the push to construct a modern, cosmopolitan capital for South Korea. First, the new capital and its iconic new districts, by positioning (South) Korea within the sphere of "modernity," represented a rupture with the nation's Korean history. Built without references to (South) Korea's past, the Kangnam of the present was recruited to stand for the nation's future, but its disarticulation from history left many concerned that the future would be stripped of Koreanness. The foreign influences in Kangnam—the sale of Japanese magazines, the ubiquitous American fast-food restaurants, the clothing boutiques on the street many called "Korea's Rodeo Drive"— attracted a great deal of media criticism. Kangnam was touted as a window on what was to come, but it was also easily seen as auguring social schisms and cultural degeneracy. Second, while for some the new neighborhoods symbolized the nation's power, importance, arrival at the threshold of modernity—this was the positive aspect of South Korea's recent experience—for others, the neighborhoods illuminated the inequitable outcome of the last decades' efforts at economic growth. This posed problems for sustaining the image of *national* bounty. Despite the immense scale of development in Kangnam and the symbolic importance Kangnam culture had taken on, only a small fraction of the South Korean population had come close to achieving a Kangnam lifestyle, and the contrast between the present circumstances in Kangnam and the rest of the country cast doubt on the likelihood that Kangnam represented a communal future.

## DISPLACED AND RE-PLACED IN MODERNIZING SEOUL

During this period of dramatic urban development, while the city and national government directed the construction of the new districts, less affluent Seoulites struggled to find their own place. This was a period of massive inmigration, particularly of young people from the countryside seeking factory jobs. Government agencies and private construction companies were focused on the construction of large-scale, for-sale apartment complexes (nearly all of the apartments were sold as condominiums) and were relatively uninterested in addressing the demand for low-cost housing during the years of expansion. New housing for low-income Seoul residents was generally on a small scale and privately built; some pioneers erected their own homes on hillsides and along canals and rail lines all over the city. The many permitless homes that sprouted on public land near the city center were the most irksome to the policymakers, who wished at least that the city core would have an orderly look. By 1970 there were an estimated 200,000 unauthorized houses in Seoul (Seoul Metropolitan Government 1992:127).

In an attempt to restore urban order, the government experimented with removing squatters to suburban developments; the largest of these was in Kwangju-gun, now Sŏngnam city—ironically, the site of the popular new town of the 1990s, Pundang. "Citizen" housing for low-income families was also built in Kuro, Map'o, Hyohŏn, Chŏngnung, Kŭmhwa as well as in several other peripheral sites, but this policy was eventually found to be a failure. People had come to Seoul to find work, and if the jobs were in the city, then the people would return there. Moreover, the disastrous collapse of one apartment building to which squatters had been resettled and fires in other neighborhoods brought unwanted attention and criticism to the removal programs in the late 1960s and early 1970s.

The construction of the new "modern" apartment districts was in some cases directly linked to the destruction of low-cost housing. Yoido and Kang-nam had been chosen as early development sites in part because they were sparsely populated areas: an airstrip, grazing land, farming villages south of the Han River. Elsewhere in Seoul, however, the process of constructing monumental new neighborhoods—Map'o, Mokdong, and later Sanggye and Sŏch'o, for example—as well as the construction of new subway lines involved removing from the path of the supercranes and swirling cement mixers existing communities that had evolved in the decades of unruly immigration into Seoul. Many neighborhoods were simply bulldozed if they were found to be in the way of progress; aerial surveillance was used to monitor neighborhoods in order to identify and target illegal housing as it appeared.

Although one could say in general that neglect, removal, and destruction characterized Seoul city's low-cost housing policies, the city did make some effort during this period to improve affordable housing. By 1969, the government had organized the construction of 2,000 buildings of "citizens" apartments for low-income households and the "improvement" (chŏngbiha-da) of another 133,000 dilapidated housing units; nevertheless, the "housing deficit" (the percentage of households without their own housing) was still calculated to be 38.9 percent (Yang 1991:17). The Economic Planning Board calculated the housing shortage in Seoul to be even higher: 45.5 percent in 1970 (cited in Mills and Song 1979:119). Households without their own units were presumed either to be squatters or to be sharing a single unit with other households. The failure of the programs of the 1960s spurred the passing of new laws to facilitate faster and more thorough urban redevelopment, particularly the Law on Transitory Measures on Expedition of Housing Improvement (1973) and the Law on Urban Renewal (1976). The U.S. Agency for International Development lent money to help fund the redevelopment of 232 districts, and by 1981, according to the ten-year construction plan, 140,000 buildings of substandard (pullyang) housing were to be improved. This proved a Sisyphean task: between 1973 and 1978 20,929 buildings were removed or improved, but sufficient replacement housing for low-income families was not constructed. The problem was intrinsic to the strategy: often, resettled families could not afford the new domiciles.[19] In the Ayŏn-2 development, for example, of those who did receive rights to new housing, more than 20 percent had no choice but to resell those rights because they needed the capital that was tied up in the future housing rights to secure housing in the present—and those families were thrown back onto the housing market (Yang 1991:18).

Although these policies failed in the sense that they did not result in sufficient affordable housing for low-income Seoulites, redevelopment did result in the reshaping of the residential landscape by pushing dilapidated and informal structures from view. By 1982, it was obvious that even the energetic removal programs of the 1970s had been futile. In the ten previous years 91,604 substandard housing units had been removed, while 79,693 permitless units had sprung up to replace them (Yang 1991:18); nevertheless, with each new apartment development project, displaced lower-income households were forced to retreat further from the space of consciousness of other city residents.

The government steadfastly presented the redevelopment aspect of its urban development plan as a program of "modernization." A 1979 publication of the Seoul metropolitan government included photos of Yŏnhŭi-dong and Donam-dong "Hillside Restoration" projects. The "before" picture shows a community of hundreds of small houses, while the "after" shows only stubby bushes and trees. The Siyoung Apartments and Housing Development (location unspecified) and the Yoido Apartments are touted as typical "modern" places to live (Seoul Metropolitan Government 1979), in an implied contrast to the single-story *hanok* structures that still housed the majority of Seoulites. Three years later, describing its approach to redevelopment, the Seoul government disingenuously stated that "as city planning is being pursued lately in a way that takes into account citizens' views to the most possible extent, housing improvement programs are also implemented very careful[ly] lest they should jeopardize the interests of citizens involved" (Seoul Metropolitan Administration 1982:52). The Seoul metropolitan administration expressed its perspective in this way:

The objective of redevelopment programs is:

 1) to, increase the economic efficiency of the city function
    through maximum utilization of land;
 2) to ensure proper urban function by integrating disorderly and
    scattered city functions into a concentric multiple type;
 3) to solve the shortage of public facilities such as roads, parks,
    and parking lots;

4) to create cheerful and efficient urban surroundings through the improvement of superannuated buildings and securing of sufficient open spaces;

5) to prepare against fire and other urban disasters by easing the excessive concentration of buildings;

6) to improve shabby dwellings and other living facilities; and

7) to prepare for the 1988 Olympics and envision the future image of Seoul through 2001.

(Seoul Metropolitan Administration 1982:51; English and punctuation original).

Like burgeoning cities around the world, Seoul struggled to modernize city housing. But commercial interests saw little profit in building new housing for poor immigrants, and the government had neither sufficient funds to establish good public housing (which, in any case, was feared to encourage further immigration) nor did it deploy the funds it did have in that sector. As a result, even a city with aspirations to planned order, such as Seoul, suffered squatter settlements. In Seoul, squatter districts came to be known as *taltongne* ("moon neighborhoods") because some of the few sites left where poor people found they could build homes were on the slopes of the many hills in the city that were too steep for most larger-scale construction—the settlements were said to be almost high enough to touch the moon. Most of these neighborhoods sprang up without the official permits that would bring amenities (publicly serviced toilets, piped water and electricity, and some security of title).

Like the curb market, which offered an outlet for the populace's financing needs unmet by the *chaebŏl*-focused formal sector but which, being technically illegal, existed only so long as the government considered it useful for its interests, the *taltongne* were tolerated by the government because commercial construction companies had distorted the housing market and left poor households with few alternatives. The superior return on investment that larger apartment units provided developers attracted construction money to projects focused on apartments of more than 30 *p'yŏng*[20] (approximately 1,000 square feet). Even government programs to provide apartments to low-income households offered units that were around 15 *p'yŏng*, significantly larger than the average size of a home in Talgoljjagi. Most Talgoljjagi homes I saw were less than 8 *p'yŏng*. Therefore, *taltongne* bridged the gap between official urban development policy and the citizens' needs.

For many low-income families the *taltongne*, despite the poor living conditions, offered almost the only refuge from the brutal price increases the real estate market experienced in the late 1980s. The very lack of legal permission of many *taltongne* homes played a part in the endurance of some settlements while the rest of the city was in redevelopment turmoil: speculative investment in untitled property was too risky for many real estate buyers even in the overheated land market of the 1980s, since there would be no guarantee that the city would not simply reclaim the property for its own benefit.[21] On the other hand, this also meant that while real estate owners in Seoul were reaping enormous capital gains elsewhere in the city, low-income owners of untitled *taltongne* property could command only limited prices for the sale of their homes. Moreover, by far the majority of low-income Seoul residents rented their homes, and they suffered disproportionately as the real estate market heated up. The destruction of existing small units according to urban redevelopment policy and their replacement with units that were more expensive because they were both newer and larger placed ever greater pressure on the lowest end of the official housing market. Between 1987 and 1991, the rental rates for the smallest housing units increased significantly more than those for larger units (Korea Housing Bank 1991). These factors held *taltongne* residents in place; for even if *taltongne* homeowners sold their property, their profits would not be sufficient to buy a home elsewhere in the city, and most *taltongne* renters could only move within the confined circuit of *taltongne* rental options.

## FINANCE AND SPACE: MOBILITY AND THE REAL ESTATE MARKET

By the end of the 1980s, Seoul had been reshaped and the population redistributed by urban policies and construction programs. New districts housed middle and upper-middle classes in modern, multistoried apartment complexes, while low-income households had been shunted to the city's periphery or clung to the city's hillsides in ramshackle neighborhoods. Between 1975 and 1985 Seoul neighborhoods became markedly more homogeneous in terms of class (Hong 1992). Through an analysis of census data, Doo-Seung Hong traced the migration of the middle class south of the river, and in particular he notes that "the middle-class households with higher education form a class group around apartment complexes" (ibid.:80), which he associates with a tendency to "protect themselves from the intrusion of lower classes[,] pursuing homogeneity in the process of housing purchase as well as in daily life" (ibid.:81).

The real estate market is both a result of this increasing class segregation in the city and is also a major factor in its persistence. Urban planners were not the only policymakers who affected the real estate market, however; financial policymakers played an important role in the reshaping of Seoul. The complex connections between industrial finance and the housing market is another important piece of Seoul's story and is a crucial backdrop to the story of South Korea's consumer development.

Ever since the truce in the 1950–53 war, real estate had been one of the investments with the highest returns in the South Korean economy. The real estate sector attracted investment capital from private individuals as well as from business investors, including the *chaebŏl*. Between 1970 and 1985, for example, consumer prices increased by 635 percent and wages and salaries[22] increased by 1,248 percent, but land prices increased by an astonishing 1,585 percent over their original value (Korea Housing Bank 1988). Between 1983 and 1988 the average annual increase for land prices was 14.7 percent, with a significant acceleration in the late 1980s (Korea Housing Bank 1990). Housing prices in particular more than doubled between 1985 and 1990, increasing by an average of 137 percent (ibid.). For those who owned property, these price increases were a windfall; for those who had not yet bought into the real estate market, it was like running alongside a train as it pulls away from the station.

Although rising housing prices had attracted attention throughout the 1960s and 1970s, public anxiety about real estate prices grew so intense in the last years of the 1980s and the early 1990s that it began to overshadow other public concerns. Newspapers carried stories of tenants who had committed suicide because they could not meet their landlords' requests for rent increases; labor unions demanded housing support in addition to and, occasionally, instead of wage hikes. The state renounced its vows (made initially in the hope of discouraging metropolitan concentration) not to construct any more new cities in the Seoul vicinity and instead announced in 1987 the plan to build two million units of new housing in five new cities ringing the capital.

The preferential allocation of financing to the *chaebŏl*, ostensibly for industrial development, had particular effects on the housing sector in South Korea. As we shall see below, South Korea's unusual rental housing market developed alongside constraints on housing finance; these constraints were also elements in the widening gap between rich and poor.

According to the 1985 census, there was a total of 2.3 million households in Seoul; 40 percent of these were owner-occupiers and 55 percent were tenant households.[23] The rental market in South Korea was itself composed of several rental payment arrangements. The majority (65 percent) of the renter households (or 36 percent of Seoul's total households) paid for their housing through the *chŏnse* system, a form of rental payment that is presumed to have evolved after liberation from Japanese rule, in a period of underdeveloped formal finance and rising pressure on the housing market (see Renaud 1993). *Chŏnse* differed in several important ways from more common monthly rental payment arrangements elsewhere in the world.

Typically, *chŏnse* arrangements required the payment of a lump sum deposit to the landlords in lieu of rent; the entire sum would be returned when the tenant household moved out. The amount of the *chŏnse* deposit was a significant sum; the average *chŏnse* deposit ranged from 30 percent to 70 percent of the *purchase* value of the housing unit.[24] Housing costs under the *chŏnse* system were understood to be the tenant household's forfeited investment income associated with the deposit. The imputed rent could be calculated by multiplying the amount of the *chŏnse* deposit by a monthly interest rate; the average interest rate in the late 1980s was 2 percent per month, approximately the rate of interest on the curb market. Rent increases were taken in the form of additions to the amount of the deposit, customarily demanded yearly.

Although there were other forms of rental payment, within the rental housing market, *chŏnse* predominated, and it could be found among almost all income ranges and in all types of housing. Renters I spoke with gave several reasons for preferring *chŏnse* to *wŏlse* (monthly rental payment)[25]: because the payment was made once a year, *chŏnse* reduced the amount of contact one must have with one's landlord around rental payments; *chŏnse* had a higher prestige than other forms of rental, perhaps originally because it demonstrated the ability to save; for households with irregular income, *chŏnse* allowed a longer period to accumulate money for rent so that if in one month the household could not put much money away for housing, the shortfall could be made up the next month without the awkwardness of asking the landlord for permission to wait for payment. Most important, however, tenants perceived *chŏnse* as a *savings* system: in contrast to "throwing away money every month," *chŏnse* renters received their money back at the end of their stay. Preference for *chŏnse* over *wŏlse* rental was unanimous. Chŏng-hae, a resident of Talgoljjagi, explained:

> *When we first moved to Talgoljjagi, we were in a *wŏlse* room. It wasn't expensive, and it was easy to make the payments, so I didn't think of moving to a *chŏnse* room. But my (older) friends (*ŏnni*) told me that *chŏnse* was better because you didn't end up just giving money to the landlord every month, and that eventually you'd have enough money to buy a house. That was true.*

Chŏng-hae was fortunate; she and her husband purchased a two-room home in 1988, just before real estate prices took a sharp turn upward. Her progress toward homeownership was a nearly ideal case. She and her husband started out their life together in a *wŏlse* room, paying 35,000 *wŏn* each month with a 30,000 *wŏn* security deposit. She quit her job because of a difficult pregnancy and moved to another *wŏlse* room with a 50,000 *wŏn* deposit but only 20,000 *wŏn* monthly payments. Two years later she was ready to return to regular work (in a small clothing factory), and shortly after that the family moved to their first *chŏnse* room, at 250,000 *wŏn*. The landlord raised the deposit twice in the three years they stayed; in the end it amounted to 350,000 *wŏn*. They progressed over the next four years to a place with a 2,000,000 *wŏn chŏnse* deposit, then a 4,500,000 *wŏn chŏnse* house. The family was dedicated to saving money and strategic moving. Finally, in 1988, they bought a 20,000,000 *wŏn* four-room home. Chŏng-hae credits her husband's dislike of drinking and the fact that they could have only one child with helping them reach their goal of homeownership.

For others, however, the hope of building their *chŏnse* deposit into a sum large enough to purchase a home was an increasingly unlikely aspiration. Another Talgoljjagi resident, Youngwŏn's Mother,[26] had recently moved with her husband and two young children into a sunny place with one very large room (about 11 feet by 18 feet) and a good-sized, sheltered outdoor platform. Her total *chŏnse* deposit amounted to 10,000,000 *wŏn*, but most of it (about 7,000,000 *wŏn*) was borrowed from her parents. She said that she needed to save 400,000 *wŏn* each month just to stay where she was: 250,000 *wŏn* in anticipation of the next rental increase, and 150,000 *wŏn* to repay her parents. Youngwŏn's Mother's household income was only 800,000 *wŏn*. She acknowledged that if she hoped to save to buy a home, she'd have to find another 200,000 *wŏn* each month to put away for that goal.

In Talgoljjagi those who were able to save money to add to their *chŏnse* deposits rarely added enough to outpace the rate of real estate price increases; in recent years, households needed to dedicate an increasing percentage of their income to saving for *chŏnse* rental hikes. Some had been unable to save enough to meet their landlord's demands for additions to their *chŏnse* deposit; they were forced to move to down-market housing for the same money.

In the late 1980s *chŏnse* deposits were increasing at a fantastic rate; a study of *chŏnse* deposits in Seoul comparing February 1989 to February 1990 showed an increase in *one year* of 26.7 percent (Kim 1990). Other statistics showed that *chŏnse* rates were increasing faster for smaller units and for lower-priced units (as the supply of these small units shrank to less than 15 percent of the housing stock by the 1980s [Kim 1993:272]), placing an especially great burden on the poorest households. This was also a time of rapidly increasing wages, but between 1988 and 1990 average wages rose a total of 35 percent,[27] falling behind the pace of *chŏnse* rate increases. Many people in Talgoljjagi found that despite more take-home pay, when their landlords demanded impossible additions to the *chŏnse* deposit, they had to borrow money from their relatives, friends, or moneylenders, adding the drag of debt at high rates of interest to their financial burdens, or find cheaper accommodations elsewhere.

In fact, despite the preference people expressed for the *chŏnse* system, *chŏnse* in reality had several disadvantages for renters when compared to a more conventional monthly rental option. Tenant households had to accumulate a large sum of money (often more than their annual income) before occupying their home (Renaud 1993:317). *Chŏnse* renters were also subject to a certain amount of risk: although there were laws on the books meant to ensure that the tenant would receive his or her deposit back at the end of the contract term, if the landlord had made a poor investment choice or if (for some reason) the landlord was unable or unwilling to have a new tenant move in, the landlord might not have access to the cash needed to repay the tenant's "loan." Most important, perhaps, the *chŏnse* system took the asset-appreciation element of homeownership and turned it *against* the tenant household aspiring to homeownership: when the real estate market heated up, the situation *worsened* for tenants, whether they hoped to buy a house or not.

The popular viewpoint that *chŏnse* was a savings plan was deeply puzzling. Sophisticated understanding of interest rates and loan risk was widespread in Seoul, across all generations and income classes. Nearly everyone I spoke with knew the current rate of interest on the curb market, and most women I asked were able to explain to me the arcane system of determining each member's contribution to the pot in a *kye* (rotating credit association)—calculations that involved complex manipulations of the time value of money and risk and return.[28] Yet few *chŏnse* renters mentioned the potential interest income they had to forgo by not investing their savings in, say, the curb market. Nor did many *chŏnse* renters mention the widening gap between the value of money and the price of real estate. It appears that the moral appeal of homeownership in some way may have overshadowed the purely economic calculation of homeownership as an investment and *chŏnse* as the only viable path to purchasing a home.

From the landlord's perspective, conversely, the *chŏnse* system was a superior form of rent collection. The landlord had the entire rent in hand at the time the tenant moved in; the landlord did not have to worry about whether the rent would be paid on time (or at all) in any particular month. In theory, the landlord functioned as an intermediary between the tenant and the curb market: imagine that the landlord invested the *chŏnse* in the curb market, returning the interest earnings to the tenants, who turned them back over to the landlord as rent. In fact, however, landlord households used the deposits in a variety of ways. I knew of landlords who had funded their children's education through *chŏnse* collections, and landlords who used the *chŏnse* to pay the costs associated with marrying off an adult child. And, with little formal financing available for home purchases, many landlords included the tenants' *chŏnse* deposit in their own home-purchasing strategy.

For example, when Chŏng-hae bought her Talgoljjagi home in 1988, the price was 20,000,000 *wŏn*, paid in full at the time of sale. Her family had 4,500,000 *wŏn chŏnse* deposit due her from the landlord of the home they were then occupying. Over the year, they had managed to save 600,000 *wŏn*. Chŏng-hae participated in a *kye*, which brought in another 500,000, and they were able to borrow about 3,000,000 *wŏn*, split between loans from their families and those taken out at high rates of interest through informal moneylenders. They had also arranged to rent one of their two rooms to a newlywed couple for a 5,400,000 *wŏn chŏnse* deposit. *Chŏnse* deposits, therefore, were critical in enabling Chŏng-hae and her family to purchase their home; they used their own returned *chŏnse* deposit as well as the one they collected from their tenants.

In fact, it was *this* use of *chŏnse* money that largely accounted for its popularity in the housing market. World Bank economist Bertrand Renaud has written that "the *chŏnse* system represents a very creative response of the household and unincorporated sectors to the inability of financial institutions to provide them with adequate services under rapid urbanization, inflation, negative real bank deposit rates, and the rigid rationing of bank loans" (Renaud 1989:11). Given the restricted access to capital in the housing sector (Park 1984; Renaud 1988 and 1989; Woo 1991; Kim 1987, cited in Renaud), the *chŏnse* system served an important role in greasing the wheels of the housing market. In 1980, for example, the total value of *chŏnse* contracts was 5.5 times that of formal housing loans, and as late as in 1986 the volume of *chŏnse* funds remained five to six times the volume of mortgages at the Korea Housing Bank (Renaud 1989:23).[29] Through the early 1990s the National Housing Fund remained the principal *formal* lending source for individuals purchasing new homes; however, with low loan ceilings and strict limits on the age and size of the housing unit to be purchased,[30] formal housing loans were relatively unhelpful and hard to come by. Households were forced to combine several sources of funds to buy a home (as Chŏng-hae had done). A 1986 survey of homebuyers conducted by the Korean Research Institute on Human Settlements showed that returned *chŏnse* deposits contributed significantly to home purchases (ranging from 13 percent to 26.3 percent of the purchase price, except among buyers in the uppermost income range) and that returned *chŏnse* deposits were more important to first-time buyers and low-income buyers. In addition, tenants' *chŏnse* deposits contributed between 1.7 percent and 7.1 percent of the price (KRIHS 1986, summarized in Renaud 1989). While many of the sources of funds required relatively quick repayment, deposits collected from tenants in a sense substituted for long-term housing loans, such as mortgages, because as long as the landlord could replace the tenant with a new renting family, the landlord need not actually think of repaying the loan.

In fact, this use of tenants' *chŏnse* money was in many ways a favorable alternative to formal *mortgage* financing for home buyers. Because of the tight housing market and low vacancy rates in Seoul, as long as the landlord household continued to rent, they had access to a lump sum of money that increased annually at a favorable rate (whether the money was invested in the property or on the curb market). In a sense, the use of tenants' *chŏnse* as home funding allowed the landlord family to make current economic use of the appreciation of the property value, to double-dip, so to speak.

During the 1980s, and in particular between 1988 and 1991, rising housing prices and the *chŏnse* system drove a wedge between these two categories of households: homeowners and renters. Those families who had not yet purchased a home saw their dream fade into the distance, while home-owning households, on the other hand, had the option of *increasing* their wealth advantage by renting out rooms or their entire house to *chŏnse* tenants and purchasing a new home for themselves. Households for whom homeownership was still an aspiration watched their savings and earning power decline relative to the increases in home purchase prices.

Low-income households suffered one further disadvantage in the South Korean housing market. Many of the newly constructed apartments were sold on a lottery basis. Prospective buyers would make deposits into a dedicated housing bank account in order to establish their eligibility for the lottery. When the apartments were finally put on the market, depositors would have a chance of having their name drawn, which would give them the opportunity to purchase the unit. While the amounts of the qualifying deposits were modest (a few million *wŏn*) relative to the cost of the housing units themselves (generally well over a hundred million *wŏn*), few low-income families could afford to put aside such sums for a few years in the hope of gaining the opportunity to buy an apartment. For those who could afford it, however, the housing lottery offered the promise of windfall profits as the prices of lottery apartments tended to appreciate quickly.

Writing in "*Kyŏngje Chŏngŭi*" (Economic justice), the journal of *Kyŏngsillyŏn* (the Citizen's Coalition for Economic Justice, CCEJ, one of the largest progressive citizen's movement groups formed after national democratization in 1987), a self-described housewife rehearsed her family's realization that they would not soon acquire an apartment:

> The dream of our four-person family is to live in a small apartment (*yŏlse p'yŏngjjari ap'at'ŭ*). It has already been six years that we have been living in the same 3-*p'yŏng* basement apartment with one sunless window. We thought that if we just bear it a little longer and endure (*chogŭm man ch'amgo kyŏndimyŏn*), the two of us, husband and wife, could earn enough to prepare one small house, but as the children are gradually growing, the cost of living is becoming unbearable. . . . Now our only hope is the housing application savings passbook. By tightening our belts, every month we can deposit 100,000 *wŏn*, and now we have done that fifteen times. But when I read the paper, I realize that I must give up that dream, too: There are more than 1,000,000 application subscribers, some of whom have been waiting eight years.

(I 1990:72)

At the same time, she witnessed how her landlord was able to benefit from the same housing policies that shut her family out. "Our landlord had one housing application savings passbook in his son's name through which he was able to buy one apartment, and he then made another housing application deposit. One person has ten housing units" (ibid.).

This process was evident in the contrast between households in Talgolj-jagi and in Yoido. All the households I spoke with in Yoido owned their apartments. A few admitted to owning others.[31] The management of the apartment complex reported that out of 744 families in the complex, 80 were *chŏnse* tenants. One of the families I knew well moved away from Yoido shortly after I completed my fieldwork; through the lottery they had gained the opportunity to purchase an apartment in Pundang (one of the new towns constructed on Seoul's outskirts in the early 1990s), and they were going to rent out their Yoido apartment. They were able to purchase the Pundang apartment using a combination of savings, a loan from the wife's parents, and the *chŏnse* from the household who were taking over the Yoido apartment. Chang-su's Mother, a housewife, spoke frankly about her ambivalence toward the upcoming transition:

*It isn't easy to move, but in some ways it will be more convenient. I'll miss my friends, and so will the boys. . . . But Pundang is not really any further from Kangnam than Yoido is, and in fact my husband will probably get to work even faster. I'm a little worried about the schools, at least for the first years, but we can make sure the boys will get the best extracurricular education. When we first considered investing in Pundang, I didn't really imagine moving, but it seems like an opportunity we can't let pass us by. There is nothing like real estate, and we'll have the *chŏnse* tenants here. And people say the air is cleaner, and our new apartment has a view of the mountains.*

By moving to Pundang, Chang-su's Mother hoped her family would be making a smart investment in new property while maintaining a valuable investment in an established Seoul neighborhood. Chang-su's Mother told me that she had set the *chŏnse* rate for the incoming tenants according to the advice of a local realtor. "*It's established. Everyone agrees as to what the correct *chŏnse* rate is.*" In 1992, that was 110,000,000 *wŏn* (approximately U.S.$145,000) for their three-bedroom apartment in Yoido. This was almost half the purchase price of their larger Pundang apartment.

The South Korean system of housing rental and finance, combined as it was with urban policies to develop the capital according to a vast, modernizing plan and situated in the context of a financing system favoring the *chaebŏl* and the project of industrialization at the expense of small-scale borrowers became one of the main mechanisms by which class differences were expressed and exacerbated in South Korea in the 1980s. In later chapters, I will look at how, in public discourse, the real estate market was tied in two ways to perceived "problems" of excessive consumption. Real estate speculation was seen as the principal source of "unearned income," which, it was said, led to self-indulgent patterns of spending. The high housing prices, on the other hand, were thought to have reached a point at which people were discouraged from long-term savings for the goal of home purchase; this despair, too, was believed to lead to present-oriented consumption.

## SPECIAL PLACES: NEIGHBORHOODS, MEMORIES, MOVEMENT

Of course, Seoul is more than a product of planner's pens or a patchwork of real estate properties; it is where ten million people live their lives, locate their memories, and imagine their futures. Seoul's native-born children must travel to the countryside and encounter as tourists their nation's historic monuments, crowded mountains, ski lodges, beaches, and rice fields or the burial mounds of their ancestors—just like those they've seen in textbooks and on television. For them, the countryside and its "traditional Korean" lifestyle is far from home. In contrast, most adults living in Seoul in the early 1990s came to Seoul from smaller settlements: a village, a town, or one of the secondary or tertiary cities.[32]

Fiction writer Pak Wan-sŏ captured the moment of awe and disappointment her narrator, a little girl, felt upon coming to Seoul for the first time, late in the colonial period, from her countryside home:

> The steep winding road was as dirty, complicated, and endless as an animal's entrails. . . . It was a strange neighborhood. Houses small as country outhouses were crowded together in a haphazard way. . . . It was dirty and messy. The paths between the houses wouldn't look as they did, if they had been planned beforehand. The paths were what people who had given up improving the conditions of their tossed-together boxes had reluctantly made to fetch and carry food. . . .

"Is this Seoul?" I asked in a reproaching voice.

(Pak Wan-sŏ 1991:192)

In Pak's story, Seoul plays a dual role as both the space of Korean hoped-for modernity and the squalid terminus collecting Koreans who have left their "proper" homes in the countryside, whether lured by temptation or forced by hunger. Many of the adults I spoke with shared their own memories of their first arrival in Seoul, often echoing this initial disappointment. Yuchung's Mother, a woman in her early thirties, spoke about her childhood as she cooked lunch for us and her two toddlers on a small two-burner portable stove in her one-room Talgoljjagi home:

> *My parents left me and my older sisters with my grandmother in the countryside [in South Chŏlla province] when I was four. I was eleven when they brought us to join them in Seoul. Our first house was on Namsan.[33] I remember from the lane behind the house I could see the river and the mountains—the view was really beautiful. Sometimes I pretended I could see all the way south to my grandmother's house when I was homesick. We were living in a little place, a Korean-style house, with two rooms. It was my family, my mother and father, my two older sisters, my younger sister, and my two younger brothers and my-self. We were all in one room. My father's cousin's family were in the other room—it was his house. Looking back, I'm sure now it must have been very crowded, but I was so happy to be with my mother again I have only happy memories. Of course, sometimes there were fights, but that's natural. We were there about two years, and then we moved to a rented house with two rooms in Sinsŏldong, just past Dongdaemun. It was much more convenient—my sister and I were working in factories in Ch'onggyech'on then—but I didn't know the neighbors, and it did-n't have a view at all. I moved out on my own soon after that.*

Other women came as wives. Suni invited me over to share a cup of instant coffee. Her husband brought in more money selling fuel than many Talgoljja-gi men, so Suni seldom had to work and could spend time with me when other women were occupied with piecework. She told me about her arrival in 1975:

> *I had never seen Seoul until the week after the wedding ceremony. I was excited about moving to the big city, after living all my life in the

countryside, but when we arrived at the bus terminal, I remember feeling so terrified and sad. We took two buses to get to the neighborhood, and although many people greeted my husband as we walked up the hill, I was not happy to be surrounded by strangers and city dirt. Fortunately, there are a lot of people here with the same history, and a few from the same province, and in the end I have made a lot of friends.*

In Yoido, many of the women came to Seoul to study. For many, the move to Seoul involved the whole family, while others came alone, mostly for college but some as early as middle school. Mi-ran, now a freelance English tutor and the wife of a wealthy manufacturer, moved to Seoul by herself in the early 1970s.

*I moved to Seoul from Inch'on for high school. I was a good student: I was usually first in my class. I took my studying very seriously, and I was proud when I passed the examination and moved to Seoul for high school. I stayed with my father's cousin, a college student, in a student boarding house in Yŏngdŭngp'o. I remember I missed my family, and that made me feel very young and lonely, even though at the same time it felt very grown up to be a student in Seoul. My younger sister moved to Seoul the same year I started college, and we rented three rooms in Ich'on to share with a cousin who was also in high school and an *ajuma* ["auntie"], a distant relative of my fathers', who watched out for us and cooked. I lived there until I was married and we moved to Yoido.*

Most of the people I spoke with had *made* a home of Seoul. This home-making was an integral part of their sense of themselves as (South) Koreans. The age at which they had arrived, the frequency of return trips to their old hometowns, the degree of difference between their hometown situation and that in Seoul as well as a myriad of other, personal details affected the extent to which any one of the "newcomers" felt uprooted. Some expressed nostalgia for what they had left behind; some were nostalgic for an imagined countryside life they had never themselves lived or had experienced only as small children. The stories of their own coming of age coincided with their coming to Seoul, and their different abilities to master the city's space shaped their sense of life success.

In order better to understand how people experienced the city, I asked people to fill in a travel journal for the previous day, noting exactly where they had gone, with whom, by what mode of transportation, how long they had been there, and what the purpose of that journey was.[34] I have thirty-eight of these travel accounts, twenty-five from women in Yoido and twelve from women in Talgoljjagi.

These travel journals showed a clear difference between the women I spoke with in Talgoljjagi and those in Yoido. The Talgoljjagi women did not leave their immediate locale, and most went to only one or two places during the day (the local market, the local play area, etc.)—many were at home most of the day engaged in sewing or other cottage industry production tasks. The Yoido respondents, on the other hand, popped in and out of their homes to the shops, to the bank, to a lunch date with a friend, to chauffeur their children around the town, to the tennis courts, swimming pool, health club, classes—one even went with her mother on a drive to the countryside to view the maples. Although only half the Yoido women left the confines of the island itself, nearly all of them made use of their car during the day.

The Yoido women also had a more developed *sense* of the city and their place in it. In structured interviews I supplied an abstract map of the city of Seoul and asked people to identify five places of personal significance.[35] I would answer direct questions about where specific places would be, but I tried not to volunteer many features myself.[36] Most people were somewhat puzzled by the meaning of the request. I was asked, "Do you mean places I often go to?" and "Do you mean places I think are important to our nation?" I emphasized that I thought each person should decide for herself[37] how she would define "significant," but that it could encompass places of personal, emotional importance, symbolic, civic, cultural, or historical importance or useful, well-frequented places. Few of the women could easily think of more than three places, but only a small number gave up before marking five *X*s on the page.

Every respondent marked her own home; most did this first. Other choices were, in order of frequency: shopping places; the location of an alma mater (high school or college); a former home; sightseeing or walking areas (usually city parks or palace grounds); the home of the woman's own parents (*ch'in chǒng chip*); her husband's worksite; the home of her parents-in-law, friends' homes, or art or cultural centers; the homes of grown children and government buildings; and (with only two women choosing each) a place of worship, a favorite restaurant, or the woman's own worksite. Some women marked and named specific sites (houses, stores, museums), while others chose neighborhoods or districts and told me what kinds of things they did there. Often, the places the women selected were places of nostalgic significance, places they used to stroll in during their school years, the neighborhood where they first lived after marriage, a childhood home. One woman drew a small circle around Chamsil, where the Olympic stadium stands, and wrote in English, "I was a volunteer at Seoul Olympic." Only two women marked on their maps places where they themselves worked to earn money, now or in the past.

I had expected a distinct class-associated difference in the *kind* of places the women would mark, reflecting differences in their daily responsibilities.[38] The maps, however, revealed more similarities than differences in this regard, and more than half the maps had shopping destinations clearly marked. Class distinctions in the type and specific location of shopping places were evident, with the large and small *sijang* (marketplaces) predominant among the women less well off, and Lotte, Shinsegye, New Core (all famous department stores) and Myŏngdong and Apkujŏngdong (expensive shopping districts) the shopping destinations of choice among the wealthy women. Friends' houses were more important to more of the women than I had expected, while the opposite was true of in-laws' homes. And fully one-third of the women felt that neighborhoods they once lived in but had left behind in Seoul were significant.[39] I also had not expected the *un*importance attached to places of work and to places of worship.

While women of both classes selected similar kinds of places, the wealthier women chose a more diverse array of sites, and some of the sites they chose were distinctive to their class. For example, the area south of the Han River, particularly Kangnam district, held significance for all the wealthier women, whereas none of the less wealthy Talgoljjagi women marked any locations south of the Han River. Several of the Talgoljjagi women marked only locations within a few kilometers of their home, and very few marked spots of *current* importance that were far from Talgoljjagi. In contrast, the wealthier women marked scattered *X*s in different neighborhoods, some reflecting personal history and some indicating present responsibilities.

Together, these two exercises revealed critical differences between the women I spoke with in Yoido and those in Talgoljjagi in their relationship to the city.[40] In Talgoljjagi most of the women I encountered worked at home during the day doing various kinds of piecework (assembling umbrellas, sewing beaded trim onto angora sweaters, stitching the shoulder seams on a

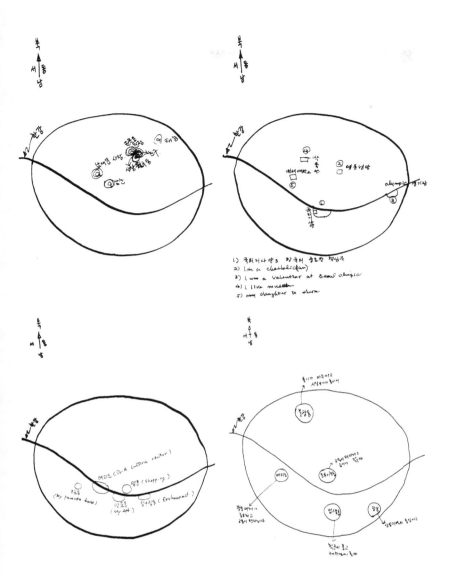

FIGURE 2.2 Personal Maps of Seoul (Four Examples)

pile of polo shirts), or they did similar tasks in small, local workshops. Some others cooked in the cafeteria of the women's college at the bottom of the hill; a few got occasional work with the progressive church, drying grains in the sun on the church's flat rooftop. Their jobs tied them to a place. Those who did move about the city (usually to visit family or to shop at Namdaemun Market) did so by the cheapest modes of public transportation: bus or subway, and often without the comfort of a seat. Women in Yoido displayed both greater mobility and a greater sense of command of the city space.

It is not, therefore, surprising that when I asked women which neighborhoods were best to live in, upper-income women answered with a sure response (or sometimes two or three), citing neighborhoods with cleaner air, smoother traffic, superior schools backed up with reasons that demonstrated previous consideration. In Talgoljjagi, on the other hand, no one I spoke with entertained real dreams of moving to a better neighborhood. Their immobility was both a daily condition and a limitation of their dreams.[41]

Women in Yoido and Talgoljjagi were ignorant, in different ways, of the lives their counterparts were conducting. Several Talgoljjagi women knew very little about other areas of the city. One day, an acquaintance told me she needed to go to the Noryangjin fish market to meet a relative but she didn't know how to get there. I told her it was near Yoido, thinking that that might be an obvious landmark. "*I don't know where Yoido is,*" she responded, and laughed a small laugh. "*Yoido is just a place on television.*"[42] On the other hand, the Yoido women, who glided through the city in private automobiles on smooth avenues, saw only those parts of the city near the new expressways and near their destinations or those shown on television. Yet, although they knew the layout of the city, its landmarks and roadways, its monuments and facilities, several of the women who lived in Yoido expressed surprise when I told them that I was conducting research in a *taltongne* north of the Taehangro district. "*Are there still *taltongne* there? I thought they were all gone by now from the city,*" said one of my acquaintances. Another commented, "*Every so often you read about poor people losing their houses, like in Mokdong or now in Sŏch'o.[43] But then the story is over, and you forget about it until the next story. In between, you never hear about it. I never know such neighborhoods exist until they're being torn down.*" While Yoido appeared on television every day, impoverished neighborhoods were largely hidden from view, separated in space and absent from the television screen so that they need not impinge on the imagined city space of Seoul's well-to-do.

## SPACE AND PLACE IN SEOUL

The spaces and places people live in are not inert environments. Since anthropology's early days, scholars have identified the meanings people bring to the ways they carve up space and the meanings spatial distinctions generate in people's lives. Emile Durkheim recognized the social origin of categories of spatial division; essentially, Durkheim believed that people divide space in order to choreograph social events (Durkheim 1995:10). Pierre Bourdieu's elegant analysis of the nested divisions of space in the Kabyle house is a famous example of the way spatial distinctions enter into the symbolic ground of a society (Bourdieu 1977:89–91). More recently, scholars have examined the ways in which political and social interest groups shape space, particularly urban space, in the context of the economic market (Lefebvre 1996; Harvey 1989). As Edward Soja writes in his call for a "sociospatial dialectic": "The production of capitalist spatiality . . . is no once-and-for-all event. The spatial matrix must be constantly reinforced and, when necessary, restructured—that is, spatiality must be socially reproduced, and this reproduction process is a continuing source of conflict and crisis" (Soja 1989:129).

Seoul's physical changes mapped and mirrored South Korea's economic and social transformation. People constantly sought points of orientation in Seoul's ever changing space. Like the old woman looking for Kwanghwamun, people found the landmarks and pathways were continuously changing shape or disappearing completely. The new shape of the city altered the terms of social interaction and created new foundations for the experience of class, gender, and nation. Seoulites created the space of Seoul through their use of the city and their interactions with the symbolic meanings the capital had accrued. Geographer Allan Pred writes about the generation and effects of place:

> Place always represents a human product; it always involves an appropriation and transformation of space and nature that is inseparable from the reproduction and transformation of society in time and space. As such, place is characterized by the uninterrupted flux of human practice—and experience thereof—in time and space. It is not only what is fleetingly scene[44] as place, a "locale" or setting for activity and social interaction. It is also what takes place ceaselessly, what contributes to history in a specific context through the creation and utilisation of what is scene as place. (Pred 1985:337)

Place is *a location for* as well as *a factor in* social and cultural practice. The modernizing dreams of planners and government functionaries created a Seoul that provided segments of the population with distinctly different access to a "modern" environment. At the same time, the city space as real estate cut a trench between rich and poor, between homeowners and renters, that not only separated people from one another in space but divided them into different social categories with different degrees of access to current and expected consumer pleasures, different ability to command the city space, different visibility within the city, and even different experiences of being "Korean."

My first year in South Korea I taught English to employees of the Samsung Corporation at the company training center in the hilly countryside an hour outside of Seoul. We teachers were assigned a car and a driver to chauffeur us back and forth daily from the city to the training center, but the men lived on campus for the entire nine-week term. Before 6 A.M. every day, they were awakened by a recording of the national anthem, and shortly afterward they were expected to assemble in the courtyard for calisthenics. They ate their meals in the canteen, and, like soldiers, they ate what they were served. A bus would come to pick them up on Saturday afternoons to bring them to Seoul for an abbreviated weekend; they were back in the bunk rooms by Sunday night.

The English training staff offered intensive language instruction along with some exposure to American and British behavioral quirks. English was recognized as the "international language of business"; European and American markets were targeted export prizes. The trainees at the center were being prepared to work with foreign engineers on joint-venture high-technology projects, to negotiate deals with visiting buyers, or to staff overseas corporate offices. The Samsung leadership was eager to have us create an atmosphere that would force the program participants to face new linguistic as well as cultural challenges. Occasionally, the training center's management (composed of regular Samsung staff) had their own ideas of appropriate cross-cultural experience; one of these was the "Western Breakfast." Nearly all the meals—there was little to distinguish between breakfast, lunch, and dinner—were recognizably "Korean-style": white rice steaming in a fist-sized metal bowl, a helping of kimchi on the side, a peppery stew, perhaps some dried fish or squid. "Western Breakfast," however, served once a term, was a puzzling composition: eight fluffy slices of white bread and a spoonful of jam to accompany the bread;

an egg fried some time earlier; and a bowl of *miyŏkkuk* (seaweed soup) with a small whole dried fish thrown in for good measure.

"Western Breakfast" satisfied no one. Those of us who were putatively "western" were not so much put off by the fish and seaweed soup—most of us had eaten Korean-style breakfasts often enough to be used to rice and kimchi in the morning—but we could not bear to look at the glistening cold egg, and the idea of consuming eight slices of Wonder Bread was a daunting prospect—for us, the mistaken western components were the disconcerting parts. The training participants, on the other hand, always complained that they were hungry without rice and that a cold breakfast was comfortless; each time "Western Breakfast" was served, someone was always bound plaintively to ask a teacher, "How can you eat this every morning?"

South Koreans were being exposed to new food habits in the 1980s. American fast-food restaurants (Wendy's, Burger King, Pizza Hut, Dunkin' Donuts, KFC—but, notably, not MacDonald's) were by 1985 well established in central Seoul and in It'aewon, the commercial strip catering to the members of the U.S. military stationed at Seoul's Yongsan base. These were areas where foreign residents and tourists congregated, but a few outposts of these chains had begun appearing in "Korean" neighborhoods, particularly in Kangnam. The Lotte *chaebŏl* had even started its own hamburger joint, the Lotteria, with a branch in the basement of the elegant Lotte department store. The few real supermarkets that existed at the time often stocked foreign-style food products, such as Danone yogurt and a cheddar cheese made by a religious community in the southern part of the country. And, of course, contraband Skippy peanut butter, Keebler cookies, M&Ms, and Mr. Peanut canned nuts from the U.S. Army base were sold from carts on street corners and in underground food stalls throughout the city (as they had been for decades). While as yet not a major factor in most South Korean diets, foreign food styles were insinuating themselves, however awkwardly, into the local environment. In the turbulence of new consumer options in South Korea in the 1980s and 1990s, changes in eating habits marked a leading edge of widespread cultural transformation.

# CHAPTER 3

# PRODUCING NEW CONSUMPTION

*Our nation's consumer culture pattern has expanded at high velocity. There are differences according to employment class and region, and it cannot be denied that, since the middle 1980s, the extent and variety [of these] has been progressing rapidly. . . . In the second half of the 1980s, the stupendous growth in consumption expenditures has been sufficient to arouse fantasies in people that Korean society had become just like an advanced nation.*

Uk-in Baek, "The secret of mass culture and Korean society"

## FOOD

Until quite recently, hunger was a common season of the year for many people in South Korea. In his ethnography of a coastal village in the mid-1960s, Vincent Brandt reported that

> the village normally has a net grain deficit. In the past this has meant that the fifteen or twenty poorest families with almost no rice land at all have had to restrict their consumption to the barest minimum necessary for survival. In the spring, after winter food stocks are exhausted and before the barley harvest in late May and June, such people usually suffer from severe malnutrition for a month or six weeks. If the crop was poor during the previous year, the number in this category reportedly rises to more than half the total population. . . . According to local accounts, poor people in other years [before the U.S. government's Food for Peace aid program] have been obliged to subsist in the spring on what they could gather along the seashore and in the mountains.
>
> (Brandt 1971:51)

Hunger is a recurrent theme in individual memory and popular representations of the past. Anthropologist Laurel Kendall's life history of a shaman includes a long passage in which the narrator, Yongsu's Mother, as a little girl discovers that her father has secretly established a second household. These are the years shortly before the Korean War. As her father withdraws from his first family, he stops bringing young Yongsu's Mother and her own mother and brother enough food for them to survive. The girl went to the second household to beg her father for some rice, but he threatened to beat

her instead. She returned to her mother to tell her the tale. The mother responded with resignation.

> "Shame on him. What's the use? If we're going to starve to death, well
> then we'll starve to death. Don't go back there."
> "My stomach is empty. Don't tell me not to go, I'm going." I was
> in a daze. A little bit later I went out again. This time I went to the shop.
> My anger was up. . . . I clutched the sack and went to the shop. "Father,
> buy us rice."
> My father's friends were there as well as the people doing business,
> so this was embarrassing for him.
> "Buy us some rice." I stood there clutching the sack.
>
> (Kendall 1988:43)

Yongsu's Mother was forced to go every day to beg rice from her father;
Kendall's text brings out the connection between her persistence and the
strength of character she draws on throughout her hard life. In my fieldwork
interviews as well, women would often reminisce about their own childhood
hunger as a period of suffering that ultimately brought them strength. In our
first meeting, Mira, a wealthy Yoido resident, told me that I couldn't understand contemporary Korean consumer issues if I didn't learn first about what
it had been like before. She had grown up in Inch'on, a medium-sized city at
the mouth of the Han River, west of Seoul.

> *At that time, almost everyone was poor. Sometimes I would find that
> my mother put a hard-boiled egg in my lunchbox, and I remember that
> as something really delicious. We ate meat soup only on holidays. Once
> in a very long while, we would eat *pulgogi* (barbecued beef) or *cha-
> jangmyŏn* (Chinese-style noodles with bean-paste sauce). Even so, think
> about it: our family was better off than average—my father was a gov-
> ernment employee, an administrator.*

Chong-hae, who moved to Talgoljjagi from a remote mountain village, was
more blunt.

> *I came to Seoul because we were hungry. The land was rough where
> we were, and it was hard to grow enough food. My village was so small
> we didn't even have a school—I had to live with some cousins in a

neighboring village to go to elementary school. After that, my family didn't have the money to keep me in school, so they sent me to Seoul to work and earn my own way. I got a job in a factory in P'yŏnghwa Sijang, and for the first time I ate enough every day, even though it wasn't good food. When I think of my hometown, my homesickness is all mixed up with memories of hunger.*

This sense of prior deprivation was broadly shared in South Korea. While many Yoido women had grown up in relative comfort, even the most indulged of the women in Yoido had few treats as children. Most of the women in Talgoljjagi had been hungry a great deal of their childhood.

Contemporary popular television and film dramas, as well as stories and novels, often showed scenes of hunger from earlier decades. Depictions of the hungry years often evoked a complex nostalgia similar to Chong-hae's, in which the pain and danger of going without enough to eat is intermingled with a yearning for a simpler time—a romantic ideal of a purer Korea. This sentiment is drawn out particularly in the many stories and programs set during the colonial period and the tragic Korean War, and through these media this sensibility is made available to people who are too young, or were too fortunate, to have shared in the privations of earlier decades. This nostalgia for the suffering of earlier years has helped to establish a sense of national unity.

By the time of my fieldwork, however, hunger was no longer widespread. A simple analysis of household expenditures on food reveals significant changes in the level of basic comfort South Koreans had attained, compared to that of a generation earlier. By the 1990s, average levels of expenditure on foodstuffs as a percentage of the household budget had dropped dramatically compared even to the Park era. This measure, known as the Engels Coefficient, is used as a general indicator of relative poverty and affluence: the higher the percentage of a household budget dedicated to food, the more straitened the circumstances of the household. In 1970 the average urban South Korean household used 40.5 percent of its budget on food; five years later, in the wake of the oil shocks on the South Korean economy and in the context of constrained wage growth and the increasingly severe labor repression of the Yushin period, that percentage had risen to nearly 50 percent. During the 1980s, however, food prices fell and overall income rose; by 1990 the relative proportion of food purchases in the average urban household budget had dropped to only 32 percent, about the level they were in Japan fifteen years earlier (Kukŭn Kyŏngje Yŏnguso 1993:18). This shift of funds away from food consumption was a crucial change in the South Korean economy: it allowed consumers to spend more on things they had earlier not even considered buying.

Simultaneously, as the population grew wealthier, the earlier grain-based semiprivation diet gave way to more varied fare.[1] Annual per-capita rice consumption dropped from 132.4 kilograms in 1980 to 119.6 kilograms in 1990 and further to 102.4 kilograms in 1997. The composition of the average household food budget changed; between 1982 and 1991 consumption of cereals (mostly rice and barley) fell from more than 30 percent to about 20 percent of the household food budget, while consumption of meat and fish, vegetables and fruits, baked goods, and soft drinks all increased (Korean Statistical Association 1992; see figure 3.1). Even more striking is the increase in the proportion of the food budget that went to meals eaten out. During the same decade (1982–1991), the percentage of an average household's food budget dedicated to eating out rose from 5.8 percent to 22.5 percent.[2] Each year during this period, households in all income categories spent an increasing fraction of their food budget on dining out; moreover, increases in the ratio of money spent on commercially prepared meals accelerated significantly after 1986 (see figure 3.2).

Indeed, by the early 1990s, the South Korean food market was varied and plentiful. Street vendors built high pyramids of apples, oranges, and pears. Vending machines sold a range of South Korean and imported soft drinks. The

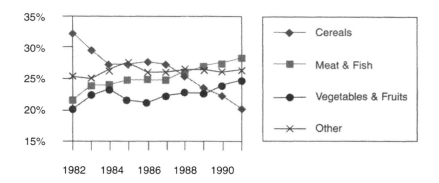

FIGURE 3.1    Seoul Household Food Budget, 1982–1991 (Excluding Meals Eaten Out): % Spent on Various Categories of Foodstuffs

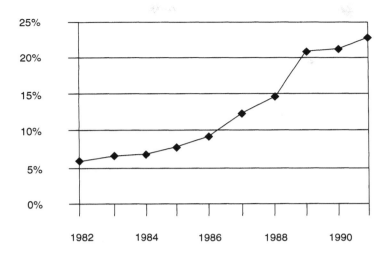

FIGURE 3.2   Seoul Household Food Budget, 1982–1991: % Spent on
Eating Out

shelves of neighborhood shops were filled with snack foods: chips, cookies, crackers, ramen, and chocolates, and supermarkets offered aisles packed with cereals, staples, snack foods as well as fresh vegetables, fresh fish, and fresh meat. Prepared meals were offered at sidewalk stalls, quick Korean-cuisine food spots, fast-food joints, and high-class restaurants. South Korea had also become relatively open to imported foods of all kinds. China sent bargain-priced shipments of sesame oil and vegetables; the United States sent luxury fruit, juices, and meats; Europe supplied bonbons and alcoholic beverages.

If amidst this plenty the thought of going hungry elicited a complex and ambivalent nostalgia for many South Koreans, Korean cuisine itself had also come to define an aspect of (South) Korean character, often specifically that of (South) Korean vigor vis-à-vis foreigners. This was so already in the early 1960s; in an essay in a well-known regular newspaper column concerning (South) Korean culture (often drawing contrasts to foreign habits), commentator Lee O-young wrote about the "true secrets of [a] civilization," which he found to lie hidden "in a country's beverages." Opening with a meditation on Coca-Cola as a representation of America's strength ("Each time I drink Coca-Cola, I think about American civilization"), he launches into a composition on a Korean drink made from pouring hot water into the

scorched rice remaining in the bottom of the rice pot, and an alcoholic bev-
erage (*makkŏli*) made from fermented rice:

> If there is a taste to scorched rice tea and *makkŏli*, it is a paradoxical
> sense of taste which must be called a "taste without a taste." It is the feel-
> ing of the hermit who does nothing but lives his whole life plainly. . . .
> Perhaps if Korean tears and laughter were put together to form one liq-
> uid, no doubt it would be like scorched rice tea or *makkŏli*.
>
> (O. Lee 1967:68)

Lee, a professor of Korean literature, saw in scorched-rice tea and *makkŏli*
the history of poverty and oppression: "We have lived for several thousand
years in the corner of a vast mainland. As we have had to live being poor,
there was no luxurious disguise, and as we always had to live in oppression,
we have not been able to expose ourselves openly" (ibid.:69).

Kimchi, a pickled vegetable side dish served at nearly every meal, has
become an unofficial cultural symbol to many South Koreans. Although
there are many kinds of kimchi, suited to different side dishes, the most common kind of kimchi, *tongbaech'u kimch'i*, is a sharply spiced recipe of shred-
ded cabbage, radish, salt, ginger, green onions, and generous amounts of
garlic and red pepper, allowed to ferment for several days to a few months as
it develops flavor. Kimchi's spicy, garlic-redolent bite is frequently presented as a metaphor for the direct, passionate behavior of Koreans, in contrast,
for example, to the bland, minimalist, exquisite cuisine of the restrained but
oppressive Japanese. Foreigners—and particularly Westerners—are assumed to dislike kimchi because of its strong odor and taste. In contrast, as
writer and epicure Yu Young-nan and food scholar Yu Tae-jong noted,
"When Korean athletes compete outside Korea, there are always accounts in
the newspapers of how they managed to eat kimchi in order to feel at home"
(Yu and Yu 1993:96). Kimchi itself, while still an important part of most
South Korean meals, is also a symbol of the connection to Korea's past (Han
1994; see also Kweon 1993). Each fall, newspapers are filled with photographs of women participating in *kimjang*, the process of preparing a store of
kimchi for the family's winter provisions. The reports paradoxically reassure
the public that this traditional practice has not been lost, but in calling attention to *kimjang* as one of Korea's remaining distinctive cultural practices,
they simultaneously point out the tenuousness of the threads linking modern

life to the past. To preserve the understanding of this national cultural treasure, a kimchi museum has recently opened.

Korean cuisine has also been portrayed as evidence of the unrecognized scientific discoveries of Korean traditional culture. Kimchi's salubrious nature is a common topic of essays, but kimchi is not the only focus of such interest. In 1992, for example, a popular women's magazine prefaced a series of sauce recipes with these observations:

> Our nation's fermented foods carry with them a history and enigmatic character that no other nation in the world could invent. They can be preserved for a long time at a normal temperature, and according to medical science they can prevent and suppress carcinogens and purify and strengthen the large intestine; their fermentation is several times stronger than yogurt's, and we cannot place a value on the still undiscovered secrets and beneficial elements of our ancestors' extraordinarily sagacious eating style. . . . You could say it is our mission to reappraise and reinvestigate the source, so that later it will be the substance that leads the world's eating culture.
>
> (I Chun-hŭi 1992:18)

This passage, like Lee's commentary, ties together an essentialized vision of Korean character, Korean history, and Korean food.

Of course, distinct class and regional differences in cooking and eating styles were historically characteristic of Korean cuisine. Chŏlla province, for example, with its fertile land, warmer climate, and many members of the *yangban* elite, was known for elaborate preparation, variety, and spiciness, while the cooler weather of the P'yŏngan region, on the other hand, contributed to the milder flavors of the cooking style there (Yu and Yu 1993). Families had distinctive styles of cooking as well; a newly married woman was expected to learn to cook in the manner of the family into which she had married. Yun-a, a fiftyish Talgoljjagi resident born in Chŏlla Province, recalled her first months in her husband's household (in the mid-1960s):

> *My parents had married me to a man in Chunchŏn Province, and one of the hardest things for me in the first months was learning to cook like my mother-in-law. At first, their food disgusted me, it had so little flavor. But whenever I cooked in my own family's style, my mother-in-

law would criticize me, and everyone would refuse to eat what I served, so I learned to cook and eat their way.*

Such variations still existed in 1992, although the large-scale migrations and the increasing tendency for newlywed couples (even when the husband is the first son) to form nuclear-family households separate from their in-laws had diluted regional and family-based distinctions. Many women now learned to cook not by studying their family's traditions (or the tastes of their in-laws) but by following written recipes featuring "regional cuisine" in magazines and by watching cooking shows on television. Older housewives lamented that not only young women but even restaurant cooks had lost the "taste" for Korean flavors and put too much sugar in their sauces.

These changes in taste and buying habits, however, did not affect all South Korean households to the same extent. At the level of expenditures, clearly poorer households still dedicated a greater amount of household resources to food. Breaking the urban population down into household income deciles, it is apparent that at the time of my fieldwork in the early 1990s, though *all* the households spent a smaller proportion of their budget on food than the average household in the 1970s, the higher the household income, the smaller the food share of the household budget. Similarly, a closer look at the importance of eating out shows that lower income deciles spent a significantly smaller fraction of their household food budget on commercially

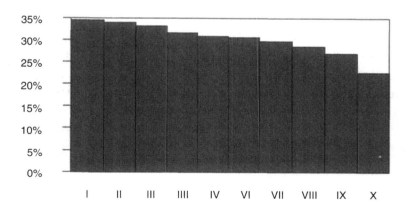

FIGURE 3.3    Percent of Household Budget Spent on Food, by Income Deciles, 1991 (all Cities)

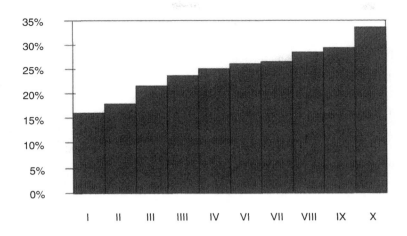

FIGURE 3.4    Percent of Household Food Budget Spent on Meals Eaten Out, by Income Deciles, 1991 (all Cities)

offered foods than did the higher-income households. (Korean Statistical Association 1992) (see figures 3.3 and 3.4). Obviously, then, poorer urban families in South Korea were still constrained in their food purchasing choices, and their food needs in turn constrained their other consumer options (by taking up a greater fraction of their budget and home labor) to a greater extent than was the case for families with higher income.

These differences were apparent in the details of the daily diet. The low-income households in Talgoljjagi ate a diet made up mostly of rice, vegetables, and fish. Talgoljjagi women shared food among different households when one family had a quantity of leftovers. With little space in their small refrigerators, Talgoljjagi women went shopping almost daily and cooked with fresh ingredients. They stuck to the Korean cuisine they knew, and they indulged in few treats: the occasional packaged dried squid, chips, instant coffee. In Yoido, in contrast, the kitchen shelves were stocked with American-brand breakfast cereals and cookies; the refrigerators were filled with condiments and side dishes of complex preparation. Growing children could hope for barbecued beef more than once a week with their rice for dinner or, on the weekend, for a pizza. Indulgent mothers sometimes worried about children who preferred foreign food to a Korean meal, and yet few denied their children their food whims. Many women enjoyed learning the art of preparing foreign recipes.

Even the experience of shopping for ingredients to make dinner varied with income. In Talgoljjagi, for example, women who were engaged in cottage-industry production would wearily put aside their umbrella-making, sweater-beading, or seam-sewing almost every late morning or afternoon and descend the hill to gather together food for the family's meal. They trudged down the hillside, taking small careful steps because the slope is so steep that even with a lifetime of practice it was still hard to shake the fear of tumbling forward. The road was rough, pebble-filled concrete, striated to provide extra traction; on either side, rugged stairs climbed up alongside the tightly packed houses. Although there were pathways cutting through the neighborhood in all directions, only five roads were wide enough for cars to pass. At the bottom of the hill, turning right at the road, past the *dong* office and the bus stop, was the tightly packed local market area. There, under the harsh light of bare electric bulbs hanging beneath heavy blue-and-white plastic awnings, semipermanent stalls set out styrofoam boxes full of ice to chill fresh fish or apples and oranges arranged in bright plastic tubs, or cardboard boxes full of onions, potatoes, squash, and seaweed. Here and there in the marketplace, some vendors steamed *ttŏkppokki*, sausage-shaped tubes of chewy rice flour in a spicy orange sauce, and occasionally customers would buy one or two, and sit at narrow tables to eat.

Suni, a woman in her thirties with two children in middle school, described her attitude toward going to the market:

> *Usually I'm so tired from working I can hardly bear to go to the market. It's not easy to go up and down this hill, especially carrying a bag full of heavy vegetables. And the prices always seem to be higher all the time. Last week they were selling apples for 300 *wŏn*, and this week they're selling apples for 400 *wŏn*. I just look for whatever looks good and isn't so expensive. It's hard to keep saying, "Give me a deal." This week we're eating a lot of *miyŏkkuk* because my parents brought back some seaweed from our hometown.*

Chong-hae was more outgoing than Suni, and although she was no wealthier, she had a different attitude toward this daily chore:

> *Usually I truly enjoy going to the market. Especially when I'm working at home[3]—I like to get out of the house and see people. At the Talgoljjagi market, I can walk up to the vendors I know and joke with them

for a while, and then they give me a good price. Then sometimes, if I have time or if there's a holiday coming up, I go to Namdaemun Market. I know some of the vendors there, too, and sometimes I've even bought them a cup of coffee in the winter. They'll give me the best quality they have, and a good price, too.*

Rice and meats were sold in small, specialized shops a little further from the street and also in another market a few blocks further north. For packaged goods (such as ramen as well as the staples of social gatherings: cookies, chips, soft drinks, alcoholic beverages—mostly beer and *soju*) there were small shops (*kage*) scattered throughout the neighborhood. In a half-kilometer radius area from the *kongbubang*, I counted eight small *kage*. *Kage* in Talgoljjagi (as in almost every corner of Seoul) were nearly always cramped, their short shelves overflowing with dusty inventory; the floors were bare concrete, and the aisles were barely wide enough for small children to pass each other. There were also two new Circle-K convenience stores, which had opened on either side of the base of the Talgoljjagi hill during the time of my fieldwork, tentacles of a trend toward brightly lit chain stores. I saw many kids run in and out of the Circle-K carrying fountain sodas, ices, and candy; few adults seemed to patronize the store even though the Circle-Ks offered many of the same products as the *kage*, but in a cleaner-looking environment. An informal count of customers entering and exiting at various hours showed approximately three-fourths of the Circle-K customers were children, teenagers, or very young adults. In my (scripted or formal) interviews I asked women whether they had bought anything at (or even gone into) their local Circle-Ks; none of the thirty-five respondents had. Shopping at these stores was perceived as both expensive and inappropriate. My Talgoljjagi friends knew that I went to the Circle-K almost daily for a large red-and-white paper cup of Diet Coke (which was unavailable elsewhere in Talgoljjagi). "*You're not Korean, you're a foreigner,*" Chong-hae told me, "*and you're just a student. Shops like that are too expensive, and they just seem foreign to me. But it's all right for you to go.*" In fact, the Circle-Ks offered some items at a discount compared to the local *kage*, but the stock was skewed toward a slightly more expensive range of products, which made the stores seem more expensive overall. Moreover, some Talgoljjagi residents resented the chain stores as foreign and as elements of new retail strategies that limited their own potential to start a business.[4]

In Yoido, on the other hand, the errand of shopping for food offered more real commercial variety to women. To do their ordinary shopping and to pick up things at the last minute, women could walk to the local supermarket, located in the basement of a small shopping center just across the street from the apartment complex. Although it had opened in the mid-1970s and was a little run-down, the supermarket had been renovated not too long before and so was only a few years out of style. Shoppers could take yellow plastic shopping carts and wheel them down the aisles to gather dry and canned goods from the shelves. Along the side and back walls of the store shoppers could find vegetables wrapped in cellophane packages with stickers marking their price, and they could choose a package of meat or ask the butcher to cut something fresh. Five check-out aisles with whirring cash registers awaited patrons' cash or charge cards. Just beyond the checkout, several independent vendors had their own stalls, some selling hot snacks. In one, goods that had been smuggled out of the U.S. military base were on sale: Chips Ahoy cookies, Jif peanut butter, and Kraft American cheese slices.

Chang-su's Mother went to the local supermarket two or three times a week; if her children were around, she liked to send them to pick up a package of this or that. She said she appreciated the convenience, but wished for a nicer atmosphere. "*It's dark and it almost seems dirty down there. It's good to have a supermarket so close, but I'd much rather go to the Hanyang supermarket, or to the supermarket in Shinsegye department store in Yŏngdŭngp'o.*"

About once a week, Chang-su's Mother (like most of the other women I interviewed in Yoido) drove to one of the newer supermarkets nearby that she mentioned, or she stopped off in the Hyundai department store's supermarket in Apkujŏngdong while she waited for her son to get out of his after-school program. Whereas even the local Yoido supermarket differed markedly from the outdoor market hustle of Talgoljjagi—the prices were set, quantities were prepackaged, and the personnel were employees rather than owners—the supermarkets Chang-su's Mother preferred put the local one in Yoido to shame. These newer supermarkets expressed the new aesthetics of the late 1980s and early 1990s: bright, white, and orderly. A wide variety of goods was displayed in colorful stacks, and foreign name brands (in Korean and Roman script) were plentiful. Like the Circle-Ks, these stores represented a new retail fashion—packaged and scrubbed clean.

In addition to the local and more distant supermarkets, wives in Yoido had several other choices for picking up the makings for dinner. As in most neighborhoods in Seoul, vendors would bring their goods from neighborhood to neighborhood on a regular schedule. On Tuesday and Thursday mornings, a truck would drive into the parking lot of the apartment complex, and a husband-and-wife team would offer fresh fish on ice for sale. There was a general consensus in the apartments that the pair offered good quality food at a fair price. (A friend living in a wealthy neighborhood near Hong-ik University told me that a popular vegetable vendor who frequented her street had in a year's time earned enough to upgrade his old truck to a new Ssanggyŏng van and had installed superior broadcasting equipment to call out his wares.) The best meats were available in specialty butcher shops a few blocks away; particularly around the holidays, women would drive the short distance and pick up large orders of beef for the family and to give as gifts to their extended family and to their husbands' superiors. Yoido housewives took care to evaluate and select the highest quality foodstuffs, and price was a secondary consideration.

Other peddlers came on an irregular basis and set up sidewalk shops around the entrance gates to the apartment complex as well: an old woman selling fruits (large apples, grapefruit, and the like) appropriate for bringing on an impromptu visit was there several days a week, while other women sold children's smocks or kitchen knickknacks on blankets spread out on the sidewalk. The residents, however, rarely purchased from these irregular peddlers, whose primary market was comprised of visitors and children.

Finally, within just a few blocks of the apartment complex there were also several 7-Eleven and Circle-K shops as well as several more ordinary *kage*, which looked entirely as dingy and crowded as those in Talgoljjagi did. The *kage* were mostly patronized by local workers buying candy and cigarettes, while the chain stores in Yoido attracted children *and* adults. One family I knew made it a regular weekend treat to walk to one of the 7-Elevens to pick up huge fountain sodas and Häagen-Dazs ice-cream bars.

None of the women I spoke with in Yoido frequented the *sijang*, the large outdoor markets (except for the Noryangjin fish market, which was nearby) to buy food.[5] Many of the women said that they had a nostalgia for the *sijang*, but that the markets were too crowded, the vendors were surly, it could be dangerous there, there was no convenient parking, the goods were dirtier and no better than they could buy in the supermarket, and few of the women enjoyed bargaining for a good price. "*My mother loves to bargain,*" Chang-su's Mother said, "*but I don't have the personality. I like to talk to people, but not to push them. Women my age [thirty-five] didn't learn to bargain in the market for food. When I think of how much more money I have than the vendor has, I feel bad asking for a few *wŏn* discount, but I also don't want to pay an inflated price. So I'd rather go to the supermarket or buy from someone I know who offers me a good price because I'm a regular customer.*"

Ignoring differences between the types of food purchased for Yoido or Talgoljjagi households and simply examining the practice of shopping for food to cook at home, it is apparent that quite distinct cultural experiences of consumption have evolved in a short time, differentiating the women of Yoido from those of Talgoljjagi. Whereas the women of Talgoljjagi bought almost everything from small-scale shopkeepers and bargained for a good price for the majority of their food, women in Yoido chose to travel to more stylish or more specialized stores, where price was less of a concern than quality, convenience, and atmosphere. In Talgoljjagi the relationships between buyers and sellers was seen as one of near equals in poverty, and the mixture, stressful to some, was a pleasant competitive game for others; the household budget depended in part on the women's social skills of persuasion. Yoido women, on the other hand, in general were distanced from the relationships of consumption, except those of specialty vendor and regular customer; the skills they needed were those of knowledge, quality discernment, analysis, and efficiency. Not infrequently, the difference between these two modes of shopping for food was described—by the women themselves as well as in the popular media—as the difference between tradition and modernity.

## BOOMING ECONOMY, BLOSSOMING MARKET

As discussed in chapter 1, South Korea's industrialization strategies during the latter half of the 1960s and throughout the 1970s, and even into the 1980s, depended upon shifting resources from production for domestic consumption to production for export. South Korea did not pursue import-substitution as its primary means of development; rather, through a combination of incentives and strictures, the South Korean government forced major industrial companies to produce goods targeted for export—despite the fact that the profit margins of export-oriented industries were significantly below those of domestic-oriented companies throughout the period. As Clive Hamilton writes, "The government had to twist arms to compel businesses to export, because there is little doubt that it was, as a rule, much more profitable to supply the domestic market than foreign ones, particularly if one were supplying the domestic market with scarce imports" (Hamilton 1986:44). The state had mapped out a long-term strategy whereby exports would largely provide the foreign exchange necessary to finance on-going industrialization. The current standard of living in the country was a consideration only to the extent that dissatisfaction threatened political stability. Some of the effects of this strategy on consumption patterns during this period were: underpricing of urban labor (which limited the funds available for private consumption); overpricing of consumer goods on the domestic market (to compensate for export losses, on the one hand, and as a result of inefficient domestic production methods or lack of competition on the other); and constraints on the supply of imported personal goods.

Unlike in many other developing countries, in South Korea even the wealthy strata were forced to accept a limited market of attractive products. Hamilton writes,

> Restrictions on imports of consumer goods mostly affected urban professionals and moneyed classes since it was they who could afford them. In most Third World countries the moneyed classes, including landlords and government officials, hold political sway often in alliance with foreign interests. . . . Here the independent strength of the Korean state, beholden not even to the industrialists, has been a powerful force. (Hamilton 1986:122)

Companies *did* produce consumer goods for the domestic market, but these were mostly inexpensive household goods and clothing. Wealthy households continued to order custom-made clothing and shoes and to spend large fractions of their income on ephemeral purchases (entertainment, weddings and other ceremonies, and gifts, for example) and investments rather than seek much satisfaction in the mass-production marketplace.

For the less wealthy, not only was the market poorly developed but supply was undependable. Shifts in import restriction policies and price controls caused swings in the availability of everyday items, often exacerbated by the public perception of shortage, as happened in 1977 and early 1978 when "basic goods such as toilet paper, toothpaste and electric fans vanished from stores as demand outstripped supply in a rash of panic buying, stoking a sense of crisis" (Clifford 1994:132). Shortages of needed inputs resulted in a curtailed supply of domestically produced goods as well.

It should be noted that one important aspect of the South Korean consumer market from the late 1940s until today has been the number of American products available through black-market sales. The widespread availability of items such as Spam, American cigarettes, peanuts, cosmetics, and European liquors have left a stamp on South Korean consumer preferences. Moreover, the black market continues to supply a significant demand for refrigerators, irons, toasters, Chivas Regal Scotch, and even rice (United States Senate 1990).[6] Black-market PX items were sold informally through connections, from push carts, and in semipermanent and permanent stalls in commercial areas, including in major department stores.

Several factors coincided to result in the flowering of the domestic market in the 1980s. For one thing, the middle 1980s marked a turning point in South Korea's export record. Growing trade imbalances between the United States and Japan had led to a meeting of the five major industrialized nations in September 1985. The Plaza Accords that resulted were, essentially, an agreement to devalue the U.S. dollar, thus making U.S. exports more competitive in price and increasing the price of Japanese imports for U.S. consumers. The South Korean *wŏn*, loosely pegged to the dollar, weakened as well. This, combined with low interest rates on foreign loans and low commodity prices, were known as the three lows or the three blessings. In addition to these economic factors, the frosty trade atmosphere between the U.S. and Japan and specific restrictions on Japanese exports of certain goods (cars and semiconductors, most notably) placed the South Korean economy in a highly favorable position for selling its products abroad. This was the foundation for South Korea's achievement of a positive trade balance for the first time ever in 1986. The concomitant economic growth resulted in the doubling of people's disposable income between 1986 and 1988 (*Korea Herald*, 19 September 1999). This translated into an actual consumption increase of 8.7 percent during this period (ibid.). The South Korean government also began to institute policies aimed at reining in the power of the *chaebŏl*. A small number of *chaebŏl* producers often had control over segments of the market. Linsu Kim reports that, "By 1977, 93% of all commodities, or 62% of all shipments, were produced under monopoly, duopoly, or oligopoly conditions, under which the top three producers accounted for more than 60% market share" (Linsu Kim 1993:363). In the 1980s this led to "monopolistic abuses such as creating scarcities, price gouging, and ruining smaller competitors" (ibid.:367), and in response the government launched several market-opening and competition-enhancing policies. The South Korean government made significant strides toward opening the domestic market to imported consumer goods, raising the import liberalization ratio (the ratio of unrestricted items to the total) from 51 percent in 1973 to 85 percent in 1984 and to 95.2 percent in 1988 (ibid.:368). At the same time, changes in the production mix of the *chaebŏl* themselves also led to a greater diversity of products in the domestic market.

These changes were dramatic and were greeted with ambivalence and wonder. The official statistics on ownership of major consumer goods provide some idea of the impressive material changes in South Korean households during this time. The Economic Planning Board's Population and Housing Census has records of ownership of televisions, telephones, refrigerators, and washing machines (as well as pianos and organs, electric gramophones, and newspapers). Between 1970 and 1985 the South Korean population underwent a significant transformation in the extent to which households were equipped with these items. Considering urban households alone, in 1970 only 14.5 percent owned a television, 8.9 percent owned a telephone, 4.6 percent had a refrigerator, and washing machines were still so unusual that the census had not yet begun to measure their ownership rates (see table 3.1 and figure 3.5). By 1985, almost every household had a television, more than three-fourths had a refrigerator, and more than half had a telephone. Though for televisions and refrigerators the largest increase appears to have come in the five years between 1975 and 1980, between 1975 and 1985 owning any of these consumer items changed from an unusual to a common phenomenon.

TABLE 3.1    Ownership Rates of Major Household Goods (by household)

| | TV | | TELEPHONE | | REFRIGERATOR | | WASHING MACHINE | |
|---|---|---|---|---|---|---|---|---|
| YEAR | WHOLE COUNTRY | CITIES | WHOLE COUNTRY | CITIES | WHOLE COUNTRY | CITIES | WHOLE COUNTRY | CITIES |
| 1970 | 6.4% | 14.5% | 4.8% | 8.9% | 2.2% | 4.6% | | |
| 1975 | 30.2% | 44.4% | 9.6% | 13.5% | 6.5% | 11.7% | 1.0% | 1.9% |
| 1980 | 86.7% | 90.9% | 24.1% | 30.3% | 37.8% | 51.5% | 10.4% | 16.1% |
| 1985 | 99.1% | 99.5% | 48.7% | 56.3% | 71.1% | 78.7% | 26.0% | 33.7% |

Source: National Statistical Office, Population and Housing Census.

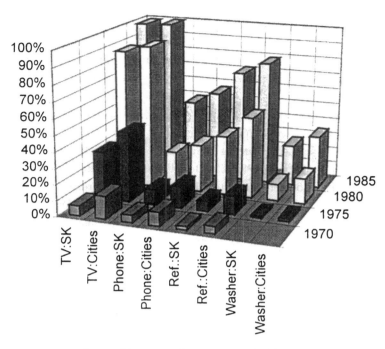

FIGURE 3.5    Ownership Rates of Major Household Goods (by household),
Whole Country and Cities, 1970–1985.

But ownership of household appliances had not simply blossomed by itself in Seoul—as in other parts of the industrialized, commercialized world,
ownership was a cultivated practice (see, for example, Fine 1995; Glennie
1995; Mukerji 1983; McKendrick, Brewer, and Plumb 1982). Radios and televisions had their attendant broadcast development support, led by state-
ownership and oversight (I 1980:151). Other expensive appliances had various kinds of private-sector encouragement. For example, during the early
and mid-1980s, some of the *chaebŏl* gave their employees company products
in lieu of their expected bonuses. As bonus payments amounted in many
cases to nearly one-third the annual salary, bonuses were an important component of employee income. Several employees I was acquainted with told
me that while at first the goods were welcome, the practice could become
burdensome. "*The first time the company gave me a microwave, I gave it
to my mother,*" said one man. "*And when I got another one for a bonus, I
saved it for when I would get married. But after that, what should I do? I

needed to save money for my wedding, so I ended up selling them to friends of friends.*" Other employees related similar stories concerning videotape recorders, televisions, and even refrigerators.

Employees were also frequently presented with gift certificates for products sold at stores owned by (or associated with) the *chaebŏl* that employed them. These stores often carried only products licensed to, imported by, or manufactured by the *chaebŏl* and its affiliates. This practice was still common during the period of my fieldwork. Hard work and overtime was rewarded by gift certificates worth as much as 100,000 or 200,000 *wŏn*; employees would choose clothing or appliances from the store's selection. Some *chaebŏl*s offered employees a choice of products they could receive as holiday gifts as well; for example, products of similar value (tape recorders and rice cookers, video recorders and televisions) were offered to employees at each level in the employment hierarchy, and the gifts were often distributed directly to the employees at their desks. These practices helped to encourage the spread of ownership of company products throughout the extended families of company employees and in effect ensured that "income" would be spent on products rather than saved, invested, or spent on ephemera.

The practice of compensating *chaebŏl* employees with goods or certificates provided direct support to the *chaebŏl*'s mission in several ways. First, the practice helped to establish the market share of the *chaebŏl* in particular areas of the market (audio equipment, microwave ovens, etc.) Second, it reduced the corporation's cash outlays. Third, it redirected salary costs to company income. Fourth, it provided an outlet for excess inventory. Finally, the distribution of goods helped to shape the wider consumer environment.

In 1991/1992 the families in the Yoido apartment complex I studied were among the best-equipped ones in the nation. Every home I visited had at least one color television (several had two); all had at least a two telephones, including a cordless phone; all owned a refrigerator, and all had washing machines. Most families owned many other major consumer goods as well; every Yoido household I visited had a videotape recorder; several had personal computers; many had elegant stereophonic music equipment, and more than half of the households with children at home had pianos.

In Talgoljjagi households were much more modestly equipped with appliances. All the houses I visited had a television, but none had more than one, and many of the televisions were obviously quite a few years old. A few were even black-and-white models. Several families did have videotape players, and video rental shops are common in even very low income neighborhoods in Seoul. Most families had refrigerators, but the models were all significantly older and smaller than those I saw in Yoido. Only about half the households had telephones. No one owned a washing machine. Nevertheless, most Talgoljjagi households, low-income though they were, had many more appliances than the *average* urban household used to have in the mid-1970s.

People gained pleasure from ownership of these things in both Yoido and in Talgoljjagi. One woman in Yoido had admired her U.S.-resident sister's Westinghouse refrigerator on a visit to Los Angeles. American refrigerators were larger than South Korean ones; size was particularly useful in South Korean households, where many side dishes are stored and reused for several meals. They also came in a range of colors atypical for the South Korean market, and their interior compartments seemed sturdier than those of models built in South Korea.[7] She had gone to the Yŏngsan Electronics Market (an expanse of nearly 3,000 independent shops not far from Yoido, where consumer electronics, including imports, were sold at fixed but discounted prices) and found just what she was looking for. She came back home pleased at the prospect of her new refrigerator. "*It's time for us to get a new refrigerator, anyway,*" she said, "*and I want us to have the best one. It will make the kitchen look much more sophisticated, and it will be easier to keep all the food in order.*" She also had plans to buy a new kitchen table and chairs in a style that would complement her new refrigerator.

Likewise, in Talgoljjagi, Miyŏng invited me in for instant coffee one morning and showed me her own new refrigerator, a Samsung model in almond color. "*My husband bought it for me last week,*" she told me, smiling. Miyŏng's husband had recently vowed to give up drinking. In the past, Miyŏng and her daughter had sought shelter at the *kongbubang* or with friends when her husband's drinking had put him in a violent mood. She was still embarrassed about my having discovered them one day hiding in a public toilet when the *kongbubang*'s door was locked and having helped them find a safe haven in the neighborhood. For her, the expensive refrigerator was assurance that her husband's intentions were good, and she wanted to show me her proof. The refrigerator was the newest and largest in the neighborhood, and it gave her a double pleasure to own it.

Yet income-correlated differences in the incidence of ownership of basic household and consumer appliances has various social effects. Washing machines are a good example. In Yoido few women did the washing for their families themselves; rather, most families hired other women to help with the housekeeping one day or more a week and laundry was the help's responsibility.[8] Thus, the possession of a washing machine benefited the domestic workers more directly than it did the family itself, making the washing machine something of a double luxury. In Talgoljjagi, on the other hand, women were exclusively responsible for their family's laundry, and without a washing machine and with few changes of clothes, laundry was a frequent and time-consuming chore. While South Korean washing machines were less than fully automated (many models required the operator to add water and to hook up a drain tube at various points in the cycle), nevertheless, access to a washing machine would free time from the demanding schedule of most Talgoljjagi women. As with food shopping, the lower-income women of Talgoljjagi expended more labor and time, and less money, than their Yoido counterparts.

Class differences in telephone ownership had more subtle effects. In Yoido women used telephones as an essential domestic management tool. Most women in Yoido had active schedules, and they made frequent phone calls to arrange events and meetings. Women phoned friends in different neighborhoods to schedule lunch appointments or just to chat. They phoned members of Bible-study circles or hobby groups to coordinate meetings and spoke with the wives of their husband's colleagues to coordinate company-focused events. Mothers, when they were absent from home for a few hours in the afternoon, would phone their children to check in, and children would phone their mothers from neighboring apartments to ask how late they could stay with their friends. Some husbands would phone to let their wives know when they could be expected home for dinner. Mothers and mothers-in-law of the women I interviewed often called more than once each day (much to the irritation of their daughters and daughters-in-law) to ask about the children, to inform the younger women about investment opportunities or extended family obligations, or to complain about some family member's inappropriate behavior. Yoido women also used the phone for utilitarian purposes, such as to order Chinese food or pizza, to call businesses to check on prices, opening hours, and stock, and to make inquiries of doctors. In most households the phone was in nearly constant use, and because of this, every family had a cordless phone, which allowed women to carry on conversations while tending to other domestic matters. The telephone was a tool that enabled Yoido women to manage their households efficiently, with full command over a range of important and timely familial and commercial information.

Telephones were much less integrated into the rhythm of life in Talgoljjagi. To a certain extent, of course, not owning a telephone was an inconvenience. There were several coin-operated telephones scattered throughout the neighborhood (and many cafés and small shops had pay-for-use telephones inside, sheltered from the elements) and there were telephones at the *kongbubang* and the *turebang*[9] so that finding an available telephone was not a real problem. Nevertheless, members of those households without phones were unable to conduct conversations of a private nature by telephone. More important, those families could not receive phone calls; on occasion, someone would phone the *kongbubang* and ask that a message be conveyed to someone else in the neighborhood. Other local shops with telephones performed similar informal message-center services. On the other hand, the lack of telephones was hardly perceived as a deprivation. Chiwŏn's Mother said she had no use for a telephone. "*Who would I need to call? Who would call me? I work at home all day, and if someone needs to speak to me, they know where to find me. My husband would never call me—if he wanted to come home late, he wouldn't ask my permission, and I'm glad he can't call to tell me what to do!*" I once asked a group of five women in Talgoljjagi how often they used the telephone; not one had had a telephone conversation in the last three days.

Nevertheless, the telephone as a material object, a status symbol, obviously had some resonance in both neighborhoods. In Yoido although the ordinary phones (where the receiver was attached to the base with a cord) were of various brands and mostly made in South Korea, with the exception of two Samsung-brand phones, every cordless phone I checked on was one of several well-known Japanese brands (e.g., Sony, National). A few women explained that the South Korean manufacturers were using Japanese components anyway, so they wanted to buy the more dependable original version rather than the copy. While this seemed to be a widely held opinion, the sense that a domestic brand product would be of lower quality appeared to be based as much on reputation and lack of cachet as on experience or evidence. Nevertheless, the purchase of the right phone was a domestic image-management decision of some small importance, and Yoido women could explain their decision process in terms of signal strength and the number of channels, hardware durability, and aesthetics. In contrast, in Talgoljjagi the family next door to the *kongbubang* had bought a cordless phone, which inspired a great number of jokes at their expense—the neighbor's house, like most Talgoljjagi houses, had only two small rooms, and it was so close to the *kongbubang* that women in the *kongbubang* were forced to eavesdrop on every phone conversation the neighbors had. "*We can hear everything they say from here. When she talks over there, we can answer her. The houses are so small in this neighborhood that two or three houses could share one ordinary phone—one phone cord could reach to all the houses easily. Who needs a cordless phone?*" observed Suni. The derision was evident in her timbre and her face, and the smiles of the other women in the *kongbubang* showed their agreement.

Well into the 1980s ownership of an item within a category of goods was enough to indicate status and to provide a sense of pride in ownership, since ownership of a microwave oven, a videotape recorder, or a color television was remarkable enough in itself. Protectionist policies kept out most foreign brands of consumer electronics and other consumer durables. Opinions differed as to the relative quality of goods produced by the major domestic producers (Samsung, Daewoo, Hyundai, Goldstar, etc.), but in practice the range of choice was limited, and the subtleties of status judgment were hardly developed. Brand awareness was more assiduously cultivated and elaborated upon during the later 1980s and 1990s, when consumer options multiplied.

## DRIVING CONSUMPTION: SOUTH KOREAN CARS

A rather extreme example of this phenomenon was the automobile market. From the 1950s through the 1960s the most common private automobile (and yet still a possession of only the very rich) was the military surplus jeep, which commanded respect and admiration. Several of the women in Yoido reminisced about romantic rides they had taken in jeeps with wealthy boyfriends in the late 1960s and early 1970s. By the late 1980s, however, a complex code of status had developed to assign a meaning to the various models of cars that were by then rolling off the assembly lines of Hyundai, Daewoo, and Kia Motors as well as to the recreational vehicles produced by Ssangyong.

The automobile market in South Korea was a clear outcome of state-directed industrial policies. The history of the industry has been detailed by several other sources (e.g., Amsden 1989; Lowry 1987; Green 1992), but the outlines are instructive and bear reviewing here. During the 1960s the local automobile industry was limited at first to assembly of foreign-made parts and then to the development of an import-substituting production capacity, with few domestic models but an increasing ratio of domestically produced parts. Total output was minimal. Then, the automotive industry was identified as a key industry in the government's 1973 Long-Term Plan for the Promotion of the Machine-Building Industry, part of the strategy to develop the heavy and chemical industries as the focus of South Korea's economy. Because automobile production was seen as a major support of both South Korean suppliers (of steel, glass, and other component materials) and its distribution and service industries, the plan designated the automobile industry as of strategic importance for increasing the ability of domestic industries to supply the domestic demand for machinery (Woo 1991:142). Although production expanded greatly in the second half of the 1970s, from 9,069 cars in 1974 to 112,314 in 1979, nevertheless, throughout the 1970s ownership of private automobiles remained at very low levels, and the annual amount of units sold varied widely with economic swings. The most significant of these swings occurred at the end of the decade. The anti-inflationary economic policies that followed the oil shock of 1979, combined with the political uncertainties following the assassination of Park Chung Hee that same year, cut the domestic demand for automobiles by half in 1980 to only 55,928 cars. In that year, the South Korean automobile industry was using only 26 percent of its production capacity. To avert disaster, the Ministry of Trade and Industry decided to reorient the industry, which had been focused mainly on supplying local demand, toward export production in order to capture economies of scale beyond the reach of an automotive industry oriented only to the domestic market. The United States, because it was a market large enough to absorb the projected output, was the export goal (Green 1992:415).

The government orchestrated a reduction in the number of automobile manufacturers, forcing Kia Motors to concentrate on small trucks and commercial vans,[10] while allowing two major *chaebŏl*, Daewoo[11] and Hyundai, full reign in the passenger car market.[12] Following the restructuring of the industry in the early 1980s, however, automobile manufacturers were still faced with a problem: production capacity was expanded well before quality production techniques were adequately developed and export markets sufficiently cultivated for export success. Moreover, South Korean manufacturers relied on subsidizing the cost of export models by aggressively seeking high profits in the domestic market. Successfully developing an export-oriented automotive industry thus depended upon nurturing a domestic market for experimentation, absorption of excess production, and subsidization of low-profit exports. The South Korean automobile manufacturers needed to dramatically expand their domestic sales.

At that time, South Korea had remarkably low rates of automobile ownership. In 1981, for example, when Seoul had a population of 8,676,037 individuals, the capital registered only 108,072 private automobiles or approximately one car for every eighty people—and Seoul had by far the highest concentration of car ownership in the country. Compared to other nations with generally similar levels of income and industrial development, South Korea was unusually short of cars. As late as 1985 there was only one car for every 100 people in the Republic of Korea, compared to one for every 50 people in Taiwan, one per 20 people in Malaysia, one per 17 in Mexico, and one per 13 in Brazil (Mukerjee n.d.:54). Automobile prices also remained prohibitively high relative to income; in 1982, the domestic price of a modest Hyundai Pony was U.S.$3,552 (Mukerjee n.d.:54), compared to average urban household wages of about U.S.$4,500 annually.

Despite the high prices, domestic sales did rise quickly during the 1980s. Table 3.2 shows the increase in the number of private cars registered as well as the number of registered drivers from 1971 to 1990 in Seoul and in the nation. In the first decade of this period (between 1971 and 1980), car ownership in Seoul had quadrupled, but the absolute rate of ownership remained quite low. In 1971, for example, there was only one passenger car[13] for every forty-two Seoul households; in 1980, there was still only one for every seventeen Seoul households. In the next few years, however, cars became more common very quickly. By 1983, the ratio of cars to Seoul households had fallen to one in nine; in 1985 it was one in seven, in 1988 it was one in five, and in 1990 there was one car for every three households in Seoul[14] (see figure 3.6). In the early 1990s South Korean automakers offset the drop-off in overseas demand by expanding domestic sales, with government assistance (Green 1992:428). By 1992, with cars lined up in nearly every alleyway, squeezed into every nook, and carpeting the avenues, it often seemed as if the population of Seoul were playing a vast game of musical chairs—if the music were to stop, it did not seem possible that all those cars would find a place to park at one time. Several newspapers carried stories of women bodily guarding parking spaces for their husbands' evening return.

There were many reasons why South Korean automobile manufacturers were successful in expanding the domestic market. Urban development played a role. The construction of far-flung neighborhoods at the edges of Seoul (and beyond) gave a new urgency to the choice between traveling the distance in crowded busses (or the subway, after it opened in 1985) or in a private car. The government sweetened the deal by improving the road network; during the

TABLE 3.2

Private Car Ownership and Drivers Licenses, 1971–1990

| YEAR | PRIVATE PASSENGER CAR OWNERSHIP (R.O.K.) | (SEOUL) | INCREASE FROM PREVIOUS YEAR (SEOUL) | LICENSED DRIVERS (R.O.K.) | (SEOUL) | INCREASE FROM PREVIOUS YEAR (SEOUL) |
|---|---|---|---|---|---|---|
| 1971 | | 26,806 | | | | |
| 1981 | 267,605 | 108,072 | | 2,202,759 | | |
| 1982 | 305,811 | | | 2,581,310 | | |
| 1983 | 380,993 | | | 2,989,401 | | |
| 1984 | 465,149 | 247,613 | | 3,487,138 | 1,105,949 | |
| 1985 | 556,659 | 296,848 | 20% | 4,088,52 | 11,384,097 | 25% |
| 1986 | 664,226 | 350,841 | 18% | 4,651,867 | 1,524,619 | 10% |
| 1987 | 844,350 | 432,638 | 23% | 5,269,494 | 1,722,385 | 13% |
| 1988 | | 547,009 | 26% | 1,985,246 | | 15% |
| 1989 | | 721,726 | 32% | 2,285,061 | | 15% |
| 1990 | | 883,415 | 22% | 2,587,227 | | 13% |

Source: Korea Statistical Yearbook 1988, National Bureau of Statistics, EPB; Seoul Statistical Yearbook 1991.

1980s, local and national government agencies dedicated massive sums to the construction of roads, bridges, and parking facilities.[15] Many executives and high-level *chaebŏl* employees were provided with company cars, complete with the service of professional drivers—a necessity for a nation with such a small percentage of the population in possession of a driver's license; in 1984, only 12 percent of the Seoul population was licensed to drive. Just as important, car ownership symbolized success, even as it became somewhat more widespread. In an essay written in 1985 (in the midst of the explosion of car ownership) entitled "Korea's Car Culture," Kim Hyŏng-kuk, professor of environmental studies, wrote: "Cars are a symbol of a person's status. . . . In our society, a person who has a midsize car is called 'Mr. Chairman,' while a person with a small car is called 'Mr. President' (Kim 1989:131)."

But in addition to indicating individual status, car ownership was also a symbol of *national* development. The sudden and very apparent advance in

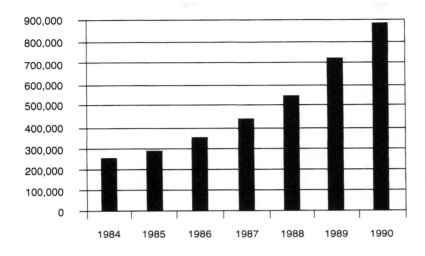

FIGURE 3.6    Private Car Ownership in Seoul, 1984–1990

South Korea's industrial capacity, visible on the nation's streets, was evidence of a leap South Korea was making toward membership in the club of industrialized nations. "'My car'," wrote Professor Kim in the same essay, "is a practical symbol of an advanced economy and can be a support of civilization. . . . It is said that the popularization of 'my car' and the development of the automobile industry is emblematic of the maturity of modernization, like the prior experience of advanced nations such as the United States" (Kim 1989:125).[16] The car industry in South Korea was presented to the general population as a national project to bring South Korea into the pantheon of "advanced" industrialized countries. Local media focused on the speedy development of improved production capacity and techniques. Coinciding with the feverish construction projects undertaken in preparation for the 1986 Asian Games and the 1988 Seoul Olympics, the expansion and development of South Korea's automobile industry was a visible and well-publicized sign that the nation was gaining the respect of the world. (The large-scale contracts won by South Korean construction firms to work in the Middle East played a similar role in the 1970s.)

In particular, Hyundai's debut in the U.S. automobile market in 1986 was perceived as proof of South Korea's membership in an elite corps of nations competing in the international auto market. Hyundai exports to the

U.S. advanced South Korea's international position on two fronts: the Hyundai Excel broke the record in the U.S. for first-year import sales (168,882 cars) and led the way to a positive bilateral trade balance; at the same time, those sales challenged Japan, South Korea's former colonizer, at its own game of selling cars to the Americans. From the domestic viewpoint, Hyundai's success was spectacular, and it led the way for the quieter entrance in 1987 of Daewoo (which built the Pontiac LeMans in a joint venture with General Motors) and Kia (assembler of the Ford Festiva, sold in Korea as the Kia Pride). Throughout the 1980s and into the 1990s newspapers and other media kept the automobile export story on the front pages, encouraging people to participate conceptually in the "national" success. This sentimental affiliation even affected a political dissident living in exile in New Jersey. In an interview with the progressive monthly journal *Mal*, Dr. Sŏ Kyŏngsŏk, a man who had been forced to flee South Korea in 1981 to avoid yet another prison sentence for his leadership role in the opposition movement, described the moment he decided to return to Seoul. In New York City one day in 1987, he saw a Hyundai traveling down Broadway and, as he put it in his characteristically wry phrasing, "while native scholars were predicting the imperialistic destruction of the subordinated economy, when I saw the debut of the Excel car in the American marketplace, . . . I realized the strength of the Korean economy. At that moment I predicted that before I die, Korea will surpass America" (Ch'oi 1992:128).[17] Soon after that he revised his earlier dreams of social and political change through revolutionary action and returned to Seoul to found a civic organization aimed at promoting economic and social justice working *within* South Korea's industrial development strategy.

Every family I interviewed in Yoido had a car, and many families had two. Nearly all the families had bought their first car in the early 1980s. (Most of the husband-and-wife pairs I interviewed were between thirty-five and fifty years old.) All but a few men drove themselves to work in the morning or were picked up by a driver; the women used their cars for entertainment and errands. For most Yoido women, cars were as essential as telephones for their daily household responsibilities of shopping, visiting family, exercising, and bringing children to after-school activities (as well as for the pleasures of meeting friends). The apartment complex, built in the 1970s, had anticipated the need to park one car per apartment unit in spaces directly in front of the buildings; in the evenings, the parking lot was filled to capacity, and new spaces had been created out of the driving lanes. This was a significantly better situation than that at Apkujŏngdong's Hyundai apartments, probably the most famous apartment complex in the nation. There, the one-space-per-unit allotment was woefully insufficient, and the security guards were frequently entrusted with the added responsibility of valet parking for those households without a professional driver. Like a child's puzzle, double- and triple-parked cars had to be shuffled back and forth one at a time in order for any one car to gain access to the roadway out or in.

In the Yoido complex, the majority of cars in the parking lot were Hyundai Sonatas. At that time, Hyundai Motors controlled almost half the domestic automobile market. Hyundai manufactured three of the four top-selling models: the best-selling Elantra, the Excel, and the Sonata. Hyundai also manufactured the best-selling luxury car in South Korea, the Grandeur, which was the car of choice for business and political leaders. Hyundai's dominance in the market helped to establish a clear hierarchy of models: from the Grandeur to the Sonata, the Elantra, and the Excel. The relatively long life span of South Korean car models at the time reinforced this hierarchy. Although some other manufacturers' models were comparable in terms of size and price, Hyundai models were preferred at every price level[18] except the most inexpensive (where Hyundai chose not to compete). In evaluating comparable cars (i.e., the Hyundai Grandeur v. the Kia Potentia, the Hyundai Super Salon v. the Daewoo Prince, the Hyundai Elantra v. the Kia Sephia or the Daewoo Espero, etc.), most of the women in Yoido stated that Daewoo models were sturdy and perhaps safer on the highway, but because they were heavy they were harder to maneuver in the city. Kia models, they said, were high quality, but their styling was poor. In each instance, however, Hyundai was the standard against which other models were judged, whether superior or inferior, and although a few women complained that little things broke on Hyundai cars (plastic parts of the interior, for example), there was general agreement that Hyundai models were the only cars that kept their value for the resale market.

There were clear standards for choosing car models appropriate to one's social position. This can be seen in the following two examples. One independent businessman told me that he was often asked by friends and coworkers and, more troubling for him, by clients why he drove a Daewoo LeMans (a car that ranked somewhere between the relatively modest Hyundai Elantra and Hyundai's bottom-of-the-line Excel). He took this kind of questioning, which called attention to an idiosyncratic choice, as a form of indirect criticism.[19] He felt that he was not only being pushed to purchase a higher-status vehicle more appropriate to his age and position but that he was also implicitly asked to clarify his status through the purchase of a model that could be more easily ranked. He admitted that he had already resolved to choose a Hyundai model next time around because he thought it would attract fewer questions. In another instance, a mother in Yoido, who had married at the relatively young age of twenty-one and had borne her two children in her early twenties, was pestered by her older son to sell her Hyundai Sonata and buy a Hyundai Grandeur. "*Why don't we have a Grandeur?*" he whined. "*Tae-yoon's mother drives a Grandeur. Bo-gang's mother drives a Grandeur.*" This boy's mother was in a difficult position. Because of her early marriage she was four or five years younger than the mothers of her son's friends, and she felt it would be inappropriate for her, a woman in her mid-thirties, to drive a Grandeur. "*You still have to respect age. Having money doesn't mean you can act like you have earned a respectful position if you are still young. It wouldn't be appropriate,*" she explained to me. She did promise her son that she would buy a Grandeur in another few years; it was as clear to her as it was to her son that a Grandeur would soon be the right car for their family.

While cars were ubiquitous in Yoido, private car ownership was only just becoming possible in the early 1990s for low-income households in South Korea. Two new very small automobile models, the Kia Pride and the Daewoo Tico, had been introduced into the marketplace to reach new market segments: newly married couples and lower-income households. Sales of the Pride were slow in the first few years after its debut in 1987, but after the even smaller Tico hit the roads in spring 1992, sales of the Pride took off. "People appear to think that the Pride is not at the lowest end of passenger cars," explained a happy Kia spokesman (*Korea Newsreview*, 18 November 1992).

One-third of the households in Talgoljjagi that completed my survey owned a private automobile in 1991–1992; of those, half used the automobile for directly commercial purposes (as taxis or trucks). The survey may have oversampled Talgoljjagi car owners: my nighttime count of cars, trucks, and taxis parked on the streets and in the few parking areas at the bottom of the hill showed only nineteen cars in an area of the neighborhood that had nearly 150 housing units. Among the group of people connected to the *kong-bubang*, the few car owners were extremely generous with their vehicles. One young man had recently purchased a Kia Pride in order to drive to work in Suwŏn, a town nearly one hour south of Seoul. Despite his long hours of work and the nerve-racking commute, he often acquiesced to the pleas of his sister and her friends to drive them to Dongdaemun for a late-night snack when he got back from his job. Although he was a shy fellow, Yŏng-il's car allowed him an opportunity to play an important role in his more gregarious sister's social life, and although no one seemed to think better of him because he had a car, he was obviously glad for the extra value he could offer to the group. Another young man, a veteran of one of the Middle East construction teams, used his minivan almost as a community bus. He drove his coworkers to construction sites when they had work, and when the neighborhood arranged a ceremony to honor the local minister's latest book, he drove eight people to the church. On several occasions he took me across town at night to the place where I was staying rather than allow me to ride the buses alone. The pleasure of riding in a car was still enough of a novelty that often two or three friends would come along for the ride, to listen to the radio and enjoy the neon-lit scenery of the city.

## LUXURIES, COMFORT, AND PRIDE

Cars were perhaps the most significant markers of South Korea's arrival at a sophisticated stage of industrial and economic development, but other signs were ubiquitous too. In the early 1990s department stores saw a surge in sales. In 1991 alone, the Korean Department Store Association reported a 45.8 percent increase in Kangnam area department store sales compared to the previous year. North of the Han River, stores registered an increase of 24.7 percent. While much of what was sold in department stores was made in South Korea, South Koreans also developed a taste for foreign goods during this period. Foreign boutiques opened in many department stores, selling internationally recognized designer brands of cosmetics and clothing, including Gucci, Bally, Burberrys, Missoni, Yves Saint Laurent, and Sonia Rykiel. In the early 1990s there was significant growth in imports of golf clubs, electronic games, and even microwave ovens (which competed directly with products made in South Korea) (*Korea Herald*, 26 January 1993). Imports of luxury food and beverages also increased dramatically; in the first three quarters of 1991 shipments of Japanese fresh fish and those of beef from the United States both doubled (*Korea Herald*, 6 November 1991). In 1992 the value of imports of chocolates in the preceding eleven months amounted to U.S.$13.45 million, 253 percent more than for the same period in 1991, and imports of grapefruits, caramels, and whiskey were also escalating. Travel itself flourished: foreign tourism was liberalized in 1988, and each year thereafter a greater number of South Koreans had the chance to see the world. By 1991, the average South Korean traveler overseas spent more than U.S.$2,000 per trip.

The expansion of the consumer market enabled South Koreans to participate in their nation's export success through ownership of both domestically produced and imported goods. This process established South Korea's position in the ranks of industrialized nations in the minds of many South Koreans. The blossoming of the marketplace also generated another comparison: that with North Korea. South Koreans were well aware that until the mid-1970s, North Korean industrialization appeared to be advancing at least as quickly as that in South Korea. By the middle of the 1980s, however, international statistics indicated that South Korea had pulled safely ahead, and the widespread availability of the material signs of national wealth helped make the statistics real. Roy Richard Grinker describes an exhibition of North Korean everyday objects entitled *Pukhan senghwal* (North Korean lifestyles) held first in 1993 in the Midopa department store in central Seoul and then moved to a permanent exhibition hall in the city of Taejŏn. The exhibition included a two-room "model P'yŏngyang apartment" set up to display a peculiar array of household objects, which included "canned foods, jewelry, books, toys, clothing . . . toothbrush, stethoscope, thermometer, after-shave lotion, door-knobs, locks, umbrellas, fans, chopsticks, knives, can openers, spoons" (Grinker 1998:57). Grinker shows that people responded to this exhibition of humble, noncommercial objects by seeing North Korean ordinary life as lost in a past that is at once almost pathetic and at the same time considered to be closer to authentic Korean culture—much like urban South Koreans view their countryside compatriots (ibid.:61). The exhibition reinforced the sense of national progress—*South* Korean national progress—toward modernity through consumer advances.

As this chapter's epigraph notes, starting in the middle of the 1980s, South Korea's market "expanded at high velocity" (Baek 1993:33). Baek points to two related phenomena: first, regional and class differences in consumer culture are increasing and, second, the rise in consumption itself "has been sufficient to arouse fantasies in people that Korean society had become just like an advanced nation" (ibid.). The elaboration of the market and the culture of consumption in South Korea was rapid and pervasive. Laurel Kendall has observed that, "The 1980s was a decade of prosperity that saw the emergence of a full-blown consumer culture, at once celebrated, mocked, and criticized. It was a time of intense national pride, but also of uneasy wondering whether, in pursuit of economic stability and a comfortable standard of living, too much of Korea's own heritage had been surrendered or corrupted by Western influences" (Kendall 1996:15). South Koreans and foreign observers alike believe that the changes have been profound.

The material environment, the consumer culture, demonstrated to South Koreans that the nation had "developed" (*paltal*). Mass marketing generated an image of mass culture, mass consumption, and consumer equality. In reality, however, consumer opportunities and choices were divergent: Seoulites were experiencing the new context in various ways, and through their experiences they generated new views of the emergent consumer culture. In the next chapter I turn to the anticonsumer backlash.

It took me a few months to find a family to live with in Seoul. In some ways I regret that I didn't have the courage to take up residence with the first family I met.[1] On the plane over from San Francisco I fell into conversation with one of the flight attendants, and she took an interest in my project. She phoned me several weeks later and offered to introduce me to a woman she thought would fit my project perfectly. She had already spoken with "Mrs. Lee,"[2] and Mrs. Lee had said she would be glad to meet me. I thanked the flight attendant, took down the phone number, and summoned up the nerve to make the call.

We arranged to meet one early afternoon in a coffee shop in the Hyundai department store in Apkujŏngdong. When I arrived, Mrs. Lee smiled and waved energetically from a seat at the counter. She was dressed in a flowing, cream-colored suit with a colorful floral scarf draped around her neck: a flattering style many wealthy women in their forties and fifties had adopted. She guided me to a table and ordered two dishes of ice cream and began to describe to me how it would be to live with her family. "*We have done a lot of traveling, so my sons are eager to learn more English. We were in California this summer—oh, but I suppose Miss Park told you that; we met on the flight. My husband is hardly ever home; he is the company director, so he is very busy. That's okay—I have fun anyway. I go out with my friend and dance, you know?*" I was still struggling to gain my sea legs in Korean, so my comprehension lagged behind the pace of the conversation. She was smiling, and I certainly believed that she was a woman who knew how to have fun. I smiled back. My own comments were sparse, but that didn't seem to bother her much. "*Are you finished?*" she asked. "*Then let's go.*" She twisted in her seat and directed the young man behind the counter to bring her a telephone. She punched in some numbers. "*It's me. I'm leaving,*" she said, hung up the phone, and got up to leave. I was a little uncertain about who should pay for the ice cream (or, to put it more precisely, I had assumed she would pay because she had invited me and because she was my elder, but she showed no signs of doing so), so I brought out my wallet from my handbag. She laughed and told me her friend owned this shop and that I should put my money away.

"*I own a little café, too, but I like this one better. The place I own is more for college students,*" she explained. We took the elevator down to the first floor, and walked out to the parking lot and directly into her waiting black Grandeur. Vivaldi's *Four Seasons* was playing on the car stereo. "*Let's go home,*" she told the driver.

The driver turned left out of the parking lot and then took the next left into the Hyundai apartment complex. We drove to one of the buildings near the banks of the Han River. The whole trip was no more than a quarter mile. The driver let us off in front of the entryway. Mrs. Lee exchanged a friendly greeting with the security guard in his booth, and we rode the elevator up to her apartment. It was the largest and most modern apartment I'd yet seen in Seoul. The entry space alone, where we wiggled out of our street shoes, was the size of some of the homes·I later visited in Talgoljjagi. She escorted me into the living room. I sat on the sofa, which was in the style of Louis-XIV reproduction furniture, creamily floral with gilt edging. She walked to the stereo and put a CD into the player before coming over to sit in one of the upholstered side chairs. She handed me the CD case. "*Do you like the Scorpions?*" she asked. She sang along vaguely to the song. "*I love their music. You can help me understand the words.*" I took out the lyric sheet from the case. "*My friend comes over sometimes to listen with me. If you explain the words, I can sing them with more feeling.*" I was studying the lyric sheet; her meaning of the word "friend" was beginning to sink in. Mrs. Lee noticed my dawning comprehension. "*You understand?*" she asked. Then she made it even clearer, smiling, using an English word. "*My '*boyfriend*',*" she said. The front door opened and the chauffeur walked in. I hadn't noticed before what a good-looking, tall, young man he was. He walked toward a room in the back. "*Listen to some music with us,*" Mrs. Lee suggested. Moments later he emerged from his room, dressed in black leather pants and silky shirt. He leaned against the archway separating the living room from the kitchen. We all wordlessly shared the music of the Scorpions for a few minutes. I did not get the feeling that the chauffeur was Mrs. Lee's boyfriend, although he seemed to be on more intimate terms than a mere chauffeur.

I looked around the living room, and noticed water stains here and there on the wallpaper. Over the following months I learned that the initial rush to construct apartments across Seoul had resulted in common leaks and warping even in luxury complexes; families appeared to spend money decorating and redecorating but not so much on ordinary maintenance of the decor. A friend asked her own rather wealthy parents about this for me, and her mother drew a connection to the war. "*Why spend so much effort on little repairs, when everything could be lost in an instant?*"

Both sons came in shortly afterward. The mother introduced me as their English teacher and sent the three of us down to the small green space behind the building, near a sandy playground, so that I could watch them during their golf lessons. I watched for an hour, and spoke a little with them in an impoverished mixture of English and Korean.[3] We played some guessing games and competed against one another to run the length of the parking lot. When we were done, I went up to the apartment and told Mrs. Lee I had an appointment and needed to get going. "*I'll drive you,*" she offered and wouldn't take no for an answer. All five of us, the chauffeur again in his working suit, got into the car, and I was escorted north across the river to the Hyatt Hotel, the closest plausible destination I could think of.

Mrs. Lee had a seemingly irrepressible sense of pleasure and entitlement to have fun. She invited me to call her when I wanted to go out dancing. Instead, I shyly retreated to Yoido.

# CHAPTER 4

## *KWASOBI CH'UBANG*: MEASURING EXCESS

*Desire and repression are an occasion for the consolidation of juridical structures; desire is manufactured and forbidden as a ritual symbolic gesture whereby the juridical model exercises and consolidates its own power.*

Judith Butler, *Gender Trouble: Feminism and the Subversion of Identity*

During the late 1980s and early 1990s public critique of the pace and scale of consumer expansiveness intensified. *Kwasobi*,[1] a Sino-Korean word meaning excessive consumption, was the term applied to the phenomenon of consuming beyond what was appropriate. Measuring this appropriateness, however, was a complex and murky matter, and the terms of propriety shifted with changing national economic and social circumstances. Appropriateness might vary with social categories such as age or class, or it might adhere to crude nationalistic interest in supporting domestic producers. More subtly, consumer responsibility might involve participating in the cosmopolitan world of imported goods, or it might require a resolution of seemingly conflicting interests of family against those of the nation, and the propriety of the cultural practice of men's consumption of women's sexual services was questioned but hardly interrogated. These concerns were not new. Appropriate consumption was a moral issue with a long history in South Korea. In this chapter, I explore the discursive field of "frugality" and "overconsumption," and examine the forms and sources of this discourse. While moral constructions of appropriate and patriotic consumption can be traced back to the precolonial period, in recent decades frugality has been represented as a strategy for national economic development, a moral practice of cultural preservation from the corruption of luxury and modernization, and a means of defending the nation from international shame and economic ruin. *Kwasobi* discourse has explicitly tied individual lifestyles to the national destiny.

## A HISTORICAL MEMORY: FRUGALITY AS PATRIOTISM

Frugality itself, as a public moral value, has deep roots in South Korea. The personal virtues of frugality and moderation resonated with some aspects of the neo-Confucian outlook of the historical *yangban* aristocratic elite (Michell 1986). During the long Chosŏn period (1392–1910), scholarship and intellectual pursuits were the privilege and the duty of the *yangban* gentlemen;[2] material and commercial concerns were, in theory at least, anathema to them (Ki-baek Lee 1984:175). *Yangban* families supported themselves primarily with the proceeds of lands to which they had been given rent-collection rights from tenant farmers, the produce of their farm lands worked by slaves as well as with government service. Money and luxury, in theory if not always in fact, were supposed to be beyond the realm of *yangban* thought. Trade was the domain of lower classes of men, *kaekchu* and *yogak* (brokers and wholesale merchants) and *pobusang* (peddlers) as well as *kongin* (licensed suppliers to the government) (Yu Won-dong 1978). It was this lower class of merchants who also performed many banking functions (lending out money and accepting deposits).

During the second half of the Chosŏn period, and in particular following changes in agricultural technology, commercial trade, and the taxation system in the seventeenth century, the social hierarchy began to blur as some peasants and merchants were able to accumulate significant wealth, while some *yangban* families descended into poverty (Ki-baek Lee 1984:228). Moreover, in the last century or so of the dynasty, excessive exactions from the peasantry by *yangban* hoping to bribe their way to a government position (or merely hoping to enrich their own coffers) intensified accusations of *yangban* corruption. These processes had several complicated effects on the concept of frugality. The luxurious lifestyles of the fortunate few were critiqued by a faction of the *yangban*, some of whom argued that the *yangban* should adopt truly productive pursuits, while others encouraged a return to a proper scholarly life. In the nineteenth century, popular culture (*p'ansori*, mask dances, and stories) mocked wicked and ineffectual *yangban*, while pretenders who had purchased *yangban* status were also targets of ridicule for their attempts to substitute riches for heritage. Nevertheless, the ideal of the nonmaterialist *yangban* scholar endured. The historian Carter Eckert notes, for example, that even on the eve of the twentieth century, the grandfather of the man who was to become one of Korea's most influential industrialists during the colonial period "is said to have considered commercial activities a violation of Confucian principles" (1991:33).

The Christian (especially Protestant) espousal of modesty in material things reinforced this message of the moral superiority of frugality. In the late nineteenth century and throughout the period of Japanese colonial domination, Christian organizations passed along a message of egalitarianism and thrift together with their support of national development and independence in their many schools and organizations (such as the Young Men's Christian Association). The role Christian organizations played in resisting colonial rule and, more recently, in protesting the authoritarian state and oppressive labor practices also helped to disseminate such Christian ethics throughout South Korea.

To the extent that they were seen, or saw themselves, as inheritors of the honor of the *yangban*, Korean capitalists have had to skirt the issue of the profit motive. In the twentieth century Korean capitalists have underplayed the importance of the pursuit of wealth as a motivation for their activities, instead emphasizing the contributions they have made to the nation's well-being through economic activity. During the years just before Japanese occupation and during colonial rule, Korean intellectuals wrestled with the need to invigorate the national economy, and Korean entrepreneurs were seen as potentially nationalist agents working for a wider political cause.[3] This pattern solidified during the colonial period, when Korean industrialists espoused a philosophy of strengthening Korea through the manufacture and sale of domestically made products. Eckert's study of business development in the colonial era shows, however, that "for a variety of reasons . . . including the dependence of Korean firms . . . on the colonial political and economic structure, the Korean bourgeoisie's commitment to nationalist principles was in fact weak to nonexistent" (1991:190) although businessmen frequently asserted their patriotism. Nevertheless, moderation as a social responsibility of the rich was from early on part of the picture of capitalism Korean entrepreneurs presented to the wider public. Eckert quotes from a 1935 interview with the eminent Kim Sŏngsu, textile entrepreneur and founder of the newspaper *Tonga Ilbo*: "There's nothing more vulgar than money, nothing more filthy than money. How could [anyone] ever say that money was the most important thing in the world? I, for one, have never once thought that money was the most important [thing]. More [important] than money are humanity and also righteousness" (Eckert 1991:225).

While Korean capitalists were eschewing the acquisition of wealth, on the consumer side strategic deployment of the small resources of the Korean populace were important cultural elements of domestic resistance to Japanese domination. By the early twentieth century, just a few decades after Korea had been opened to international commerce, Japan had maneuvered the Korean nation into a huge debt to its looming eastern neighbor. The

Movement for the Redemption of the National Debt (*Kukch'e Posang Undong*) was formed in 1907 to collect funds to pay off the debt in an attempt to regain national independence.[4] The movement (albeit ultimately futile) was popular and widespread; men gave up smoking and donated the money they had saved, while women sold their jewelry for the cause (Eckert et al. 1990:235), setting a precedent for a patriotic practice of frugality among ordinary Koreans. In 1909 a short-lived movement to support native industry, known as the "Love Korean Products" movement, was established (Wells 1985:828), also to little effect.

In the context of a new colonial cultural policy allowing for some greater freedom of assembly for Koreans in the 1920s,[5] several strategies for achieving national independence through acts of economic patriotism (for example, savings clubs and temperance societies) developed. Cho Man-sik, a Presbyterian elder and secretary-general of the P'yŏngyang YMCA who had already been an active participant in the patriotic movement (he was imprisoned for ten months for his role as an organizer of the 1919 March First uprising), established the largest of these, the Korean Products Promotion Society, in 1922.

The society was based on the idea that Korea had fallen prey to Japanese domination because Koreans had not established a foundation of self-sufficiency; any patriotic resistance to colonial rule would have to establish first the economic basis of national prosperity. Japanese colonial policy had constrained the development of Korean industry; the small output of Korean manufacturers was dominated by cheaper and higher-quality imports of consumer goods. The Korean Products Promotion Society's program called for the purchase of domestic goods and the rejection of imported products, the establishment of local businesses and industrial cooperatives to manufacture and supply the population with native clothing and food, and an attempt to hold on to the land. "In order to promote Korean Products we must make it our aim to buy and use goods made by Koreans, and also unite to manufacture and supply those goods we need. Unless we come to our senses and exert ourselves in this way, how can we expect to maintain our livelihood and develop our society?" asked the society's manifesto (quoted in Wells 1985:838). Underlying the movement was a sense that a new form of self-support and self-sufficiency[6] was essential. Historian Kenneth Wells paraphrases the society's philosophy that took the peasant household as its model: "The former *self-sufficiency* of the home unit had vanished, replaced by a short-sighted, suicidal opting for present convenience. It is easier, at first, to let others produce goods and simply to buy them—but after that, the deluge: no land, no nation. *Self-sufficiency* meant being responsible for one's own and the nation's economy" (Wells 1985:839; italics in original).

Although the movement ultimately had little impact on the development of a native industrial base,[7] Cho Man-sik himself and the movement more generally were popular symbols of an ethical nationalism incorporating both spiritual and practical elements. At the time, Cho was regarded as a "Korean Gandhi" for his frugal lifestyle and exemplary moral leadership. In the 1990s Cho's example was revived and used as a reference point for South Korean consumer nationalism.

Following liberation, in the second half of the twentieth century members of the South Korean industrialist class (along with other upper-income individuals) still found themselves in a difficult position. In a nation dependent on economic growth, business owners were judged by the public according to the degree to which they apparently put the interests of the nation as a whole ahead of their own prosperity. Eckert observed that capitalistic development in Korea lacked an underlying historical or philosophical basis for seeing the pursuit of self-interest and personal profit as a social good.

> Capitalism [in Korea] as a conscious strategy of national development antedated its development as a socioeconomic system, and the original formulation of what might be called a Korean capitalist morality came not from a bourgeoisie, which did not exist at the time, or from an intellectual elite who, like Smith and Locke, were themselves enmeshed in an already developing capitalist society, but rather from late Chosŏn reformist scholars like Yu Kilchun (1856–1914). Such men were steeped in a long neo-Confucian tradition that emphasized communitarian values and were interested in capitalism primarily as a way to augment the wealth and power of the country to save it from imperialist domination. Ideas of Confucianism, nationalism, and capitalism thus all fused in the late nineteenth-century Korean intellectual milieu to produce a moral vision of capitalist activity stressing national needs and goals and denigrating the purely private pursuit of wealth.
>
> (Eckert 1993:117–118)

These sentiments were still current after the division of Korea into two countries. Economic activity that strengthened the Republic of Korea was essential to the defense of the nation (in particular during the 1950s and 1960s, when North Korea's social and economic development appeared to be at least keeping pace with that of the South), but the pursuit of profit for personal gain was not portrayed—as it often is in, say, the United States—as the ultimate motivation, the beating heart, of a healthy capitalist economy. In the United States the public benefits of capitalism are not viewed as outcomes consciously engineered by any agents acting in the interest of *society*; yet public discourse in the U.S. expresses an expectation that the sum of all the agents pursuing profit will result in benefits for all. South Korean entrepreneurs need to tell a different story. In his ethnography of a South Korean *chaebŏl*, Roger Janelli notes that the official company history highlights the founder's nationalism, and company managers assert that the *chaebŏl* still contributes to the welfare of the nation (1993:112–113). Eckert argues that the South Korean bourgeoisie has been unable to attain a position of hegemony, in part because of this culturally distinct perception of the moral position of capitalist enterprise and in part because of disappointed expectations that the upper class, like the *yangban* in an idealized past, would take care of the working masses: "the class continues to be surrounded by an aura of public disapproval and illegitimacy" (Eckert 1993:110).

Repeatedly during the period following the establishment of the two Koreas, rich and ambitious men, along with their families, (women were seldom singled-out in the early years of the R.O.K.) were brought before the public and symbolically pilloried for their profiteering. Shortly after Park Chung Hee came to power in the 1961 military coup, his government established a revolutionary court to put on trial, among others, people accused of "illicit wealth accumulation"—mainly those who had profited through unproductive (and/or corrupt) activities during the Syngman Rhee regime (1948–1960). Jung-en Woo lists the activities that could result in a charge of profiteering, among them activities that were explicitly illegal (such as "illegally transferred their wealth abroad" or "illicitly earned profits totaling more than 100 million *hwan* [an old unit of currency] by either purchasing or renting publicly owned properties,") but also activities that were not so clearly beyond the bounds of legality, such as "obtained loans or purchases of more than $100,000 worth of government- or bank-owned foreign exchange." Woo comments: "In other words, it was a crime to have indulged in the political economy of the Rhee era" (Woo 1991:83). The arrested included fifty-one owners of the largest businesses.[8] Later administrations followed Park's example: Chun Doo-hwan (later himself convicted of similar charges) started his rule by purging from his administration public officials who had profited from their positions. Kim Young-sam as well tried in his first months in office to establish his moral high ground vis-à-vis the dense webs that had evolved between business and government.

The issue was not as simple as "corruption." Throughout the 1960s President Park spiced his speeches with references to "corrupt businessmen, who in the past pursued an exorbitant profit through tax evasion and non-productive speculation, or . . . would-be industrialists who had their factory make noise only during the time when a government fund was on its way to them" (Park 1970:137), as he did this New Year's message of 1968. But while there is ample evidence that many South Korean industrialists eagerly—and sometimes overly so—sought personal profit, it is important to recognize how widespread and pervasive the censure of the pursuit of enrichment was throughout the period of industrial expansion. Speaking directly to the business community in 1966, Park reminded his audience that

> our total effort put into achieving the historic task of modernization of our fatherland is not for the benefit of certain individuals, not of certain groups. It is for the benefit and glory of the present as well as our posterity. . . . In this sense, I urge you to think of the society and the nation before temporary excessive profits or the profit of "my company" or "my factory." . . . You must be aware at all times of the fact that those who pursue immediate gains in complete disregard of our current task of building a self-sufficient economy will be judged by the public as they deserve.
>
> (Park 1970:154)[9]

This kind of discourse meant that if business owners dared to engage in conspicuous display, they made themselves vulnerable to criticism of their patriotism as well as their social consciousness and their propriety.

These messages may have been aimed explicitly at business leaders but the implied audience was wider, and many less wealthy individuals imbibed the notion that personal indulgence was improper. During South Korea's lean years in Park's early tenure, quotidian frugality was ideologically transformed into an act of popular patriotism. During the early years of the industrial push, Park placed the burden of responsibility for the success of national development strategies on the shoulders of individuals in all their daily economic decisions. Shortly after he assumed command, his Supreme Council of National Reconstruction imposed rations on rice at restaurants and outlawed the sale of goods on the black market (Lie 1998). In his 1968 New Year's message, he said,

> If each of our 30 million people wastes 10 *wŏn* a day, the daily loss will amount to 300 million *wŏn*, and if the daily waste continues year round, a huge sum of 100 billion *wŏn* will be lost. The latter figure corresponds to half of the national budget. . . . When a frugal spirit permeates homes, schools, and offices, making all citizens watchful against waste and loss, no matter how trivial it may be, this will display formidable power in economic construction: as the proverb says, "Little and often make a heap in time." It should be recognized deeply that a frugal life, doing away with waste and practicing economy, will act as a "hidden force," benefiting not only housekeeping in individual homes but the whole national economy.
>
> (Park 1970:134–135)

The women I interviewed clearly recalled the patriotic campaigns during the Park era to save electricity and to collect scraps of metal and paper for reuse during their school days,[10] and while South Koreans generally dismissed such campaigns as powerless to affect their opinions, most people also easily recalled many patriotic slogans and activities dating from several decades ago. Except for the youth, memories of these messages haunted the contemporary discourse about frugality.

## CONSUMER MORALITIES

As we saw in the previous chapter, after decades of privation, consumer opportunities blossomed in the 1980s. Many South Koreans welcomed the chance to fill their lives with new furniture and appliances, gadgets and automobiles, works of art, expensive hobbies, jewelry, music, and nights out on the town. To a greater extent than ever before, however, these new opportunities to own objects and purchase entertainment underscored the economic gap between prosperous and impoverished households in South Korea. A discursive backlash was generated, addressing several points: a culture of immoral indulgence, the social and moral problems arising from the conspicuousness of differences between rich and poor, and the material impact international trade (in particular, the import of foreign goods) might have on the domestic economy.

The Seoul YMCA had a long history of involvement in consumer issues and held seminars, organized citizen groups, and conducted research into what it believed were unwholesome consumption patterns. The chief of the Department of Civil Society Development at the Seoul YMCA explained to me that the YMCA's involvement in the anti-*kwasobi* campaign stemmed from a desire to promote clean living, and their program was launched in 1986 with a seminar entitled "Social Forum for the Cultivation of the Consciousness of a Wholesome Consumer Lifestyle." This exploration of South Korean consumption patterns focused on problems generated by the sudden successes of the South Korean economy in the middle of the 1980s. In the seminar's introductory remarks, the president of the Seoul YMCA stated that the extreme speed of economic development demonstrated the resourcefulness of the South Korean people, but that

> on the other hand, following the rapid economic improvements many problems have arisen. . . . The accumulation of U.S.$48 billion of international debt is shaking the foundation of our independent economy with several problems; first and foremost we might mention the impoverishment of the agricultural economy, the insolvent mass-production companies, and the gap between rich and poor; following the ideology of the power of money (*hwanggŭmmannŭng chuŭi*) inverted values destroyed our social ethics and even public discipline, giving rise to all kinds of social diseases and immorality based on abuse of connections.
>
> (Seoul YMCA 1986:7)

In particular, the seminar focused on solving the problems of "relative poverty and the sense of class incongruity" and on reestablishing the independence[11] of the South Korean economy from foreign debts through increasing the savings rate and national investment funds. The seminar participants were clearly extremely concerned about the importance of the foreign debt[12] (one section was entitled, "The Nation's Debt, the Citizen's Debt, Precisely My Debt: The Debt I Must Repay"). Equally troubling to the conference participants was what they saw as the increasingly conspicuous difference between rich and poor—made visible in large part through new consumption patterns.

Seoul University professor Son Bong-ho articulated the conference's critique and plan:

> The key is asceticism. . . . Nowadays our society's consumer trend is developing toward extravagance (*sach'i*) and an all-out dedication to pleasure (*hyangnak ilbyŏndo*) because the general recognition of the value of abstinence has been erased; this is something that makes our culture and our human nature extremely superficial.
>
> (Seoul YMCA 1986:25)

Son identified several reasons to embrace asceticism: the ability to suppress instincts sets humans apart from animals; extravagance and waste uses up resources and creates pollution, "a sin against all humanity" (Seoul YMCA 1986:27); and, finally:

> asceticism is a great contribution to the materialization of social justice. Even if people say that the social structure promotes the enrichment of the rich and the impoverishment of the poor (*pinikpin puikpu*), if in particular the people who live the lifestyle of the upper class practice asceticism, this will greatly diminish the injuries of this structure. However high one's income, if we eschew excessive consumption, the proper portion of that income can be saved and used to promote production of benefit to the entire society.
>
> (Seoul YMCA 1986:28)

In this early conference, the Seoul YMCA's argument for frugality is rather vague, based primarily on three arguments: that conspicuous consumption makes poor people feel uncomfortable, that personal restraint and asceticism is a humane virtue, and that domestic savings—achieved through the rejection of consumption—are necessary for a healthy national economy with few foreign debts.

This initial conference was held when the South Korean economy was at the threshold of its first flush years. From 1986 through 1989 South Korea experienced a positive trade balance for the first time in its history. South Korea successfully hosted the Asian Games in 1986; popular protests brought about the end of authoritarian rule and the beginning of democracy in 1987; and in 1988 the world convened in Seoul for the Olympics. But the international successes of the mid-1980s had generally receded by the end of the decade. In the late 1980s strikes, skyrocketing real estate prices, and the threat of competition from countries in Southeast Asia with cheaper labor eroded the sense of celebration, and the South Korean national economy slipped back into the red in 1990.

Three years after the Wholesome Consumer Lifestyle conference, the Seoul YMCA published another booklet, this time to report on research it had conducted into the "pleasure (i.e., sex) industry" (*hyangnak sanŏp*). While the "pleasure industry" was certainly nothing new to South Korean culture, it attracted a great deal of public attention in the late 1980s. Using a medical metaphor, the booklet opened with a summation of some unsettling economic "symptoms" (*chinghudŭl*):

> In particular, lately our economy has several characteristics: (1) the rate of economic growth has been reduced from the original plan of 8% to 6–7%, (2) the consumer price index has risen from the original 5–7% to 7–8%, (3) the quarterly growth index fell to 5.7% and within that the manufacturing sector's growth index fell to 1.0%, (4) in the private sector, money and assets dropped 14.2% while consumer outlays increased and borrowing grew to 123.2% and in the last year during the same period, the individual savings contribution to funds for enterprises was insufficient, falling from 110.8% to 58.8%.
>
> (Seoul YMCA 1989:6)

Staying with the the medical imagery, the report's prognosis was that if the spread of *kwasobi* and the rise in prices were to continue, "these will be a harmful influence (*yŏnghyangŭl kkich'ilgŏt*) on the healthy development of the national economy." Therefore, the YMCA conducted a survey to provide information for action.

> It is apparent that the extravagant places of pleasure (*hohwa yuhŭngŏpso*) and the pleasure industry continue to prosper, and it is also certainly the fact that the prosperity of the pleasure industry, not captured by the official statistics, is an important part of the unreported aspect of the tremendous rising of the national propensity to consume. . . . Through this survey . . . we can examine the actual costs of using extravagant places of pleasure and the ratio of the income and market consumption expenditures of the pleasure industry and we can clarify the overconsuming character (*kwasobijŏk sŏnggyŏk*), and indicate how large these economically, socially, and culturally unproductive expen-

ditures are, and later we present the basic material for regulating the pleasure industry.

(Seoul YMCA 1989:6)

The survey looked at room salons, stand bars, adult discos, "high class" (*kogŭp*) saunas, massage shops, and decadent (*t'oe p'ye*) barber shops[13] to survey the price of specific alcoholic beverages, side dishes, tips, music and singing, "sharing a bed" (*tongch'im piyong*, which was broken down into the price of the room and the price of the *kisaeng*, the woman), cover charges, bathing, massage, sexual service massage, and barber services. Commenting on the report, Koryo University sociology professor Kim Mun-cho pointed to what he thought was the most significant causes of this "pleasure culture":

For the most part, in the past discussions of the reasons for the trend toward luxury and pleasure took such psychological issues as our innate pleasure principle or the spirit of sudden riches or also the dismantling of traditional ethics as the topic of discussion. . . . But luxury and the pleasure industry are no less than the extreme form of *kwasobi*, and if what we call *kwasobi* is recognized [as part of the] inclusion in Korean society's industrial capitalism [and as] a universal problem of capitalistic society, we can see the need for a diagnosis of the cause [considering] the transition of capitalism and the connected structural explanations.

(Seoul YMCA 1989:20)

Kim's analysis points back to the underlying suspicion of the culture of capitalism with its attendant emphasis on the individual. In his discussion, Kim expands from a condemnation of the popularity of the "pleasure industry" to a condemnation of luxury itself. Ultimately, this report indicates that perhaps the impulse to experience pleasure is an urge people ought to suppress.

Improper spending, such as expenditures on sexual services, was discursively tied to the way in which an individual had earned the money spent. In 1990 the Seoul YMCA reported on its Citizen's Campaign to Eradicate Pleasure Culture (*hyangnak munhwa ch'ubang simin undong*). This campaign pointed to "unearned income" (*pullo sodŭk*), which was defined as income from investments, assets, and income transfers from others[14] (Seoul YMCA 1990a:10), as one of the main factors behind the continual growth of the pleasure industry. "In our society an absurd amount of income . . . from real estate investments and stock investments is concentrated in the hands of investors. To demonstrate, in 1987 the profits generated from the rise in the price of land was 34 thousand trillion *wŏn*, which was 85% of the income from labor in that year" (Seoul YMCA 1990a:12). Nevertheless, however important the economic causes were,

> the social atmosphere is shown to be crystallized in the disorder of society's morals. If society's morals were wholesome, the patrons of the pleasure industry would not be as plentiful as they are, and however limited the employment opportunities got, there would not be as many women working in pleasure industry places as there are. We cannot fail to overlook the point that in the process of economic development, people's values have degenerated to the worship of mammon.
>
> (Seoul YMCA 1990a:13)

The concerns of YMCA publications and studies shifted subtly in the early 1990s. The most pressing issue was no longer how best to adjust to the new conditions of affluence but how to restore South Korea's competitive strength. Rather than continuing to focus on the questionable moral status of personal indulgence, the Seoul YMCA turned to practical issues of how to defend the domestic economy. In this later period, the Seoul YMCA issued pamphlets discussing where to buy good domestic products (Seoul YMCA 1991), the proper frugal conduct at *Ch'usŏk*, a major gift-giving holiday (Seoul YMCA 1990b), improving the relations between consumers and farmers by buying South Korean produce (Seoul YMCA 1990c), the quality and desirability of foreign products and the significance of brand names (Seoul YMCA, n.d.) as well as a general consideration of the *kwasobi* issue (Seoul YMCA 1990d). Nevertheless, even after this shift, the Seoul YMCA approach encompassed both structural and sociological analyses of the causes of *kwasobi*, and it did not abandon its strong moral criticism of indulgence on the grounds that it did direct harm to the domestic economy, that it endangered the harmony between the classes, and that it was unwholesome in the first place.

The YMCA was a leader in the frugality movement, but other organizations (such as the National Council of Consumer Protection Organizations) were significant actors as well. A central issue was the defense of domestic agriculture. The 1970s were hard years for South Korean farmers, with rising rates of rural poverty and of tenancy.[15] During the 1980s economic conditions in the countryside continued to worsen. Government agricultural price supports were cut, while imports of foreign agricultural products were increased during the early years of the Chun Doo Hwan administration. Farmers' incomes rose during this period, but so did their indebtedness; by 1986, the average debt of farming households was one-third the value of the household's income (Hart-Landsberg 1993:257).

In the 1980s farmers organized to protest these conditions. Farmers demonstrated for such issues as irrigation tax relief, land ownership for tenant farmers, reductions in agricultural imports, resistance to further opening of the agricultural markets, democratization of agricultural cooperatives, and an increase in the price of rice (Hart-Landsberg 1993:258). The farmers' complaints were received with sympathy in many quarters of Seoul. A large fraction of Seoul's population was born in the countryside and had first-hand experience of farming life; many others visited relatives in their family hometowns on holidays. There were obvious contrasts between the cosmopolitan city and a countryside that appeared to be stuck in history. At the same time, popular culture portrayed the farmers (both historical and contemporary) as "authentic" Koreans. Some of the most potent ideas of the main political opposition movement focused on the *minjung* (the people, masses) and particularly the farmers as the source of a common, unifying, pure culture that could empower radical political action spread to popular music, literature, drama, and public performance (Choi 1995).[16] The symbolic importance of farmers to the urban vision of the national well-being lent added weight to the farmers' protests against the economic difficulties of the farming life.

The moral connection between farmers and city dwellers was reinforced directly through the protest actions themselves. Anthropologist Nancy Abelmann (1996 and 1995) has written extensively about the Koch'ang Tenant Farmers' Movement, in which farmers, along with students and other outside organizers, struggled in the mid-1980s to gain ownership of the land they cultivated as tenants. The Koch'ang farmers brought their protest to Seoul itself (from their homes in North Chŏlla province), where more than two hundred representatives of the movement occupied the headquarters of their landlord, the Samyang Corporation, demanding the opportunity to purchase the land. Abelmann's study explores in particular the relations between the farmers and student activists, who traveled to North Chŏlla to conduct *nonghwal* (agricultural action) in which students and farmers worked together, with the ultimate goal of awakening the farmers' consciousness that they were the subjects of history. Through actions such as these, urban residents and activist farmers came in direct contact with one another,[17] bolstering the emotional force of the farmers' protests through personal connections with urban residents (or members of their families).

Many of the farmers' protests were directed against U.S. pressures on the domestic market for agricultural products. The U.S. was the major source of agricultural imports; for a time, South Korea was the largest *per capita* importer of U.S. agricultural products (Hart-Landsberg 1993:257). The need to defend the nation's farmers in the face of the Uruguay Round negotiations (beginning in 1986) of the General Agreement on Tariffs and Trade (GATT) had generated a sense of desperation in response to international pressures to "rationalize" agricultural trade. A national Movement to Stop Importation, focused on agricultural products, was founded in 1986; in 1987 farmers tried to attack the U.S. Embassy in Seoul to protest American pressure to pry open the agricultural markets further. In 1990 the National Federation of Farmers Organizations was established to more effectively resist imports of farm products.

Beef was a focal issue for local activism and international tension. In the 1970s and 1980s the South Korean government had helped to promote the development of the domestic beef industry, providing expansion of credit to cattle farmers and producer incentives for female calves as well as restricting slaughtering to mature cattle. The beef cattle inventory nearly doubled between 1982 and 1986. The buildup, however, led to falling domestic beef prices (from 1.57 million *wŏn* to .92 million *wŏn* per head between 1983 and 1987), reducing the profitability of the domestic industry. Although beef imports steadily increased in the early 1980s, the South Korean government employed a variety of mechanisms to limit the import of beef under these circumstances. Between May 1985 and August 1988, the government stopped all commercial imports of beef. In 1988 beef imports were placed under the administration of the Livestock Products Marketing Organization (LPMO), working under a framework of quantitative restrictions established by the Ministry of Agriculture, Forestry, and Fisheries. Prospective foreign beef exporters would bid on parts of the quota; the lowest bids won the right to export a limited quantity of beef to South Korea, and the LPMO would auction the beef to South Korean buyers. In 1988 the United States charged South Korea with GATT violations in its treatment of beef imports. South Korea argued that the restrictions it placed on beef imports were legitimate exceptions allowed as special measures to stabilize the nation's balance of payments (General Agreement on Tariffs and Trade 1989). In November

1989 the GATT Balance of Payments Committee sided with the United States, and South Korea agreed to revise its beef importation practices, with the goal of a full opening of the market by July.

In this context it is hardly surprising that the campaigns to protect domestic agriculture—and the lifestyle of farmers—often employed the language of siege. A pamphlet published by the "Pan-National Movement to Obstruct the Livestock Market Opening" in 1992 provides one example. The pamphlet opens with these words:

> Citizens!
> We absolutely must defend our Korean beef.
> If we give way on Korean beef, [then] pork, chicken, and all other kinds of our livestock will vanish. . . .
> We are going to fight until the end. . . .[18]

This pamphlet provided a pointed expression of the atmosphere of "economic warfare." It clearly identified the enemy: "Without [due] regard, the United States and other advanced nations are selling a lot of beef to our country, [in] what is known as the Uruguay agricultural negotiations [they are] applying continuous pressure for market opening." The farmers' protests asked consumers to choose their foods based on patriotic considerations. Similarly, in response to the opening of the cigarette market (previously a government monopoly), a campaign for patriotic smoking ("use our tobacco with love for our country") developed in the early 1990s.

Private as well as government-funded consumer agencies contributed in various ways in the background to the campaign to defend domestic agriculture. For example, in summer 1989, after four years of geometric growth in grapefruit imports (which by then had reached $10 million annually, with about three-fourths of that from Florida), the South Korean government's Agricultural Chemical Research Institute reported that tests of grapefruit shipments from the U.S. for pesticides showed a residue of alar, a suspected carcinogen, to be estimated at 0.5 parts per million. An international dispute arose over the test results and their effects. The executive director of the Florida Department of Citrus complained that the lab test, which could not measure alar at concentrations of *less* than 0.5 parts per million, was "equivalent to a finding of no alar." He explained that "alar is not used on, and has never been used on grapefruit." While the South Korean government lab admitted that this could be the case, the Citizens Alliance for Consumer Protection of Korea picked up the issue and announced a nationwide campaign, coordinated by seventy regional consumer organizations, to warn people against eating imported grapefruit. Forty-three South Korean trading companies that were the major importers and sellers of grapefruit became the targets of a consumer boycott. A Citizens Alliance spokesperson said, "As Korean consumers, all we want is safe fruit. . . . We are not convinced American grapefruit is safe." Grapefruit sales plummeted, and the U.S. Embassy fumed (*Korea Herald*, 7 July 1989).

The U.S. did not pose the only threat to domestic agriculture.[9] While the U.S. primarily pushed at the luxury pole of South Korean farm output by providing less expensive or higher quality substitutes for items grown in South Korea (such as beef) and by offering novelty products (such as grapefruit) that might tempt consumers away from their usual choices, in the early 1990s the People's Republic of China began to export inexpensive, familiar fruits and vegetables to South Korea. This new menace to South Korean farm livelihoods ignited new protests. The healthfulness of Chinese imports was questioned frequently. Three years after the grapefruit incident, the major South Korean consumer affairs magazine, *Sobija Sidae* (The age of the consumer), published a review of domestic and imported agricultural products under the title, "Agricultural and Fisheries Products: How to Distinguish Between Imported and Domestic Goods." The article looked at such food products in daily use as peanuts, sesame, and green peas.

> These days, even if one goes to the neighborhood markets, one can see plentiful imports of agricultural and fisheries products. . . . Because of complaints about the remains of pesticides, imported agricultural products have been sold at a high price under the guise of domestic products; many housewives were deceived in this way. This is an investigation of the essential points of distinction between imported goods and domestic goods, by looking closely at the distinguishing features and differences that are hard to identify and that are not [usually] possible to sort out
> (*Sobija Sidae* 1992:58–59).

In other words, *Sobija Sidae* was claiming that because South Korean consumers were suspicious of the safety of imported foodstuffs, cheap imports were being sold in the markets at inflated prices to fool housewives into thinking they were buying safer, domestic goods. The report was illustrated with several photographs. The photographs of sesame seeds compared an abundance of tawny domestic seeds with a paltry pile of dark Chinese imports; other photographs showed the imported goods at a smaller scale or at a cruder resolution than their South Korean counterparts, leaving readers with the impression that imported goods were comparatively scrawny and unwholesome.

Other media picked up on the themes of frugality and patriotic consumption and broadcast them far beyond the community of consumer activists. Many books and articles analyzed South Korean consumers. Newspaper coverage of the Uruguay Round focused on sensitive topics, such as the rice issue. An editorial commented, "Rice has been the very backbone of the country's economy as well as its culture. It is under such circumstances that the idea of opening the market to foreign rice arouses emotion-charged controversy" (*Korea Herald*, 20 October 1991). An essay focused on wastefulness reports on Mr. Kang's "bad memory" of his recent wedding celebration: although "it is natural" that he spent more than two months' salary on food for his guests, he regretted the large amount of food that was left behind and had to be thrown out. The same article then mentions a restaurant that was popular because it did not serve side dishes that had already been offered to earlier patrons.[20] Because of this wasteful practice, "In this restaurant they throw away so much food in one day that they can fill three 10-kilogram containers, each as big as a little child" (Kim Hong-mok 1991:143). Building savings was a key theme. An editorial in celebration of the twenty-eighth National Savings Day in 1992 stated, "For an individual or a nation, the need to save both for economic reasons and for decency of lifestyle is unassailable." What concerned the author was that the savings rate "for the first six months of this year was down to 33.8 percent [from a high of 38.1 percent in 1988], a sober reality indicating that our consumption is by far outpacing the actual growth of the nation's economic capabilities." Newspaper stories lamented the growing "tourism deficit": South Koreans traveling abroad were spending a total sum larger than foreign tourists spent in South Korea. In spring 1992, just before one of the principal traveling seasons, the Korean Customs Administration announced that travelers bringing in more than $5,000 worth of goods would face criminal charges (previously the limit had been $10,000) and that "frequent travelers" would be stringently monitored. At around the same time, one of the state-owned television networks broadcast a program focusing on the spending habits of the very rich similar to the U.S. program "Lifestyles of the Rich and Famous" yet designed to inspire not envy, but scorn. One friend recounted how she had been appalled watching an episode that followed South Korean tourists in Hong Kong. "*All they did was spend money. They went from one store to another, buying watches and electronics and clothing and back again.*"[21] Another newspaper story noted that the confectionery makers Lotte and Haitai were accused of "indiscriminate import sprees of foreign-made cookies and chocolates." In an editorial focused on the broader problems of the South Korean economy, the writer blamed the trade deficit on "a blind preference for foreign things" and noted that virtue is as important as industry in getting the economy back on track:

> A steep rise in conspicuous domestic consumption has caused a rapid increase in imports, giving rise to imbalance in all sectors of national life. . . . To revitalize the nation's once thriving exports, the competitiveness and productivity of manufacturing industries must be strengthened. For example, a curb on pleasure-oriented and consumption industries, which have been absorbing manpower from manufacturing fields, is required. To overcome the present challenges, we should first establish proper values supplanting the wanton self-indulgence of excess. . . . That virtue is as important to our unique socioeconomic requirements as the economic mechanism. It is now a time of soul searching for all of us.
>
> (*Korea Herald*, 11 September 1991)

The call for a return to virtue was common in the anti-*kwasobi* discourse, although often, as in the editorial above, the exact nature of that virtue was left unspecified. Its opposite, though, was clearly wantonness. *Kwasobi* culture was blamed for what was reported to be a growing "crime psychology." On the one hand, the visible disparity between rich and poor was seen as provocative of crimes of revenge. In one highly publicized incident, a jobless man kidnapped a woman in the parking lot of the Hyundai department store in Samsong-dong in Kangnam; when he was caught, he explained that he committed the crime "out of disgust for the luxurious lives of the rich" (*Korea Herald*, 3 November 1991). On the other hand, the abandonment of asceticism was linked to lax morals and a more general loss of discipline. An editorial commented on the story of a thirty-one-year-old woman who had jumped from a window to her death a few days earlier because, the report said, she suffered "a severe mental disorder after being raped ten years ago":

Our community has become too complacent about the current wave of sex crimes. . . . A moral campaign to contain excessive permissiveness and decadence is in order. . . . A trend toward greater liberty and toleration in reaction to the too rigid and aescetic traditions of the old must be guarded against. We can hardly reverse the drift toward pleasure-seeking or merely try to return to the days of Confucian puritanism, but the time has indeed come for us to draw the line and restore a measure of discipline and propriety.

(*Korea Herald*, 14 September 1991)

For several weeks in summer 1989 local newspapers focused on sexual violence: a female college student bit five centimeters off a middle school boy's tongue in self-defense to fend off a rape attempt, while another college student leapt from a hotel room to escape her assailant. Several stories focused on what was feared to be an epidemic of kidnappings of children and women for sale to the sex industries; there were tut-tutting reports of the tendency for sex industry proprietors to squeeze more than their due cut from women sex workers, and in late July President Roh Tae-woo announced a crackdown on flesh trafficking and drug peddling. These reports presented an image of Korean society as gone awry through sexual indulgence. Even a newspaper article on the rising divorce rate contributed to this notion: "It is certainly a pity to see many young people inclined to regard marriage as just an expedient way to fulfill sexual desires. They fail to grasp the vital spiritual value of marriage, which serves to bind couples together in a genuine partnership that successfully outlives merely earthly motives and material pursuits" (*Korea Herald*, 7 July 1989).

From the Seoul YMCA to farmer's organizations to newspaper articles and editorials, criticism of consumer practices and the linking of the phenomenon of *kwasobi* to erosions in South Korean morals, deterioration of the South Korean economy, and disunity among South Koreans were commonplace in the late 1980s and early 1990s. One of the most pervasive voices in this discourse was that of the South Korean government itself.

## CORRECT LIVING CAMPAIGN

In the early 1990s the South Korean government's Public Information Office (*Kongboch'ŏ*), issued a series of posters in an anti-*kwasobi*, proper lifestyle campaign. These posters amplified selected themes from the popular movements, creating a unique voice in the discursive field. The public anti-*kwaso-bi* message depended upon popular perceptions of the *kwasobi* problem, but also redirected the terms of consumer patriotism. The Public Information Office emphasized the importance of patriotic frugality in a general effort to pull the nation back into a positive international trade position. Frugality became a key to both economic success and to salvaging South Korea's international reputation.

In autumn 1991 one striking poster in a Seoul subway car drew my attention to the South Korean anti-*kwasobi* campaign. On the right side of the paper was a cartoon of three bright green frogs in a lily pond. The two smaller frogs squat with their big mouths open, eyes bulging, horrified at what may be the death throes of the third, much larger frog. Stomach grotesquely distended, the big frog reaches back to support its bulk by leaning on the lily pad. The frog's unmatched eyes protrude, one saucerlike and bloodshot, the other shaped like a projectile launching from its socket. Foam bubbles from the frog's sagging jaw. The enigmatic headline reads:

MAMA FROG IMITATING A BULL
ISN T THIS EXACTLY OUR IMAGE TODAY?

The poster's text then goes on:

Income level 6,000 dollars—
Consumption level 20,000 dollars—
This is not someone else's story but exactly our own image today.
Now is not the time for us to be extravagant like the blustering,
    crowing mama frog.
We should all once more tighten our belts and

* Be thrifty consumers in the family with a frugal lifestyle
* Resume a diligent appearance in the office

Healthy family, let's make a wholesome society together.

This poster, produced by the Public Information Office, referred to one of Aesop's fables—although I was not familiar with the story, most of my South Korean friends and acquaintances were.[22] Two young frogs leave the safety of their pond one day and hop to a nearby field. There they see many wondrous sights, but the most amazing of all is a huge bull stamping in the meadow. They have never seen anything so marvelous before, and they quickly hop back to the pond to share the story with their mother. The mother, who herself knows nothing of the big world beyond, cannot imagine there exists anything so large and to prove that she is as grand as whatever the little ones saw, puffs out her belly and asks her children, "Do you mean this big?"

"Oh, no, mama," they reply, "it was much bigger."

Not easily discouraged, she takes another, deeper draught of air and asks, "Like this?"

"No, mama. It was much, much bigger."

You can imagine the end: The frogs repeat this colloquy until, inevitably, the mother frog explodes. The moral of the story, I was told, is not to transgress one's appropriate station in life.[23]

The most banal lesson for the harried subway rider whose eyes might come to rest on the poster in an effort to distract his or her mind from the unbearable pressure of the rush-hour crowd was that each household must resist the temptation to overreach a sensible budget or risk personal ruin. The foolish mother frog not only destroyed herself but left her little ones alone and unprovided for in her idiotic display.

The frog poster played in many subtle ways on a sense of insecurity about the South Korean national image in an international context. The text opened with a comparison of income and consumption presented not in the domestic currency, the *wŏn*, but in the currency of a foreign nation: U.S. dollars. If the intention had been simply to point out a dangerous discrepancy between household income and household expenditures, these statistics would most appropriately have been shown in the local currency.[24] The use of dollars as the unit of measurement invited comparison with other nations, obviously but certainly not exclusively the United States. The poster suggested that a household budget of $20,000 may make sense if you live in a nation with the power of a bull, but not in a nation that has yet to outgrow its small $6,000 pond. Other reports in circulation at the time used similar figures, generally comparing per capita GNP or per capita income to household consumption or to per capita share of national consumption, which included imports of capital goods and other nonconsumer items. For example, a newspaper reported, "It is not only up to business enterprises but also the responsibility of the government to properly guide the nation's economic course and all the Korean people, who are now spending $15,000 a year while earning only $5,000, local commentators said in unison" (*Korea Herald*, 19 September 1991).

In other ways the language of the poster heightened the sense that South Korea must be on guard against appearing foolish to outside observers. In linking the repulsive image of excess, a bloated frog choking on its own vomit, to the question, "Isn't this exactly our image today?" the poster asked its viewers to imagine their consumption being watched and judged by someone with a more sophisticated understanding of appropriate behavior. The word *mosŭp*, meaning image, form, appearance, occurred three times in this brief poster. "Isn't this exactly our image today?" "This is not someone else's story but exactly our own image today." "We should . . . resume a diligent appearance in the office." The message was not simply about the material dangers inherent in extravagance; the poster warns that unwarranted extravagance is being *observed*. There were others, members of the international community of income earners and consumers, who were ready to mock the ridiculous sight of South Korea puffing itself up with a lifestyle it could not digest. Whether or not one had the individual or household means to support a high level of consumption, one's personal responsibility should transcend these considerations and extend to the effect one's own spending behavior would have on the outside world's perception of the nation. In fact, what may appear to *you*, as a South Korean citizen, to be appropriate, may be as distorted as the judgment of a frog in a pond—or, in the Korean idiom, a frog in a well.[25]

Other posters in this Public Information Office series evoked similar feelings of anxiety. One poster that appeared a few months later showed a young male office worker in a smart gray suit, holding an attaché case in one hand and leaping forward with his tie flapping behind him. The headline proclaimed, "Come on! Let's dash again. Now is not the time to hesitate." The text continued:

At one time, Westerners paid the Korean people's diligence the compliment: "There is no one in the world who can beat the Japanese except the Koreans." But the instant we averted our gaze, nations that had better tended to their affairs [have raced ahead] showing [us] the heels of their shoes, and we are tottering. For a nation with nothing else but its human resources, there is no other way to live well than to work diligently. . . . We are a nation that has put its confidence and important experience in hibernation. Now the world is dashing ahead. Come on! Let us get up and dash again.

Another poster showed a drawing of four people paddling a boat and warned, "If one person rests, forty million will be late."

"KOREA" won the world's praise and envy. Let's seek that glory again. Hasn't the selfishness that says "I'm just one . . ." called excessive consumption (*kwasobi*) and the pleasure tide (*hyangnak p'ungjo*) made it difficult for the nation's livelihood of forty million? Now we must start from exactly "me" myself and with one mind gather our energy and vigorously advance.

In this poster, the word "Korea" appeared in Roman letters, capitalized, as if to demonstrate the perspective of the outside world (again, particularly Westerners) on the nation (which, in Korean, is called *Han'guk*[26]). A fourth poster showed a photograph of kimchi, radish sprouts, and fish stew with the headline, "We are wasting too much precious food" followed by the explanation, "Food waste [amounts to] approximately 8 trillion *wŏn*." Although the caption states the monetary value of food waste in *wŏn*, the body of the poster text explains how that translates into U.S. dollars: "That is calculated to correspond to 10 billion dollars. Even if we cut this only in half, that will have the effect of a 5 billion dollar reduction in our trade deficit." Note, again, that the calculations employed here are unreliable: the implication is that all the food saved would be food not imported, whereas much of the wasted food was grown in South Korea.

These and similar posters commissioned by the Public Information Office to advocate consumer modesty, increased savings, and longer work hours appeared in subway cars, on trains, and in abbreviated form outside train stations during the early 1990s. In addition to the poster series, the Public Information Office placed advertisements in newspapers and arranged for short broadcast messages on television and radio and in the subway. On the electronic billboards that flashed the time, weather, news headlines, and advertisements at major intersections, one of the most common messages in 1992 was "Work 10 percent longer—Save 10 percent more." The telephone information exchange, 114, played a short message about savings and hard work while the computer searched for the requested phone listing, and similar messages played on several government-affiliated switchboards. The official newsreels shown before feature films in local theaters often included documentary footage of luxurious living, extravagant shopping, and waste.

Even children were targets of the message that saving more and spending less was a duty. From an early age, South Korean schoolchildren were taught the importance of disciplining their own consumption. In a textbook[27] on "Correct Living" (*Parŭn Saenghwal Iyagi*) for young elementary school children, the following story, "Mina's Pledge," introduced the concept of using money sparingly:

Mina came home from school. Her mother was sitting in front of the desk writing something.

"Mom, what are you doing?" Mina asked.

"I'm recording all the money our family spent."[28]

"Mom, do you record the money I spent?"

"Of course, do you want to take a look?"

Mina looked at the things her mother had recorded. Not one penny of the money Mina had spent was left out.

"I've been eating a lot of snacks," Mina said, a little embarrassed.

"The crayons I lost and had to buy again are also here."

Mina saw that she used more money than her older brother. Her older brother really hadn't used very much.

"Mina, if the family isn't frugal, it's hard to manage the household. If from now on you only buy the things you truly need, you will use money sparingly and save," said Mina's mother.

"All this time I haven't been using things sparingly and I've misplaced a lot of things. I'm going to try to be frugal like Mom." Mina arranged her drawer a few times and made this pledge.

(Education Ministry 1990:32–35)

Girls (and women) in particular were encouraged to cultivate the habit of thrift, although boys (and men) were not exempted. A story that appeared in the textbook for children one year older focused on a boy, Suyŏng, learning to shed his embarrassment at the reputation his grandfather and father had as misers (*kudusoe*: literally, "shoeleather"). In this story, however, in contrast with Mina's lesson, Suyŏng learns that frugality is a family honor. After breaking up a fight between Suyŏng and another boy who had called Suyŏng's grandfather "Shoeleather Grandfather," the grandfather tells Suyŏng how they got the nickname:

Suyŏng's grandfather calls Suyŏng and says, "Suyŏng, are you so embarrassed by that nickname of your grandfather's and your father's? It's
not an embarrassing nickname. Listen carefully to my story," he began.
"When your grandfather was as young as you are, our house was extremely poor. But I worked diligently and used each little thing sparingly, and so we lived. So I taught your father to live the same way.
Your father also works industriously, and he is even more frugal than I
am. You could say that it is thanks to this that we can live as well as we
do now. Suyŏng, do you know the meaning of the words hanging there
on that wall: 'Diligence, Sincerity, Frugality'?"

"Yes. It means, 'Be hardworking, do the work you take on well, and
use things sparingly.' "

"Ah, our Suyŏng is all grown up. These are our family precepts.
That's why you can hear the nickname "Shoeleather" applied to your
grandfather and father."

"They are family precepts?"

"Our family follows them."

"Ah, like our school precepts?"

"Yes, they are called that because we must keep each of the precepts."

Suyŏng felt that his grandfather's nickname was something to be
proud of. "Grandfather, I want to keep the family precepts so that I'll
get the nickname 'Shoeleather.' How about, 'Kind-hearted, neighbor-
helping Shoeleather?'"

"That's very good."

Suyŏng's grandfather smiled broadly and took Suyŏng's hand.

(Education Ministry 1991:50–55)

The government did not restrict itself to inundating the people with
such messages, but had played an active role in the suppression of what it
viewed as excessive consumption in earlier decades. In the late 1960s and
early 1970s, for example, the Family and Ritual Code (1969, revised 1973)
placed restrictions on the ways families could engage in common ceremonies (weddings, funerals, sixtieth-birthday celebrations). Wedding invitations, for example, were banned under this code. In 1986 a new directive
specifically targeted the exchange of wedding gifts (Kendall 1994). For various periods, the government outlawed certain kinds of extracurricular tutoring of school children, ostensibly to preserve the integrity of the public

school system, and foreign travel was banned until the late 1980s. In the 1990s, however, watched by sharp-eyed international observers, government actions to reduce consumption could no longer be so bold and were often somewhat circuitous.

In April 1990 the government initiated a comprehensive anti-import movement. People who purchased foreign-made cars were notified that their taxes would be scrutinized. The Bank of Korea launched an investigation to discover those people who spent more than U.S.$3,000 on their credit cards while traveling abroad, in violation of foreign-exchange regulations. One weekend in the summer, all the major Seoul department stores suddenly eliminated or drastically reduced their displays and promotions of foreign products. The Hyundai department store even eliminated an entire floor of shops selling imported goods (Hart-Landsberg 1993:245). The American Chamber of Commerce in Seoul (AmCham) cried foul and accused the government of ordering the department stores to curtail their sales of imports, but AmCham was unable to prove any government involvement in the matter.[29] The department stores announced that they had simply been responding to the demands of their customers. At around the same time, several newspapers' editorials called for a spontaneous economy drive, including a drive to buy local products rather than "luxurious" imports. In the English-language *Korea Herald*, one column read:

> Such an economy drive should be spontaneous and largely moralistic. The United States and several other Western nations have registered complaints over the possible intervention of the Seoul government to encourage and organize the campaign. There is no ground for the suspicion. It is entirely up to individuals and private interest groups to refrain from patronizing imported goods stores. The government ought to clarify its noninvolvement in such a movement that might give a false impression of unfair trade practices for curbing free imports and the free market.
>
> (*Korea Herald*, 16 July 1990)

Given the influence the government still had over the major media, their call to stop buying imports only added to AmCham's suspicions.

The South Korean government continued to add to the discomforts associated with certain kinds of consumption. In September 1991, 300 public officials who had traveled abroad for personal reasons during the summer without prior authorization were threatened with "heavy punitive steps" (*Korea Herald*, 7 September 1991). Newspapers reported that people who had purchased foreign cars were to be investigated on the suspicion that they had gained the foreign currency to acquire their cars through smuggling. The insult to one's reputation was as bothersome a piece of this news as the threat of investigation. As in the case of the disappearance of foreign boutiques from department stores, the prosecution announced its investigation as a response to "criticism from the public" of "the widespread use of foreign luxury goods . . . among the well-to-do . . . [who] caused the sense of social incompatibility" (*Korea Herald*, 7 September 1991). Perhaps most irksome for foreign companies attempting to export consumer goods to South Korea was the institution of a price tag system "to help consumers instantly recognize price differentials between import prices and final consumer prices." A total of 102 items, including video cameras, headphone stereos, leather bags, water purifiers, sweaters, radios, and humidifiers were required to be tagged. Tariffs and consumption taxes plus the high margins added to foreign goods often tripled or quadrupled the import costs; foreign companies charged that consumers examining the tags were discouraged from purchasing goods with a consumer price so much higher than their dockside value. Finally, some things, such as all Japanese popular cultural products, were banned entirely by law.

AmCham served as the watchdog for suspected fair-trade violations in South Korea. In 1993 AmCham continued to complain in its annual report to the U.S. Congress:

> The Korean anti-import drives (also called "frugality" or "austerity" campaigns) have a significant detrimental impact on trade between Korea and the United States. Touted by the government as "grass-roots" campaigns, these frugality campaigns, via demonstrations and extensive media coverage, urge Koreans not to buy imported products. Ostensibly, the campaigns are organized by the various Consumer Protection Groups in Korea; however, many of these groups are funded all or in part by the Korean Government. Big ticket items like travel abroad, automobiles and home appliances have been the primary targets of the campaigns. The campaigns do have a significant chilling effect on imports as a whole, especially because imported goods represent such a small part of the consumer market.

> (American Chamber of Commerce 1993:8–9)

Clearly, AmCham had grounds for its complaints, but just as the government was not the sole agent in the frugality campaign, so imports were not the only targets of government intervention in the consumer market in the name of *kwasobi ch'ubang*. One of the most heated issues in the early 1990s was that of the sale of bottled water. Foreigners had long had access to purified mineral water, but the sale of mineral water to South Korean citizens was forbidden by law. Only two percent of Seoul's residents had faith in the potability of the tap water; yet, on the grounds that it would further undermine faith in the city's water system, the Seoul city government resisted South Korean national Ministry of Health and Social Affairs' 1992 announcement that they would legalize the domestic sale of mineral water. The law was widely flouted: by the time of my fieldwork, all the households in Yoido purchased bottled water somehow, and many offices also supplied water coolers with purified water. Poor households still relied on tap water, which they boiled in an attempt to kill bacteria. Fear about water-borne diseases and other contaminants in the water as well as inconsistencies in the supply of water meant that the distinction between those who did and those who did not have access to bottled water had implications beyond simple convenience. The controversy over government policies regarding the sale of water was seen as emblematic of ineffective programs aimed at reducing the disparity between rich and poor that was now apparent in the most mundane details of daily life.

During the early 1990s *kwasobi* and consumer responsibility was a pervasive field of public discourse. The major themes were the danger imports posed to domestic producers, the danger consumer spending posed to the domestic economy (by directing money away from investment), the danger indulgence itself posed to Korean social morality, and the danger that conspicuous consumption posed to the harmony between rich and poor.

It is not surprising that the flight attendant introduced me to Mrs. Lee when she heard I was hoping to study consumption. Mrs. Lee appeared to be the embodiment of *kwasobi* itself! Mrs. Lee lived in the most famous apartment building in Seoul, and she owned a shop in one of the city's most well-known department stores. She indulged herself with clothes and admirers, and she spoiled her boys with sweets and golf lessons. On holidays, she took her family abroad, draining *wŏn* from the national foreign exchange reserves. *Kwasobi ch'ubang* was not just a government propaganda campaign. Existing ideas about the symbolic and material importance of household frugality as participation in the development of a healthy national economy formed the basis of a renewed discourse of economic consumer patriotism. In the next chapter, I will look at the gendered aspects of *kwasobi* criticism. One the one hand, the multiple elements of this discursive field opened the possibility for consumers in a variety of positions to feel *they* were consumer patriots, while "others" were not. The existence of women like Mrs. Lee provided an essential contrast for many affluent women: at least their expenditures were appropriate, responsible, and for the pleasure of the family, not for themselves. At the same time, the social constructs of women and mothers in South Korea have themselves become enmeshed in the issues of consumption, overconsumption, and the moral value of pleasure.

On an autumn afternoon, just at that hour when electric lights become perceptible in the waning daylight, I am strolling through Myŏngdong. This shopping district is in the geographic center of Seoul, a few minutes' walk from Seoul City Hall, across the street from the Lotte and the Chosun hotels and the Midopa, Lotte, and Shinsegye department stores, at the foot of Namsan (South Mountain), not far from Namdaemun Market.

Myŏngdong, "Bright Ward," is a financial center for securities trading, and middle-aged women stand in foot traffic handing out business cards or crouch in the streets offering immediate curb-market lending and foreign exchange services from their bulging purses; it is a boutique district where Bennetton, Timberland, Levi's, Calvin Klein, and the most fashionable mass-market apparel manufacturers in South Korea have dedicated stores; it is a center for plastic surgery and beauty services; it is an entertainment district with opportunities to see live theater or films or to engage in eating, drinking, and dancing. Three of my favorite coffee shops are here: the sleekest has only a dozen small glass tables but features a dj spinning international hits; another is decorated in a nautical theme, with heavy ropes draping from the vast ceiling and portholes and knobbed steering wheels hanging on the walls; the last, three narrow stories high, seems left behind in mid-1980s fashion: the plush chairs, upholstered in a cream-and-red floral pattern, are shaped like those found in the cheapest tea houses, but the effect is cozy, and the management serves pancakes and whipped cream with the coffee. KFC has two busy outlets in Myŏngdong; on hot nights there is a line out the door of Baskin Robbins 31 Flavors; down narrow alleys tiny restaurants serve Korean meals to the cognoscenti. Fashion and food are found at ground level; nightlife and business above, accessible by tight stairways and discrete doorways, or below in basement nightclubs. Myŏngdong's atmosphere is redolent with consumer pleasures. Music pulses in the streets; people, mostly young, throng the lanes to slip in and out of buildings, peek into shops, and look at one another, massing, flowing, jostling in the glow of walls of display windows. I always look at the clothes in the windows of Myŏngdong, wishing I had enough money to buy something, indulging in the ordinary fantasy that the right outfit would make me stylish. Months of living among the images of groomed allure dished up in Seoul have left me feeling dowdy. As I pass by a series of windows, I notice that one advertising theme is shared by several shops. Mannequins, dressed in miniskirts, bell-bottomed jeans, and go-go boots, adorned in beehive hairdos, thrust one hip forward behind the legend, in English, "Nostalgia 1960s."

What kind of nostalgia is this, I wonder. I recognize these images and these styles from my own family photos, from my own New England memories of my 1960s childhood dreams of becoming a hip teen. But South Korea entered the decade of the 1960s as one of the world's poorest countries, with a per capita income estimated at less than $150. Half the population still lived in the countryside, and most of the city residents worked long hours for poor pay in factory jobs or worse. I have spent more than a year hearing stories from women about the privations of their youth, *their* 1960s, and about how it is not possible to understand today's consumer choices without understanding South Korea's past. Perhaps even more to the point, the consumers targeted by these boutiques were as yet unborn in that hardscrabble decade—they have no memories of the sixties, they *cannot* experience this nostalgia. "Nostalgia 1960s" is a slogan that evokes in them a nonmemory of a fabricated era.

Others have shown how history and memory are manipulated, generated even, in the process of making subjectivity and community (see, for example, Dirks 1990; Spivak 1988; Fischer 1986; Hobsbawm and Ranger 1983). It has become almost a truism in social theory. Pieces of reality are patched together to consolidate themes, justify outcomes, select among possibilities according to perceived continuity. Memories are reconfigured in new contexts, and even forgetting becomes active. Obviously, the reformulation of memories and histories is part of making meaning in the present.

What is more often overlooked is how envisioning the future enters into this same process of generating community identities. In South Korea, consumption, the future, and national identity dance together within the discourse of *kwasobi*.

# CHAPTER 5

## ENDANGERING THE NATION,
## CONSUMING THE FUTURE

*But to women of conscience and insight the ends of living will always be a part of the problem of spending money. . . . There is a scheme of values embodied in every housewife's work, whether she knows it or not, and this scheme affects for good or ill the health, the tastes, the character of those for whom she cares and those with whom she associates.*

Wesley C. Mitchell, "The Backward Art of Spending Money"

In early November 1991 the edition of *Newsweek* magazine distributed in East Asia featured an article entitled, "Too Rich, Too Soon."[1] The article opened with the question: "South Koreans are celebrating their economic success—by going shopping. But now times are tough. Are they living beyond their means?" In the first paragraph, the article reported on the government's campaign to reduce conspicuous consumption. "Officials of President Roh Tae-woo's government recently called in the wives of a number of army generals and delivered a stern lecture: stop spending so much money. Stay out of fancy hotel restaurants. Don't frequent luxury stores. Any failure to heed these recommendations could hurt your husband's chances for promotion" (Emerson 1991:12). The five-page article featured the following consumer marvels: a woman "overheard gushing to her companions, 'She bought a 500,000-*wŏn* ($660) pair of panties!'"; another woman reported her cousin's 17-million-*wŏn* ($23,000) trip to a clothing boutique; "young female office workers and retired couples" heading off on expensive foreign tours; the "bustling market for aphrodisiacs such as deer blood, cobra stew and bear bile, which can cost as much as 500,000-*wŏn* for a 10-cc shot";[2] "ambitious young brides-to-be [accumulating a dowry] . . . of at least 100 million *wŏn* ($130,000) to land that perfect doctor or lawyer"; and "one middle-class Seoul housewife" who used the profits she made from her real estate investments to lend out at high interest on the curb market and then took those proceeds and paid $3,000 each month to hire a tutor for her son. In addition to these anecdotes, the article was illustrated with seven photographs.[3] One of the pictures, of a protest against conspicuous consumption, showed (only) men engaged in the protest; the only other man in any of the photographs was a photographer himself, setting up a shot of a bride in a lavish white gown. The rest of the pictures featured women: shopping, assisting shoppers, or demonstrating ownership of expensive goods.[4] One caption below a photo of five young women walking out the gates of Ewha, South Korea's most prestigious women's university, proclaimed, "'Slaves to money.'"

This article provoked an angry response in South Korea. *Newsweek* enjoyed a wide circulation among South Koreans working to improve or maintain their English-language skills, and so a surprisingly large number of people either read the article themselves or heard about it from colleagues and friends; numerous South Korean print and broadcast media also reported the gist of the *Newsweek* article. Despite the fact that "Too Rich, Too Soon" contained little more than a repetition of criticisms already ubiquitous in the South Korean press,[5] the embarrassment of international humiliation in such a high-profile foreign magazine was intensely felt. "From the ashes of war, the miracle on the Han, the myth of the Olympics . . . Korea now has descended so far as to be the nation that is the laughing stock of the international community," wrote one commentator. "Of the four dragons, one has deteriorated into an earthworm" (*Tonga Ilbo*, 26 November 1991). For several weeks that November, friends of mine brought up the topic of the *Newsweek* article in conversation, and many reported that in their own places of employment the article sparked heated discussions among coworkers.

There were several elements entangled in these responses: embarrassment about the "truth" of the level of overindulgence of contemporary South Koreans (compared to imagined international standards or to memories of earlier Korean lifestyles), recriminations and resolutions that South Koreans should live more frugally, and indignation that *Newsweek* should focus a spotlight on a weak point of South Korean society rather than on South Korea's successes. In almost every comment I myself heard or read, two examples in particular from the article were repeated and provided a central focus of discussion: the photograph of the Ewha students, and the 500,000-*wŏn* pair of panties. The following comment, made to me by a young woman who was at that time attending Ewha herself, expressed a core ambivalence many people felt: "*There *is* a problem in our country if someone is spending 500,000 *wŏn* on a pair of panties, and it *is* true that Ewha students are well-known to spend too much money on clothes. This is a weak point in our society and in our economy. But why did *Newsweek* write a story about it? There are many positive things they could write about Korea.*"

The *Newsweek* article had obviously hit a nerve. On the one hand, no one seemed ready to deny that some people in South Korea were spending

large amounts of money on trivial indulgences, and many apparently believed that this was a serious social problem; on the other hand, the piece was
widely perceived as an affront to the South Korean nation. Exacerbating the
sense of insult was the photograph of the Ewha students, with the "Slaves to
money" caption—Ewha students, the flower[6] of South Korean female college students, had been put on display for the amusement and derision of the
international community. At the same time, it was hard to resist the conclusion that, with women buying 500,000-*wŏn* panties and spending 17 million
*wŏn* at a time on boutique clothing, women themselves had left the entire
South Korean nation vulnerable to this ridicule. Often when commenting on
the article, people acknowledged, as my Ewha friend did, that they, too,
knew women (or, tellingly, knew *of* women) who spent similarly outrageous
sums on clothing and beauty treatments.

Despite the public outrage, the *Newsweek* article was not, in fact, a blunt
censure of South Korean extravagance. Rather, the article was structured as
a journalistic *inquiry* into whether South Koreans were slacking off from
work and indulging themselves too soon for their own good, and it also reported on South Koreans' reactions to this phenomenon. In addition to the
opening vignette recounting President Roh's warning to the generals' wives,
*Newsweek* cited MBC-network[7] broadcasts on the theme "We can't go on
like this," editorials in the *Korea Times* and the *Chosŏn Ilbo* newspapers, and
diffuse popular feelings of class resentment ("*weehwagam*" [*sic*]: a feeling of
incompatibility or disorder), fear, bitterness, and jealousy. Not simply a foreigner's critique, the article with its moralistic tone was a product of
*Newsweek*'s editorial perspective *in combination* with the reported judgments
of many South Koreans themselves.

The *Newsweek* article and the local responses to it reveal some important
points about the *kwasobi ch'ubang* campaign and about the meanings of consumption in South Korea. First, however paranoid the internationalist sub-
text of the Public Information Office *kwasobi ch'ubang* campaign poster series may have *seemed*, the *Newsweek* article provides evidence that the
apparent paranoia had some foundation in fact: the world *was* watching what
South Koreans were doing with their money.[8] *Newsweek* added a new, less
directly interested Western voice to the whining reports of the American
Chamber of Commerce and U.S. government trade representatives about
unfair obstacles to the South Korean market and about South Korean government meddling in civic consumer movements. South Korean local arguments and contestations about consumer propriety were indeed implicated in

national image-making processes on a global stage. Struggles to redefine (in a radically new context of affluence, democracy, and shifting international competition) a national mission and national character were not sheltered from the critical gaze of international observers. Indeed, the actions of South Korean consumers and consumption critics partook of and contributed to larger, international themes of patriotism and consumer responsibility. One might ask where the Buy American or the Green Consumer movement starts and the *kwasobi ch'ubang* campaign ends: the spectacle of multiplying patriotic consumer movements played to an international readership and audience in the 1980s and 1990s.

The article also reveals the tendency, shared by South Korean, European, and North American popular and scholarly thought, to associate women (as a simplified social category) with consumption and consumerism. At the turn of the last century in the United States, economist Wesley C. Mitchell published an amusing article entitled, "The Backward Art of Spending Money." In the vein of efficiency analysis, Mitchell explores the imbalance between the knowledge and skill people bring to the task of *making* money, whereas "Important as the art of spending is, we have developed less skill in its practice than in the practice of making money. . . . To spend money is easy, to spend it well is hard" (Mitchell 1912:269). Mitchell centers his analysis on the division of labor in spending: "the women bearing the heavier burden of responsibility" (ibid.: 270), and he attributes the backwardness of this area of economic practice to the dominance of women and the structure of society into disconnected nuclear families. Veblen, too, believed that in the industrial era, as men were increasingly forced to demonstrate their worth through *vicarious* conspicuous consumption and leisure (as they became more entangled in professional obligations), consumption of "food, clothing, dwelling, and furniture by the lady and the rest of the domestic establishment" (Veblen 1994:43) and the "performance of conspicuous leisure, in the way of calls, drives, clubs, sewing-circles . . . and other like social functions" (ibid.:41) came to stand in for men's own actions.

Daniel Miller addresses (and adopts) this phenomenon directly in his essay, "Consumption as the Vanguard of History":

The quintessence of power in the modern world lies objectified in the image of the First World Housewife. Indeed, I termed the housewife a global dictator in recognition of the sheer authority that the collective decision-making, which she stands for, now exercises. . . . I recognise, of course, that consumption is not synonymous with housewifery. There are many men who are primary consumers for households, and much infrastructure and provisioning that is purchased by institutions rather than individuals. Nevertheless, while in most cases not the consumer, she continues to stand as image for consumer decision-making. In many countries the housewife is far more than a figure of speech.

(Miller 1995b:34)

In Miller's view, "the First World housewife" wields power as a member of an aggregate economic force of demand that affects the livelihood of individuals and communities far from the site of consumption. At the same time, Miller's iconic female consumer is the household provisioner, seeking low prices as well as the opportunity to transform economic value into a moral and social relationship with her family. The historical development of the European and North American figure of the housewife as consumer has been traced in many other works, taking into consideration such factors as colonial circuits of trade, new urban technologies of selling, and transformations in the distribution of household labor within a changing labor economy (see, for example, McKendrick 1974; McKendrick et al. 1982; Hall 1992; Laermans 1993; Leach 1984; Williams 1982). Several of these studies have demonstrated the critical importance the expansion of consumer opportunities and the commodification of basic life support have had on the reconfiguration of gender categories, roles, and relations.

While it is important to be clear about the distinctions and interrelations between the shifting material contexts that gave rise to the social function of "housewife," the symbolic meanings of "housewife" and the varied effects the idea of "housewife" has had on gendered social dynamics, my point here is that the image of the housewife as the archetypal consumer—an image common to (though not identical in) North America and South Korea[9]—begins to equate women as consumers and women as housewives, and it is also part of the process whereby men's consumer practices become invisible. Moreover, the kind of consumption that women conduct as "housewives" (or as women who take on the domestic task of providing food and comfort to the household) is a special case of consumption: women-as-housewives-as-consumers assume a *responsibility* for a *collective* interest. This kind of consumption is far from the celebratory, subculturally creative, or resistant forms of consumer practice that have formed the basis for the majority of studies of consumption in recent years (e.g., Hebdige 1979; de Certeau 1984; Gilroy 1987; Hall and Jacques 1990). The dominance of the image of women-housewives-consumers foregrounds, for women consumers in particular, a moral distinction between responsible consumption and personal indulgence.

This leads to a consideration of the second gendered aspect of consumption: the danger potentially inherent in consumption. Just as the Public Information Office's frog, in her maternal guise, was held up as the warning image of the self-destructive consumer or consuming nation, respectively, the women in the *Newsweek* article were seen by the foreign correspondents and by many people who discussed the article as the ones who, through their acts of consumption, made the nation vulnerable to economic failure, social unrest, and loss of authentic culture.[10] The imagined inability of women, as a class, to restrain their desires is seen as leading to the social disharmonies of conspicuous consumption, the financial ruin of spending beyond one's means, and the corrupting adoption of foreign ways and things. The importance of restraining oneself for the larger good is deeply embedded in Confucian ideas of propriety, as is the sense that men are better endowed than women with the capacity for moral restraint.[11] Moreover, the incomplete and narrow perspective attributed to women is believed to at times lead to mistaken excesses thought to be in the interest of the family but in fact endangering the community. This sense that the nation is made vulnerable through its women-as-consumers seems almost sexual, metaphorically related to the idea that the nation's women need to be protected from the predations, or temptations, of foreign men.[12]

In this chapter I examine the focus in the *kwasobi ch'ubang* discourse on women as consuming subjects, and I will look at the responses, in speech and in action, of South Koreans—focusing on South Korean women themselves—to these images. As other anthropologists have been concerned to show elsewhere, women in South Korea are actively engaged in the maintenance as well as the transformation of cultural ideas and practices. *Kwasobi* discourse takes much of its power from themes and assumptions carried into the contemporary context from earlier moments. Thus, in the late 1980s and early 1990s women, charged with enacting the ideals of proper consumer patriotism, found themselves on the front lines, facing the incongruities between the present and the past. The responses of the women I spoke with to the irresolvable conflicts between responsibilities and to the incompatibility between images and experiences gave rise to new possible visions of responsible motherhood, patriotism, and national community.

## WOMEN AND THE CRIMES OF AFFLUENCE

The gendered responsibilities underlying the *kwasobi* discourse should be placed in the larger context of popular contemporary views of women and wealth. Eunhee Kim Yi found that middle-class wives in Seoul were seen (by themselves and their husbands) as responsible for creating a domestic environment that would restore their husband's vitality so he can face another workday: "The home is a place to rest" (Yi 1990). This entailed not only cultivating calm at home but also ensuring that the husband had confidence that essential domestic decisions (regarding children's education, furnishing, budgeting, etc.) were in capable hands. In the context of changing standards and shifting opportunities, this was an increasingly complicated task. For example, Laurel Kendall notes the skill needed to negotiate a pathway through conflicting criticisms of excess and inadequate ceremony in wedding arrangements, where the requirements of frugal propriety and properly ceremonious conduct of ritual are juxtaposed (Kendall 1996). In a shifting environment, the wider public and even their own families held women to old standards; just as in the Chosŏn era, in middle- and upper-income households in contemporary South Korea both men and women would assert that the sexes were in charge of complementary spheres. The outer world belonged to men, while the domestic sphere was the responsibility of the wife, who took charge of the prosperity and propriety of the household (just as heaven ruled over the earth, *yin* and *yang*).

Most households in South Korea require more than the income from a single paycheck. In working-class families, young women may work in factories (as they often did during the years of the industrial "push"), and married women may divide their time between work at a factory and piecework done at home. They may take jobs in the service industry, cleaning, selling insurance, peddling, or serving customers. In families that aspire to the ideal of a working husband/father and a housewife at home, the wife/mother is generally more circumspect about the ways she brings in income. Tutoring children is one acceptable occupation, and occasional part-time work is often tolerated. More common, however, is the attempt to generate additional income through investments.

Women's domestic roles, so defined, left them vulnerable to harsh judgment. Women's active participation in the ballooning real estate and stock markets were well-publicized: the image of the housewife wheeler-dealer took on the quality of a hero or a monster, depending on one's viewpoint. In

the early 1980s the questionable actions of two women in particular established the image of female greed in the public media. President Chun's wife,
Lee Soon Ja, was an infamous real estate speculator much disliked by the
public. Another woman, Chang Young Ja, known as "Madame Chang,"
gained a huge fortune through her control of the curb market. Before she
was arrested in 1982 it was estimated that her activities alone accounted for
approximately 13 percent of all currency in circulation (Clifford 1994:195).
Yet many women with moderate incomes engaged in various methods of investment for the enrichment of their families. Women's home management
was often a critical source of family asset development: side jobs, buying and
selling real estate, bribing teachers, lending money, *kye* participation, and active management of a stock portfolio were common activities of South Korean "housewives." One pediatrician I met, a woman in her midforties, told
me that compared to the families of her old college friends, her family had
fallen behind economically because her full-time job prevented her from focusing on investment strategies. A World Bank publication noted that differences between households in terms of *wealth* in South Korea were much
greater than differences in terms of *income*, indicating that these activities
were critical to the family economy (Leipziger 1993). All these methods of
investment, however, fell under the rubric of *pullo sodŭk* (unearned income),
and some were in fact illegal (tutoring, ownership of multiple properties,
bribery), so that while women felt compelled to engage in these activities as
part of their good management of the household finances, they were vulnerable to public criticism. Such women were seen as "pushy"; Cho Hae-jŏng
lists eleven terms used to express this negative image in the 1980s, including
*ch'ima param* (housewives attempting to influence the public sphere through
informal power), *k'unson* (women with informal-sector money dealings),
*Madam Ttu* (women who busied themselves with marriage arranging), and
*pokbuin* (Mrs. Realtor) (Cho 1995).

   Speculation in real estate drew the most virulent vitriol because the investment activities of the women of one class appeared to directly impinge
on the dreams of families of another class. In 1990 the Minjung-Minjok
Movement's research institute stated, "the sirocco wind of speculation in
housing, land, and other real estate and the sharp rise in the national labor
price was by far exceeded by an absurd amount of unearned income; . . . Because of this, many people gave up the dream of preparing their own house
and gave themselves up to a condition of despair" (Minjung-Minjok Undong Yŏnguso 1990:9–10). In Talgoljjagi, most women associated *kwasobi*

with the rising real estate prices. "*Some people buy two or three or four apartments, and they just get richer and buy more, and we can't afford a one-room home,*" Suni complained. When I asked Suni if she thought *kwasobi* was a cause or an effect of the rising real estate prices, she replied, "*Both. People who own houses can spend more money, and people who can spend more money can buy gifts for the right people so that they can keep buying investments.*"

To drive the point home, the media offered up morality tales featuring affluent women and their debauched lifestyles. These wealthy women were generally depicted as selfish, indulging in alien forms of leisure, starkly contrasting with "traditional" ideals of female chastity and modesty. Several stories circulated concerning rich women and their gigolos in Kangnam-district spas and hotels; it was rumored for a time in 1992 that one young man, a swimming instructor in a posh health club, was HIV-positive and had possibly infected several rich "housewives." Such stories were passed along in a tone that plainly implied that the women deserved what criticism or punishment they attracted. This perspective became part of the common background of *kwasobi* discourse.[13]

In the very same month *Newsweek* published its "Too Rich, Too Soon," a leading South Korean progressive monthly magazine, *Mal* (Word), carried an article entitled "*Kwasobi* and the Five Thieves of the Nineties." The title referred to a well-known poem, "Five Thieves," published in the early 1970s by dissident poet Kim Chi-ha. Kim's poem had taken aim at the corrupt and greedy members of the rich and powerful strata; as a result, the poet and his editor were jailed for inciting class struggle. *Mal*'s "*Kwasobi*" article examined how the contemporary *kwasobi ch'ubang* messages that pervaded daily life paradoxically distracted people's critical focus from powerful and culpable individuals and groups and instead created a sense of an *endemic* and individual moral problem of overindulgence. The author, Ch'oi Chong-uk, a philosophy professor, used the article to argue that the resurgence of anti-*kwasobi* propaganda was a distraction from the larger causes of economic inequity in South Korea (*chaebŏl* domination, government corruption, etc.).

Ch'oi's skepticism of the anti-*kwasobi* campaign did not, however, render him sensitive to the gendered foundations of the *kwasobi* discourse. Midway through the article, the professor included a personal commentary on a newspaper report of a well-publicized sexual assault on the wealthy wife of an unnamed company president. He wrote that the journalist was shocked by the crime of sexual assault, but that Ch'oi himself was more astonished by the value of the jewelry the woman reported stolen at the time. Ch'oi went on to list the jewelry that had "covered her body":

> A 40,000,000-*wŏn* [approximately $50,000] three-karat diamond ring; a gold Rolex watch (18,000,000 *wŏn* [approximately $22,500]), a diamond and gold bracelet, and about five pearl items, all worth about 70,000,000 *wŏn* [approximately $90,000]. That's about two times the value of the *chŏnse* deposit on the apartment I live in carried like something trivial on the wrists and neck of that woman. It seems absolutely impossible to imagine the ultraluxurious lifestyle of such a woman.
>
> (Ch'oi 1991:151)

Ch'oi also saw fit to transmit the information that the assailant had met the woman in a hotel cabaret, seduced and attacked her, and then stolen her valuables. Ch'oi concluded this anecdote with the following observation:

> But this overconsumption, extravagance, and waste are not merely the vanity of this kind of woman of leisure. The world of children is also being polluted by the fashions of overconsumption and waste. Such things as 110,000-*wŏn* German-made dolls, life-size Japanese-made toy M-16 rifles, and 460,000-*wŏn* U.S.-made wooden playhouses are selling like hotcakes.
>
> (Ch'oi 1991:151)

Ch'oi exploited the story of the woman and the violence she suffered as the frame on which to hang his commentary on the problem of extremes of wealth in Korea. In the 1980s, he wrote, many criminals were Robin Hoods, while "the crime of the 1990s has changed from theft to sexual assault, and the target is extravagance" (Ch'oi 1991:151). While Ch'oi may not have meant that sexual assailants were, like Robin Hood, countercultural heroes, he said nothing to counter this implication.

The media also reported on the spread of a crime known as "destruction of the family." This was a variation on house burglary in which the burglars, gambling that housewives had reason to fear that their husbands would reject them if they did not protect their chastity, would break into a home during the daytime, steal the household valuables (televisions, jewelry, money), and rape the wife to discourage her from reporting the crime. Although it did not appear, from the stories, that these burglars targeted the very wealthy, these were reported to be crimes inspired by the rise in national affluence and the growing materialism of the national ethos as well as by the spreading gulf between rich and poor. Moreover, many of the comments on such crimes, such as the following newspaper quote, pointed to those wealth-generating practices conducted primarily by well-to-do women (real estate investments in particular) as the "cause" of unrest: "Experts . . . point out that the government should try to eliminate real estate speculation and other ills which widen the gap between the haves and have-nots, thus spreading crime psychology" (*Korea Herald*, "Crimes down 2.7% since Oct. 1990, but Citizens Feel Unsafe," 12 October 1991).

The *kwasobi ch'ubang* campaign must be seen in the context of these crime stories,[14] where not only the "crime-provoking" divisions between rich and poor were made visible by material goods (associated in most of the news stories with women), but where the breach was blamed on investment activities that were themselves strongly associated with "housewives," and the victims of these crimes were almost always women, generally housewives. Many of the affluent women I spoke with brought up the issue of crime and of their sense of insecurity in the large marketplaces and old alley neighborhoods, where they felt their wealth made them conspicuous. Most believed that *kwasobi* created tensions between rich and poor; many were critical of their own indulgences (although few said that they had altered their own habits of adornment or consumption[15]), and they looked even more severely at the excesses of other (imagined) women. The effect of these crime stories was to show that prosperity made women at once vulnerable to crime and left them undeserving of compassion.

## MOTHER-PATRIOTS AND THEIR CHILDREN

While the guilty pleasures of women of leisure provided one focus for popular *kwasobi* criticism, lack of extraordinary privilege did not exempt other women from reproach. *Kwasobi* discourse pitted the interests of the family against the interests of the nation and demanded that wives and mothers take responsibility for choosing between these priorities. In particular, the responsibilities of motherhood placed ordinary domestic errands within the sphere of moral consumer choices.

Although the *kwasobi ch'ubang* campaign assumed that women's primary role was domestic and that they had principal responsibility for domestic matters, the emphasis on the social and national stakes in consumer decisions drew women's domestic activity into the public sphere, disrupting the simple association of women with household or family. Married women are still referred to as *chip saram* ("house person") or *ansaram* ("inside person").[16] In its archetypal construction, the division between inside and outside in Korean gender ideology implies that a well-run household will function well for the community if the woman of the house focuses on the interests of her domestic circle, while the man of the house should see that the family and kin's interests are in harmony with broader social needs. A mother should not need to weigh conflicting interests; in taking the right action for her family, she would be taking the right action for her community. Moreover, traditionally, "It was the wife's task to keep the customs pure. This was a heavy responsibility, for the purity of the customs as they were cultivated in the domestic sphere was directly correlated with the rise and fall of the dynasty" (Deuchler 1992:232).

As I discussed in an earlier chapter, this concord between public and domestic long-term interests was often invoked by President Park Chung Hee during the "industrial push" years of the 1960s and 1970s. Frugality was portrayed as essential for the welfare of each household *and* for the nation. In Park's speeches, frugality was not so much an end in itself, a proper manner of living, but a strategy for achieving abundance. Park often made the explicit association between diligence and parsimony in the present and prosperity in the future. For example, in his "New Year's Message" for 1967 he used a rural metaphor: "What we require is the patience and wisdom not to divide seed grains among us and consume them, but to wait until they have increased to a harvest of 10 *sok* [a Korean measure of volume]. . . . I must appeal to you all to endure a little for the sake of a better tomorrow" (Park 1970:173). Implied in this rhetoric was a promise that even if the present adult generation may not see the fruits of their sacrifices, parental renunciation would pay off in the children's affluence. For several years after Chun Doo Hwan's ascension to the South Korean presidency in 1980, household frugality continued to appear as a government concern. In 1984, for example, the Ministry of Health and Social Affairs circulated a pamphlet on efficient housekeeping carrying this message: "In order to build a self-reliant economy, government, business, and households should collaborate. Especially, it is of foremost importance for the housewife to manage the household economy frugally and save for the formation of domestic capital" (quoted in Moon 1994).

The promise of future prosperity was all the more convincing for South Korean women because it accorded with what Cho Hae-jŏng (1986) has called "mother power." Cho has explored the complex intersection between women's familial responsibilities and the wider social domain, arguing that structural and cultural characteristics of South Korean society encouraged the strong identification of mothers with their children (particularly their sons). In this environment women identified with the success of the *next* generation rather than their own and thereby reproduced the dynamic of the coexistence of "mother power" (in the home) and male dominance. She argued that while women might exercise considerable autonomy and authority in making decisions about family and home matters, this would not translate into broader social gains for women; in fact, it would act as a deterrent to women's engagement in feminist movements. "Mother power basically stays at the personal level and has a conservative tendency. Mothers are able to defer gratification so much longer than wives or sisters that they, although discontented, tend to hold on and endure with a vague hope in the future of their children" (Cho 1986).

In the 1990s, however, the public exhortations to frugal living were being made in a changed context: the foundation for envisioning a simple harmony between household and national future interests through present domestic frugality had in a sense been undermined by the nation's achieved material successes. By the 1990s, the promise of general national prosperity had been fulfilled, but it was increasingly apparent that the distribution of wealth had not been impartial. The nation's children as a whole may have benefited, but many particular children had not. In fact, the greater affluence of some individuals and families had obviously bought them favors and profits, as stories of corruption, bribery, and lucrative real estate investments saturating the media showed. But the material aspirations of urban laborers, for themselves and for their children, had come to seem more and more chimerical. What persuasive force the discourse of future rewards had held for earlier generations was undermined by the evidence that for some families and individuals, the prosperous future had already arrived. While public posters might proclaim that "now is not the time to rest," and the media echoed the phrase, "It's not yet time to pop the champagne cork," the very proliferation of consumer goods and services that were the rewards of decades of work and savings shook people awake from the dream of an equitable future society.

It is not surprising then that consumption centered around children became the focus of a particular strain of *kwasobi* criticism in the early 1990s. Newspaper photographs of overweight children who preferred pizza and ice cream to rice and of children who took taxis to school visually criticized overindulgent mothers who spoiled their children. Children were considered particularly vulnerable to the seductions of smuggled-in Japanese comic books and electronic games and to the Japanese television shows for the reception of which well-off families bought satellite dishes. The legal prohibition on the import of Japanese popular culture was widely ignored, particularly in Kangnam, so the government initiated a targeted crackdown on the sale of foreign magazines near schoolyards to shield South Korean youth from the seduction of alien fashions and ideas. While the specter of Japanization of South Korean children loomed, the American cultural influence was equally troubling. A rash of editorials declaring that the sensuality of Michael Jackson's performance was inappropriate for South Korean youth followed his stop in the country on a world concert tour in the early 1990s.

Moral corruption, and especially sensuality, was a particular worry. Prudish condemnation addressed young women wearing short skirts, shorts, or sleeveless tops both for their own loss of modesty and for the temptation they posed. A pamphlet published by the Seoul YMCA warned that it was no longer only men who indulged their carnal desires: "this same tide has also infiltrated family, sex, and every generation to reach even women and youth. It is reported that housewives and middle school students are drug addicts, and the selling of women without hiding their age is not stopped; it can be said that this is concrete proof of the expansion of the atmosphere of indulgence that promotes exactly this depraved pleasure" (Seoul YMCA 1989:19). The *sinsedae* (new generation) were characterized as egoistic, individualistic, materialistic, hedonistic, superficial, and corrupted by foreign influences.[17] The dating games and openly suggestive behavior of the *orenji chok*, wealthy teens and young adults who frequented the bars and dance clubs of Kangnam, were focal points for media criticism and for private anxieties about where the nation was heading.

Another concern was, simply, that youth and young adults were developing new and unwelcome consumer habits. As one journalist commented, "Nowadays the new generation doesn't know how to use things sparingly, and they lack a frugal character" (Chae-ryŏng Chŏng 1990:35).

Clearly part of the message was that mothers were neglecting to teach the new generation the importance of frugality as a national cultural trait and as a national responsibility. Mothers' failures to do this threatened the stability of the nation. Recall Professor Ch'oi's association, in the article in *Mal*, of expensive children's toys with the licentious behavior of women of leisure. Mothers were faced daily with the conundrum whether by making their hardworking children happy with treats, games, and excursions they were destroying the fabric of the nation's future generation.

The dilemma in which women found themselves—choosing to honor family or national interests—was felt most pointedly in the issue of education. As in Japan, college admissions depended upon performance on an entrance exam, and high school students with college aspirations studied marathon hours for many years to prepare for this exam. Anecdotal evidence seemed to show that educational achievement could indeed lift a pauper to the middle class or beyond, but while hard work was a critical element in scholastic success, members of the affluent classes understood that mothers had the responsibility to devote both money and their own energy to ensuring that their children had the greatest chance of seeing their studies pay off.

Mothers were responsible for ensuring that their children had the best assistance with their school work and for providing the best foods to keep their children's minds active and bodies fueled, for staying up late with their children as they studied, for monitoring their children's study habits, for assisting with their homework (some mothers took classes themselves to improve their understanding of their children's curricula), and for disciplining their children when their levels of achievement were not satisfactory. In addition to these measures, mothers could choose from a variety of commercial study aids that increased the price of educational success. Formal extracurricular classes in specialized institutes were available in a range of quality and price options, and private tutors could instruct and drill children individually. Together, these two practices were known as *kwaoe*, extra lessons. Quietly paying an extra sum to the teacher might ensure that one's child would receive more attention or a better seat in class (classes often had forty to sixty pupils). The choice of residential neighborhood was important too: The popularity of Apkujŏngdong was in part due to its collocation with the eighth school district, where attendance at the elite Kyŏnggi High School, formerly accessible only by examination but now the neighborhood school, through alumni networks offered access to many of the most powerful men in South Korean business and government.

Many media stories focused on extracurricular education as a *kwasobi* problem. The Korean Education Development Institute estimated that 1990 expenditures on private education of this type reached 9.4 trillion *wŏn*, more than the 8.7 trillion *wŏn* spent on public education (*Korea Herald*, 23 June 1992). The cost of educational assistance had been a sensitive public subject for more than a decade. Given the ideal of individual social mobility via accessible education and personal effort and intelligence, the potential for wealthy families to buy educational success was a serious threat to the vision of an equitable future. Extracurricular institutes for middle and high school students were outlawed in 1980 and not legalized in Seoul again until 1992, and most private tutoring was also illegal during this period. Despite the ban, use of extracurricular education was widespread. As one might expect, the percentage of students attending extracurricular schools tended to vary with the social class and income of their parents and with the sex of the children; in a Seoul-wide survey of middle-school boys, for example, three-quarters of the boys in schools located in middle-class neighborhoods were enrolled in outside study programs (I 1992:72). Moreover, professor Kim Young-Hwa found that mothers had a strong tendency to want their children to attain a higher level of education than they had themselves (Kim 1992); initial class-related differences in women's educational attainments were therefore likely to be amplified in their children.

Costs varied widely, but media coverage of the high end of the market linked *kwaoe* with *kwasobi*. In fall 1991 the Seoul police arrested a forty-four-year-old man for charging "too much" to tutor two students to prepare for the college entrance exam. Each student's parents had paid 8.5 million *wŏn* (about U.S.$10,000) per month for the tutoring services (*Korea Herald*, 30 October 1991). Another article reported:

> Figures released by the Economic Planning Board on a set of cases over Koreans' conspicuous consumption showed that Korean parents spent 7,129.5 billion *wŏn* for providing their children with extraordinary schooling last year [1990], up 113 percent from 3,340.4 billion *wŏn* in 1985. . . . An increasing number of parents competitively let their pre-school children or primary pupils learn such out-of-school lessons as piano, abacus, and fine arts.
>
> (*Korea Herald*, September 1991)

The mothers in Yoido struggled daily with the expense and the logic of extracurricular education. Every mother with school-age children told me she paid for some supplementary training outside of school. The amount of money spent and the kinds of education purchased varied widely according to the age of the children, the sex of the children, and the personal interests, values, and experiences of the parents and the children. Yun-sun, for example, was a woman who had spent several years in the United States with her family. Her son and daughter had studied in American elementary schools, and they fondly recalled the freedom of a childhood without the pressures of extracurricular school. The daughter, her younger child, was enrolled in art classes in the afternoon; she had asked for the classes because all her friends went directly to the art school (in an institute in the shopping center across from the apartment complex) after school. Art was an examination subject in elementary school. The son, however, had resisted extracurricular studies until he came home with a low grade on a math test, so she enrolled him in an institute for supplemental math instruction. These were the only lessons Yun-sun selected for her children. "*I don't know if I'm doing the right thing, but there is no easy decision. I think childhood should be a time when children have plenty of time to read and play and enjoy their friends. If they fall behind in their studies, or if they ask for extra tutoring, I'll think again. I may have been too influenced by my American experience.*" The total expense for Yun-sun's children was 150,000 *wŏn* per month.

Many other women in Yoido voiced similar concerns about the pressures on small children to study rather than play. Sang-hun's Mother, a mother of two boys (ages nine and twelve), told me, "*My boys have a lot of energy. The younger one is a scamp—he's always making up new games. The older one is more serious, and he goes through phases: last year he loved to play the violin, and this year it's art. They both do well in school, but I worry that it's not good enough. I wish I could allow them more time to play, but it's my responsibility to make sure they have a bright future.*" Sang-hun's Mother admitted that she herself had not been a star student, and she felt that she wasn't up to monitoring the boys' studies herself. The older boy was already ambitious: he told me that he wanted to be a doctor and that if he didn't get into Seoul National University, he would settle for Harvard. Sang-hun's Mother had enrolled her boys in what seemed to be an average extracurricular load for the Yoido community. The younger son had art lessons two days a week, piano once a week, English conversation twice a week, and he subscribed to a mathematics workbook course. The older son also had art lessons (but at a more prestigious art institute near one of Seoul's art colleges) once a week and piano lessons with the same neighborhood instructor (a woman who lived in the apartment complex) as well as formal English and math instruction at an institute in Apkujŏngdong. Sang-hun's Mother spent three afternoons or evenings a week driving her older son to his lessons. She spent about 350,000 *wŏn* on extra schooling for her two sons each month.

The most extreme case in the apartment complex was Chi-sun, the ten-year-old daughter of Suk-hi. Chi-sun was a poised and extremely intelligent girl. Like Yun-sun's children, she, too, had spent time (first and second grade) studying in the U.S., but she had completed her transition back into Seoul school life. She was class president, an honorary position that generally recognized leadership and scholastic ability,[18] during one of the terms I was living in Yoido. Chi-sun started three mornings of the week with tennis lessons at 6:00 at the nearby courts. When she came home from school, she studied piano (with the neighborhood teacher) as well as Suzuki-method violin (lessons one afternoon a week and Saturday mornings, in another neighborhood south of the Han River). She was enrolled in the art institute in the nearby shopping center together with her friends. She practiced her English conversation with me once a week, and she also participated in a conversation group at school for children who had had English-language experiences abroad. She was an active member of an astronomy club as well. The total cost for Chi-sun's lessons was not outside the norm (about 220,000 wŏn), but Chi-sun was much more tightly scheduled than the average ten-year-old girl. Near the end of my fieldwork, Chi-sun decided to quit her morning tennis lessons. "*I think I'm a little too busy,*" she observed.

One woman who had moved from Yoido to Mokdong a year earlier found she was spending more in Mokdong on extracurricular expenses, in part because her children were a year older and in part because she trusted her local schools even less than she did the Yoido school. "*Every month I spend 1,000,000 wŏn just for one child, and I have two children. They both take piano, art, tennis, math. My daughter also studies English, and my son also takes guitar. Then last year my daughter was the classroom vice leader, and that cost me a lot of money. And of course I give the teacher gifts. It's all very expensive.*"

Middle-income mothers had various concerns about kwaoe. In addition to their worries about the pressures on their children, they were also concerned that their children would become dependent upon coaching to study. Were they undermining their children's ability to achieve on their own by accustoming them to tutoring? Mothers, after all, were responsible for ensuring that the next generation would be strong and effective. The cost was another consideration. Mothers in Yoido discussed frankly their ambivalence about paying such sums for their children's education even though the children attended public school. A few women directly addressed the financial impact the extracurricular schooling had on their own family's budget.

"*I tutor neighborhood high school students in English,*" explained one mother of middle school children. "*I used to enjoy it, but I don't really anymore. I can't quit, though. This is the only way I can earn enough money to pay for my own kids' extracurricular schooling and still be home for them most of the time.*" Another mother commented, "*My mother is always phoning me with schemes for money—'Put this in your bank account,' 'Buy this stock—I just got a tip that some big investors are about to get in.' It always seemed so shady, and I still don't like to think about whether all of it is strictly legal, but she knows what she's doing, and I can bring in an extra 500,000 *wŏn* a month this way. That's how *I* pay for my children's lessons.*" Other women who did not mention their efforts to earn money commented on the need to budget wisely to afford the extracurricular lessons.

In a group conversation a friend in Yoido arranged for me, however, most of the women focused not so much on the expense from the perspective of their own household budget but on how their expenditures on their children's education related to the *kwasobi* problem and the growing gap between rich and poor. Many saw the need to spend money on private instruction as a result of public-school failings. "*Because the schools aren't very good, students need to study outside school. That's what creates the problem between rich and poor around tutoring,*" said one mother of two elementary school boys. Some mothers complained that many teachers no longer take pains to present the groundwork of material in class, since the teachers know that many of their students are already ahead of the class in their after-school lessons. Yun-sun noted that her son's poor performance on the math exam was not just because he had fallen behind in the United States. "*He told me that the teacher had just skimmed over that part of the lesson, because the other students had already studied the material at their institutes.*" This puts those mothers who might ordinarily opt out of extracurricular education in a bind. "*I never had a tutor, and I don't think my children should need extracurricular classes, either,*" explained one mother, who attributed her own class mobility from a working-class childhood to an affluent present to educational success. "*I know they are smart, and I can help them study. But the other students learn everything ahead of time, so if I don't enroll my kids in an extracurricular program, then they'll be behind in school. This is a real problem, and not just for me. Think of those families who can't afford extra lessons!*" Yoido mothers were more tight-lipped about the "white envelopes," gifts of money they paid to public school teachers, but those who would discuss it were clearly unhappy not just with the expense but also with the social implications. "*There is a going rate. Everyone knows it. We talk about it. You have to pay, or the teacher won't pay any attention to your son or daughter. I feel badly for the mothers who don't have enough money to pay, but there isn't anything I can do about that,*" one woman explained. Women felt pressured by the teachers themselves. One woman told me that she felt self-conscious about her address because the apartment numbers correlated to the apartment size; she was sure her son's teacher knew she lived in a (relatively spacious) 45-p'yŏng apartment and that he expected her to be generous with her white envelopes. Another observed, "*Sometimes a young teacher refuses to take the envelopes [of money]. This can cause real problems, because then you don't know how to secure the teacher's attention for your child. The system is bad, but at least we can do something for our children.*"

The middle- and upper-middle-income women I spoke with in Yoido and elsewhere in Seoul regarding these expenses were clearly struggling to construct moral frameworks for decisions that apparently forced them to choose between their children's interests and those of the nation. This often led them to ask questions about the role of the public education system in reproducing class differences, and it pushed many of the mothers to the conclusion that the only welfare they could affect was their family's. Some rationalized that, ultimately, the nation would benefit from their efforts to provide their children with the best education possible, but few of the women of the comfortable classes felt sanguine about the intersection between *kwasobi* and *kwaoe*.

Mothers in Talgoljjagi were positioned very differently with respect to the *kwasobi* discourse focusing on extracurricular education, as few had the money to purchase even the most basic study aids, and many were themselves only newly literate. When I asked whether they thought extracurricular schooling was a *kwasobi* problem, Won-sŏ's Mother laughed bitterly: "*I hear some mothers give money to teachers to show their gratitude or to ask for their attention. I gave my son's teacher an envelope to get her to stop beating him. That's all I can afford with my money.*" Miyŏng expressed her own despair: "*My daughter studies hard and she does well in school, but my son isn't interested and he never does his homework. I sent him to a local extracurricular school, but I don't think he learned anything. I can't help him study, and I can't afford to pay for good lessons, so I just hope he learns something and stays out of trouble. And I wish I could help my daughter more. I know it will be harder for her when she gets to high school.*" Their recognition of the difficulties of doing well in school contrasted with the hopes many mothers had for their children. When I asked about their ambitions for their children, most women said they hoped their children would have white-collar jobs and that they hoped their children would finish high school and even college.[19] Obviously, though, the women themselves recognized the chasm separating their dreams from their present reality.

Despite the inequities Talgoljjagi women themselves noted in their children's access to educational opportunities, few of the Talgoljjagi women criticized richer mothers. I mentioned the newspaper story about the tutor who was arrested for charging 8.5 million *wŏn* a month for his lessons and asked if the women thought this was *kwasobi*. "*Of course it's *kwasobi*,*" Chong-hae remarked, "*but it's in the newspaper because it's so *uncommon*. That's why they call it *kwasobi*.*" Youngwŏn's Mother said, "*8.5 million *wŏn*—I can't imagine that. That's too much. But as for extracurricular education, it's the mother's responsibility to help her children. They are doing the right thing.*" On the other hand, many of the women said that it was part of the *pinikpin puikpu* (the poor stay poor while the rich stay rich) phenomenon. In essence, many Talgoljjagi women viewed the problem of extracurricular educational expenses in terms of social structure, rather than as one of individual culpability.

The *kongbubang* ("study room") in Talgoljjagi helped to provide some of the scholastic support Yoido mothers bought commercially. Part of the wider Minjung-Minjok movement, the *kongbubang* had been established a few years earlier by a pair of dedicated, feminist sisters in order to provide literacy training to local women and school support to the neighborhood children. Volunteers from the neighborhood and local colleges, including the small women's university at the bottom of the hill, staffed the classes and study groups. In the "Mother's School," adult women could study basic reading, writing, Chinese characters, English, arithmetic, and hand acupuncture. Several of the women I spoke with had gained confidence in their reading and writing ability for the first time while studying at the *kongbubang*;[20] often they were first motivated to sign up for reading lessons when they found they could not help their children with their homework. Children were grouped by age, and the classes for children offered a combination of scholastic assistance and drills in basic school subjects as well as confidence-building activities. For adolescents, Korean farmers' music, badminton, and art were optional classes. The *kongbubang* was seen as an invaluable community resource. It provided a safe space and a place for women to discuss the difficulties they faced with their families, and for many of the children it was the only place where they could find adults to help them with their schoolwork or where they could simply study quietly.[21] Many women expressed a deep feeling of loyalty and gratitude to the *kongbubang*, and they contributed to the *kongbubang* by bringing food and presents and by volunteering for various activities.

Other mothers in Talgoljjagi took personal pains to provide their children with a home environment conducive to study. Chong-hae was able to make sure her daughter, an only child, had quiet study hours at home in the afternoon after school. "*I check her homework every night, even though I can't tell if it's right or wrong,*" she said. "*I didn't learn to read even *han'gul*[22] until I was thirty, but my daughter wants to be a teacher. I'll do what I can to help her.*" Youngwŏn's Mother, who herself had finished only the sixth year of elementary school and had recently completed the *kongbubang*'s reading and writing program, filled her one-room home with books for her daughter, age four, and her son, who was not yet two years old. "*I always wanted to finish high school, but I started work when I was twelve. I tried to commit suicide when I was sixteen. I was so lonely and tired, and I didn't think anyone would ever marry someone like me. I wasn't pretty, and I was just a factory girl. I got on a train, and I was planning to go to the eastern sea to kill myself. But a Christian woman on the train started to talk to me, and she helped me see the possibility for a better life. Since then, I've been involved in social movements, and I have a vision for the future of the community and my children. I know there is a power in being able to read and write and to study many things. It's a power we need to have, personally and politically. That's what I want for my children, and for all the Talgoljjagi children.*"

For many Talgoljjagi mothers, the *kwasobi ch'ubang* campaign was a distant rumbling.[23] They dealt with the inequities of the national economy at the level of making quiet spaces and keeping their children safe in the school room. They nourished their hopes for their children's future in the collective space of the *kongbubang*. For these women, government promises of future prosperity seemed empty; they had little money to save (but they saved what they could) and saw no reason to expect or ask richer families to practice frugality for their sakes. "*If I had money, I would do just what they do,*" was the most common perspective on the spending practices of the wealthy. They would do what they could to make their children's future better, without expecting much benefit from economic development at the national level.

## QUESTIONING *KWASOBI*

While *kwasobi* discourse was pervasive, not everyone was persuaded by it. First, the boundaries of *kwasobi* were unclear. In Talgoljjagi, Chong-hae dismissed the idea of *kwasobi*. "*If I had so much money, I'd buy a large apartment, and a car, and beautiful clothes. I'd go to Australia for a trip. Anyone would do the same.*" I said that I thought in part the campaign was concerned that *kwasobi* was demoralizing for people with little money and that *kwasobi* would cause trouble between rich and poor. Miyŏng laughed, "*Kwasobi* is not the problem. Who cares what a rich person buys? Of course, rich people drive in their Grandeurs or their imported cars. The problem is we cannot afford to buy a house. Do you know the phrase *pinikpin, puikpu?* That's just the way it is.*"

In Yoido the issues of *kwasobi* struck closer to home and demanded constant response. Often women associated *kwasobi* with impropriety. It was hard for me to bring up the topic without appearing to imply that I thought the woman I was then speaking to was guilty of *kwasobi*. When I asked if *kwasobi* was a problem, one woman told me, "*I spend too much money on gifts for my husband's bosses.*" It was just after *Ch'usŏk*. "*We bought beef for his superiors, and I spent almost 1,000,000 *wŏn*. Then we got beef from my parents and my parents-in-law. They received so much they had to distribute some to us. I had to buy an extra-large freezer just for this season. There is so much waste in our society!*"

When I asked what the women in Yoido thought was the most serious issue around *kwasobi*, many said that they thought conspicuous consumption would cause poor people to envy rich people. "*Yesterday I saw an old grandfather waiting for a bus, and some student drove by in a black Grandeur. Can you imagine? Such a big car, for a student! I wondered what that grandfather thought about it. It just didn't seem polite.*" Another woman commented that because, in her estimation, many people had become rich suddenly,[24] they didn't know how to behave properly. "*If poor people see that other people no better than they are are enjoying themselves, they will think, 'Why should I work hard?' That is why we have the problem of the three Ds.*" It was said that few people were willing to take on dirty, dangerous, or difficult work any longer and that this was causing problems of productivity.

For women in Yoido, however, the sensitive issue of propriety was an element in their consumer choices and hence in their sense of who was guilty of *kwasobi*. Almost all of the apartment interiors in the complex had been altered and furnished according to the interior design ideas of the women of the house. One apartment had a sunken living room; several had removed or reduced the walls between the kitchen and main sitting areas to form a more open plan; most of the bathrooms had been newly tiled and refitted. Women took cues and inspiration from one another, but they also measured the efforts of their neighbors. When I admired the spacious feeling of Chang-su's Mother's redesign, she responded with pride: "*I was the first one to take the verandah over and glass it in to bring it inside. Everyone else followed my example.*" But at another time a woman in a neighboring building listed the apartments that were, in her opinion, overdone. "*Chang-su's Mother is trying to make a 45-*p'yŏng* apartment out of one that's 35 *p'yŏng*,*" she observed. Women also measured their own consumer choices against multiple unspoken scales. When one woman went with her mother to look at new furniture, she came back in an irritable mood. She pulled out a catalog of elaborate rosewood pieces. "*My mother wants me to buy Chinese-style furniture. Of course it's beautiful, but it's for older people. We're too young to have a set like this. People would think it was strange. It's not appropriate.*"

Many of the families in Yoido had traveled or lived abroad and nearly a third had close relatives living in Europe or North America. These cosmopolitan experiences had awakened a desire in many to participate in the world's marketplace by owning imported fashions and imported furniture. Rarely did someone return from foreign travel without presents of cosmetics and liquor; one family had a sizable collection of XO whisky on display. Owning foreign-made products linked them to the international world of consumers they encountered in the media, if not in person. The issue of foreign cars, however, was more problematic. Cars were particularly visible symbols of consumer propriety (recall the young mother who felt she could not yet buy a Grandeur because of her age, and the business man who had chosen the "wrong" car for his position). The role of the car industry in the export successes (and weaknesses) of South Korea's economy in the 1980s and 1990s intensified the sense that buying a car was a matter of patriotism. By buying a Hyundai (or, to a lesser extent, a Daewoo or Kia), the purchaser participated materially and imaginatively in the success of Hyundai Motor's trade strategies. Owning a foreign car seemed almost traitorous.[25] In the parking lot of the Yoido apartment complex, the only imported car was a solitary Mercury Sable. A friend of the owner defended him: "*He works for Kia Motors, and they import the Sable. It's not his choice, his office told him to drive a Sable.*"[26] In 1992, however, when Hyundai was holding a surplus of Sonatas that originally had been intended for North America, their release onto the domestic market was a success. One woman in Yoido who purchased a Sonata Gold told me the cars were sturdier and better designed and that she got the advantages of buying a foreign car as well as the pride of buying a Korean-made car. But another woman had bought a Mercedes for her father-in-law, an international businessman, after the 1988 Seoul Olympics when foreign cars that had been brought in for the games were sold off to private owners.

> *My thought was that now that our country had successfully held the Olympics and was succeeding in the international marketplace, we could all show that we don't need to be afraid of foreign things. I wanted to give the best car to my father-in-law, so I chose the Mercedes. What a mistake! Not very long afterward, we started getting audited by the Tax Office because we were owners of a foreign car. I thought, 'This doesn't make sense. We didn't import this car—we bought a used Mercedes. Why are they bothering us?' But anyway, after two or three years, we sold the car so the Tax Office would leave us alone.*

In these consumer choices, women of relative wealth were constructing for themselves a sense of what level and style of consumption was appropriate so that they could escape the charge of kwasobi. In the public media, too, writers occasionally raised questions about kwasobi. Some expressed impatience with the campaign itself. In a column entitled "One Woman's Way" in the English-language Korea Herald, Choi Jin-young suggested that the government should stop complaining about kwasobi. Only a few years ago, she wrote, "it was the government and the media that propagated without discretion the news that we had more dollars in reserve than ever and we could splurge. And splurge we did" (Korea Herald, 28 September 1991). Yi Sung-ho, in a letter to the editor, also blamed the government. "I have yet to know anyone who has earned his money the hard way and who is indulgent in lavish spending. Then who is to blame for the loudly cursed overspending spree? . . . The culprits are the government or the politicians who fail to set up law and order or social justice in this society" (Korea Herald, 5 September 1991).

Others addressed the issue of kwasobi from a rationalist perspective and questioned whether it really was a serious problem for the South Korean economy. Columnist Yoon-yul Kim argued that *kwasobi* "ugly and distasteful as it is and unworthy of defense, is nowhere near the main cause of the serious trade deficit and social disequilibrium we are experiencing now." He noted that while less than 1 percent of shoppers are overspenders, all consumers have "every right to buy or consume what they please" and that "the present campaign seems to have several related issues mixed up, either purposely or out of ignorance, causing its militancy to be misdirected" (*Korea Herald*, 19 September 1991). Another columnist commented, "Everyday consumers vote with their money. . . . Viewed in this manner, the phenomenon, inappropriately called *kwa-so-bi*, should be understood as a clear signal that the Korean consumers now prefer higher quality items and service (and are sometimes willing to pay grossly exaggerated prices for them). That our producers are unable to satisfy such demands is a huge failing on the part of our economy. . . . [But the *kwasobi* movement] since it will do absolutely no good in the long run, . . . should be banished from our society" (*Korea Herald*, 19 September 1991).

Foreign economists, too, disputed the notion that excessive spending was endangering the nation. South Korea's private savings rates were among the highest in the world; in 1990 the rate was 30.7 percent.[27] In 1994 Susan Collins observed, "Koreans appear to have responded to above-average income growth as transitory and to have saved most income gains" (Collins 1994:244). She noted that there had been a "slow adjustment of consumption patterns over time, with household consumption for given current levels of real income based on historical or societal norms" (ibid.:255) rather than responding directly to the income increases. This was confirmed by the National Statistical Office; during the period of the most heated *kwasobi* rhetoric, average urban household expenditures consistently rose more slowly than average urban household incomes, leading to greater savings margins (*Korea Times*, 9 October 1991).

The contrast between the high rates of savings and the charges that consumer spending was undermining the national economy formed one basis of skepticism about *kwasobi*. Conflicts between one campaign and another also opened a crack in the discourse of *kwasobi*. The woman who had bought her father-in-law a Mercedes—in response, she explained, to government encouragement—gained strength for facing the charges of a *kwasobi* lifestyle through her experience with needless government harassment. *Kwasobi's* link to *pullo sodŭk* through the easy-come-easy-go explanation[28] rankled some Yoido women who believed the income they generated through investments was hardly "unearned." Other women constructed a critique of *kwasobi* rhetoric through other personal conflicts. Suk-hi gained her cynicism in the following experience.

In the early 1990s foreign travel had become one of the central foci of *kwasobi* criticism.[29] Many Yoido families had relatives abroad, and a large number of the families had either recently gone to visit them or were planning a trip for the next school vacation.[30] Other women had lived abroad in their twenties, studying at graduate school or accompanying their husbands' foreign scholastic pursuits. Foreign travel, however, posed one of the starkest conflicts for well-off mothers between the interests of the nation (as set forth in *kwasobi* terms) and the interests of the family. In spring 1991 Suk-hi made plans to travel with Chi-sun and Chi-sun's eight-year-old brother Il-hyŏng back to the town in California where the family had spent two years, 1987 and 1988. Suk-hi was looking forward to catching up with old friends, and she had a brother of whom she was quite fond who lived in Los Angeles. Chi-sun was excited, too, although Il-hyŏng, who no longer spoke any English, said he was worried that he would feel stupid. Still, Il-hyŏng had been promised a trip to Disneyland, which seemed to distract him from his fears. But just a few weeks before the end of the semester, Il-hyŏng came home from school and announced that they would have to cancel the trip. The boy reported that during school assembly that afternoon the principal had explained that foreign travel was an example of *kwasobi* and that students should discourage their parents from taking them abroad. Indeed, the principal forbade students to travel to foreign countries. Rather, he suggested, Korean families should travel in their own country, visit the mountains or the shore, or tour the national historical monuments. Suk-hi told me about her reaction.

> *I was surprised by how Il-hyŏng's announcement affected me. You know that I usually see through all the government propaganda, and I was furious that the government was so obviously trying to manipulate families through our children. But at the same time, I thought about giving up the trip anyway. For one thing, I didn't know how to explain to Il-hyŏng that it would be all right if I disobeyed his principal, and Il-hyŏng himself has very strong patriotic feelings, which I think is a good thing, especially given his experience abroad. But what was even more surprising for me, I started to worry that this trip really was more of a personal indulgence than the national economy should have to bear right now.*

In the end, Suk-hi decided not to cancel the trip. For one thing, she said half-jokingly, the plane tickets had already been purchased, and she wasn't sure she'd be able to get all her money back—surely *that* would be unfrugal behavior. Suk-hi also believed that the children as well as the nation would benefit in the long run from more international exposure and practice with the English language.[31]

One interesting factor in Suk-hi's decision-making process was her anger at the escalation in antitravel propaganda. Suk-hi clipped for me some of the articles that had appeared in the English-language press (similar articles were carried in vernacular papers): An editorial in the *Korea Times* (12 June 1991) commented, "there are an increasing number of indiscreet and well-to-do families who are deplorably sending their newlywed children on honeymoons overseas and even their elementary and secondary school children on overseas study programs to learn foreign languages." The same editorial opined that "a recent government decision to regulate overspending on foreign tourism and check wasteful overseas tours by young students in particular is appropriate in view of the nation's vital need to improve its foreign exchange holdings. As a result, unqualified students whose records at school are poor will be banned from making overseas trips to take foreign language courses. And those who have run up large bills with their traveler's credit cards will be subject to regular monthly checks by the Bank of Korea." In an article entitled, "Gov't to Tighten Curb on Students' Overseas Travel," the *Korea Herald* (21 June 1991) reported that the Education Ministry had decided to ban student group tours, including visits to foreign sister schools, and to require students and teachers to report their travel plans to their school principals in order to curtail "frivolous" use of foreign exchange.[32] Suk-hi told me, "*I was reading these articles, and one day my anger grew bigger than my guilt and fear. If I think the best thing for my children is a trip to California, and if we can afford it, what right does the government have to threaten me? We live in a democracy. We have the right to travel now. We have our passports. Something shifted for me.*"

Suk-hi's story illustrates one of the effects of the *kwasobich'ubang* campaign's discursive pressures: many of the women in Yoido had grown frustrated with the conflicts between their social and family responsibilities—so frustrated, in fact, that they attained (however occasionally, however partially) a new perspective on proper action as patriotic women and mothers. Two elements of the *kwasobi* discourse and of recent history created this opening. First, archetypal *kwasobi* appeared to be carried out elsewhere: in Apkujŏngdong, in Hong Kong, by women they met at church; few women in Yoido saw their own lifestyles as excessive, with the possible exception of the nearly involuntary expenditures on gifts and on extracurricular education for their children. Moreover, the message of frugality as necessary to ensure the nation's prosperous future had aged badly. For women with a comfortable income, earlier decades of frugality had succeeded: years of scrimping *had* brought wealth to the nation and to their families. There was no persuasive argument for further restraint for an even more prosperous future. And since the point of frugality appeared to be to create a better future, spending money on one's children could be considered as spending *for* the future. Suk-hi reached the breaking point over her trip to California: she rejected a direct order from her son's school principal and made a conscious decision to choose for herself what would be best for her children and her nation. Other Yoido mothers, while less articulate about their choices, shared in this rebellion against a discourse that denied the possibility of correct action.

## CONSUMER PATRIOTISM

It is important to keep in mind that membership in a national community is experienced differently by differently situated persons. While in theory all individuals who meet the threshold criteria for membership in the national community can claim national identity, not all members of the nation can behave as patriots in the same way. Patriotism is thus implicated in the cultural processes of making distinctions between people within a nation. The allocation of different positions within a national community often reinscribes preexisting categories (Williams 1990), and in contemporary South Korea gender was just such a critical distinction. Men were offered the opportunity to prove their patriotism during their mandatory service in the military as youths, and this experience was reenacted ritually for the rest of their lives in nostalgic preferences for food eaten by soldiers (including small animals caught in the mountains and a soup made with tinned meats), remembered in conversations, and reproduced in militarized structures of behavior in South Korean commercial offices and the state bureaucracy (see Janelli 1993:48). Men of various classes were offered (economically) productive roles in the patriotic development of the South Korean economy: farmers, factory workers, and white-collar office workers all appeared in government images of people making their contribution to the national good by dint of hard work.

Roles broadly deemed appropriate for South Korean women in maintaining the nation and claiming national identity by right of patriotic living were distinctly gendered (although in many instances women performed the same labor functions as did men[33]) and almost always referred to heterosexual female or maternal roles. Other scholars have noted the symbolic roles women in the abstract are relegated to in this question of national identification: as facilitating relations between men, bearing the marks of ethnic tradition, reproducing the nation as mothers, and depicting the limits of the nation through men's erotic fantasies about foreign women (see Smith 1996; Williams 1996; Ebron and Tsing 1995:396; Parker et al. 1992; Stoler 1991). In South Korea, the sexual use of "foreign" women (of Korean women by Japanese and American men, of Southeast Asian women by South Korean men on business and pleasure trips) demonstrated the strong sense that power at the level of the nation affords men of those nations the ability—if not always the right—to buy the sexual services of exotic women from other ("less developed") countries. It was less widely known that the South Korean government had, for years, served as overseer in the last instance of the settlements of prostitutes established around the U.S. military bases in that country. During the 1960s and 1970s, representatives of the South Korean government told the women in lectures that they were performing a patriotic service, contributing to the security of the nation and adding to the stores of foreign currency (Moon 1997). This opportunity to demonstrate feminine patriotic devotion was, of course, not widely recommended to the South Korean female populace.

Women who have participated in anticolonial struggles, too, have often found that their own participation is seen as limited by their gender and that their perception of this constraint is one pathway to personal awakening (Jayawardena 1986). When women patriots are often seen as oddities or as minor figures in the struggle, how do women in their day-to-day engagement with the ordinary world perform and imagine what national identity means to them? South Korea provides an opportunity to examine national identity and patriotism as it was experienced through a specific, gendered aspect of life that had become part of the public discussion of national responsibility: the act of consumption. New ideals of consumption were generated in private practice and in public propaganda. Disputes about the meaning of the nation and how to balance conflicting affiliations (to nation, family, class, and—for some—to the international strata of sophisticates as well as to the past, the present, and the future) had both verbal and enacted elements. Ideology, consciousness, and explanation were not always congruent with the material circumstances. By listening to women discuss consumption as an abstract phenomenon and as a concrete part of their lives and by observing the choices they made in the marketplace, we gain some perspective on how ideas of national identity differed among women and how those ideas expressed the gendered character of South Korean society. These are cautionary insights, warning us away from assuming a universal aspect to the phenomenon scholars have been calling "national identity."

Other scholars have examined the coevolution of specific gendered political frameworks and the development of consumer culture in various places. David Kuchta has traced the development of an aesthetic of masculine austerity as a foundation for bourgeois male authority (as opposed to the authority of the aristocracy) to the late seventeenth century in England. "By associating modest masculinity with political legitimacy, . . . men used a cultural construction of gender to define the character necessary for participation in the polity. . . . Political participation in the nation, then, was defined in terms of masculine renunciation of luxury, and this definition explains why vanity and luxury were such dominant definitions of femininity" (Kuchta 1996:65). European women were recruited to particular styles of consumption as part of the nation-making process. In nineteenth-century France, "the notion of the importance of the bourgeois women's role in the making of the nation through tasteful consumption was born" (Auslander 1996:95). Control of women's consumption was a consistent theme, from directing women's "natural inclination" to seek frivolous novelty toward domesticity and away from coquetry in eighteenth-century France (Jones 1996:38) to austerity in Germany in the early years of World War I, when women with sufficient resources to spend money were seen as "the inner enemy in the economic war" (Davis 1996:292) as well as in Mussolini's Italy: "Starting in the second half of the 1930s, with the shift to autarchic economic strategies, the dictatorship tried to exercise firmer control over consumption habits. With the aim of rallying public support for austerity, fascist propagandists targeted 'luxurious' women as enemies of the state. Fascist women willingly went along with attacks on things foreign" (de Grazia 1996b:351). The South Korean experience confirms these studies. Consumer practices and consumer images have become distinctly gendered, and these gendered images feed back into the definition and allocation of social and political roles and responsibilities.

A focus on consumption also addresses a particular set of insights generated by recent theorizing on nationalism. Several studies have pointed out the difficulties of making national cultures, nationalist sentiment, and national identities in a global environment where people, goods, capital, aspirations, dangers, information, pollution, and images flow with unprecedented freedom across transnational space (Hannerz 1989; Appadurai 1990 and 1991; Ferguson and Gupta 1992; Featherstone 1990). The congruence once assumed for territory/space and society/nation/culture is now undercut by a recognition of the importance of "border crossings . . . differences *within* a locality . . . the question of postcoloniality . . . [and postcolonial] hybrid cultures . . . [and] interconnected spaces" (Gupta and Ferguson 1992). Travel, encounters with visitors, international news, the Korean diaspora, and the import and export of goods—as well as national division—have all contributed to the destabilization of the notions of "Korea" and "Korean."

The "crisis" of the late 1990s has not dramatically altered these conditions. While many serious analysts look both within South Korea and outside to political, structural, and business reasons for the near bankruptcy of the nation's economy, others blame the usual suspects: extravagance, waste, and personal indulgence. In the next chapter I explore these themes and place them in the context of 1997 and beyond.

At rush hour, inside one of Seoul's still-new subway cars, we stand so close together that I cannot shift my feet to gain a more stable stance in the rolling train. I do not know if it is a hand, a knee, or a briefcase pushing at the back of my thighs, and my face is pressed so tightly into the shoulder blades of the tweed coat in front of me that the air I take in smells of sweaty wool. At each stop along the line, as we get nearer to the center of town, unimaginable numbers of people squeeze and shove their way into tiny crevices, while those of us who are knocked off balance by the incoming wave cannot stifle the moans and grunts our bodies themselves voice as we fold ourselves into smaller packages to accommodate the newcomers. The windows, looking out into the black tunnels of Seoul's netherworld, are gauzy with the steam of hundreds of lungs hurtling toward the center of modern Korea. At the next station, Chongno Sam-ga, I am buffeted by people shoving their way toward the exit, and only by grabbing onto the poles near the doors do I manage to stay inside the car; keeping my grip firm, I defend the prime space in the tidepool just to the side of the door. This is my favorite spot on the subway. Perhaps it was designed for the huge bundles tied in flowered nylon the *ajumŏni*s[1] heave-ho into the car as they enter at the Chongro O-ga stop, below the East Gate market, but at rush hour I try to make my way into that corner. Here, standing next to the row of seats, I can breathe a little more freely and survey the scene.

From this vantage point, looking over and past the shiny black-haired heads of commuters lucky enough to have claimed a seat, I can see the colorful array of posters displayed above the luggage racks near the car ceiling. The posters provide me with a simple, cost-free language lesson, and I scan the walls for unfamiliar vocabulary. I have seen most of them before: One poster explains that the brand of underwear the handsome businessman is wearing gives him confidence; there are several advertisements for private extracurricular drilling practice to prepare children for school exams, showing in two rows black-and-white photographs of the teachers in charge of English, math, Korean; perky models smile holding bottles of alcohol, shampoo, kitchen cleanser, cooking oil; and one last poster shows a drawing in pastels of a few bright apartment buildings nestled in verdant hills, and suggests that these are the homes of your dreams.

# CODA

As per capita GNP comes to exceed U.S.$5,000, our nation's consumers have also slowly come to show a variety and individuality in shopping patterns and lifestyles. At the same time, the opening of the market according to the Uruguay Round negotiations will lead to the penetration of the domestic distribution market and, of course, the domestic distribution industry as well as the manufacturing trades by the immense capital strength and the well-developed management know-how of the advanced nations; we must anticipate that we will be faced with the enormous influence of more advanced national economies. It seems that in order to prepare for these changes in consumer desires and the market opening, it has become necessary to establish scientific and systematic methods of marketing.

Han'guk Yut'ong Chosa Yŏnguso (1991)

## UNDERSTANDING CONSUMPTION

Arjun Appadurai has suggested that "we treat demand, hence consumption, as an aspect of the overall political economy of societies. Demand, that is, emerges as a function of a variety of social practices and classifications, rather than as a mysterious emanation of human needs, [or] a mechanical response to social manipulation" (Appadurai 1986a:29). In South Korea throughout the period we have been examining, there was, in fact, significant social manipulation of demand emanating from the government and from its key partners in development, the chaebŏl. South Korean consumers responded, but by no means mechanically. Expanded consumer options brought new tools for expressing old social distinctions and envisioning new ones. Many people took genuine pleasure from the new market: in things themselves, in the act of shopping, and in consuming new services and new consumer environments. Certainly, too, people felt envy and frustration at the limits of their ability to achieve their consumer aspirations. Some of the new consumption reinforced a sense of national purpose. A great deal of consumption was status-differentiated and status-marking, but much was not and some was ambiguous.

Scholars of the culture of consumption have elaborated several identifiable broad perspectives on the importance of consumer practices. Ben Fine and Ellen Leopold (1993) provide a useful analytical overview of the disparate approaches to the study of consumption in a variety of disciplines: the focus on utility maximization of independent, rational consumers in economics, consumers as information processors in psychology, and the interest in what consumption communicates in sociology, anthropology, and history.[1] Fine and Leopold's principal novel contribution is to emphasize the interrelations between aspects of systems of provision that include production, distribution, and consumption; they point out that

> the implied preference in the literature for either a demand side or a supply side explanation has the critical effect of diverting interest away from the changing history of the relationship *between* them. The divergent paths taken by different industries may ultimately owe as much to the emergence of agencies mediating supply and demand (like distribution networks in the clothing industry) as to the development of either set of forces on its own.
>
> (Fine and Leopold 1993:95–96)

This is an excellent point, yet Fine and Leopold, in dismissing one-sided studies of consumption, pass somewhat too lightly over the way material culture enters into the making of meaning in contemporary societies. Within the field of consumption scholarship focused on the meanings embedded in acts of consuming, I draw a division between those who view consumption as conservative, and those who see consumption as expressive and even potentially liberatory.

On the one hand, the consumption celebrators often overemphasize the potential for consumer practices themselves to overturn existing social hierarchies. For example, in his study of urban malls, Rob Shields writes that the act of window shopping turns malls into places where

> people may take the opportunity to elaborate more complex behaviours, to engage in more roles, even to contest the economic rationale and rationalized norms of the site. Hence the genesis of a site of cultural change, of social experimentation, a theatre of everyday life. . . . Discrepancies arising from economic class differences are met with compensating cultural inventions, lack of political power is displaced by superior "performance" in a site which endorses a certain theatricality in which all participate at the same time as forming an audience.
>
> (Shields 1992:7)

Schields claims that "in the process, hegemonic systems find themselves undermined" (Schields 1992:2) by people strolling in the mall. Similarly (if more persuasively), Dick Hebdige sees in subcultural styles the possibility for "the subordinate class (the young, the black, the working class) to . . . embellish, decorate, parody and wherever possible to recognize and rise above a subordinate position which was never of their choosing" (Hebdige 1979:139), and Michel de Certeau believes that consumption is the realm in which society's weaker members exercise their tactics of resistance (de Certeau 1984). While these observers highlight behaviors and activities that may indeed give expression to rebellious disdain for dominant cultural systems, rarely do the studies of consumption as political resistance draw a clear connection between the ludic or expressive consumer practice and any transformation or effective undermining of aspects of social structures.

The opposite camp includes work from more diverse perspectives, including those who believe consumption's pleasures obscure "reality" or generate "false" consciousness by distracting consumers from their oppressive social reality (e.g., Ewen 1990; Tomlinson 1990), those who believe consumption marks and reproduces (generally preexisting) distinctions (Veblen 1899; Bourdieu 1984), and those who focus on the seductive babble of the consumer semiotic code or the ways consumption draws people into the superficiality of commodified postmodern culture (Baudrillard 1975; Jameson 1984). Such studies often illuminate fascinating details regarding the processes of defending the status quo, yet the dour message of eternal social replication, of the inescapability of hegemony, ignores the creative dynamism of social complexity.

Clearly, elements of both perspectives are illuminating, but neither alone fully captures the meaning and effect of consumer society. As Fine and Leopold note, consumption is a cultural practice that engages and affects the entire economic system. When Stuart Hall asks, "Can a socialism of the 21st century revive, or even survive, if it is wholly cut off from the landscapes of popular pleasures, however contradictory a terrain they are?" (Hall 1991:62), he is pointing to the important place consumption has as a practice of individual and group expression and meaning-making, a practice seated in an existing context and yet with the potential to illuminate and change the social landscape. Consumption assumes a new significance in politics for Hall:

There has been an enormous expansion of 'civil society,' caused by the diversification of the different social worlds in which men and women can operate. At present, most people only relate to these worlds through consumption. But, each of these worlds also has its own codes of behavior . . . [which] allow the individual some space in which to reassert a measure of choice and control over everyday life and to play with its more expressive dimensions. . . . Such opportunities need to be more, not less, widely available across the globe.

(Hall 1991:62)

In South Korea in the 1990s, consumption was an evolving cultural and political ground, experienced differently from different social positions, with both unifying and dividing effects. Income and wealth were marked by different consumer patterns and possessions and influenced the capacity to consume. For example, according to a report issued by the National Statistical Office, homeowners spent a much larger fraction of their income on personal consumption than did renters (81 percent compared to 68.7 percent in 1989) (*Korea Times*, 24 September 1992), presumably either because renters needed to save more, or because homeowners had higher incomes, or both. As we have seen, the act of shopping often generated experiences of class difference and inscribed differences in skills utilized, outlooks, behaviors, and the places consumers chose to shop. But not all South Korean consumption was focused on Veblenesque "emulation" and the assertion of status. Some goods worked well as markers of status (car owners, for example, appeared to cooperate in maintaining the clarity of the map of social distinction within that realm), but other goods did not. I was surprised to find that when I showed interview participants and friends a set of photographs I had taken of a wide range of people on the street in various places in Seoul and asked them to tell me all they could gather from their dress, people drew few conclusions about class or occupation from the images. Although there were some class-marked ways of dressing (designer or imported clothing, college-coed fashion, or the hip-hop look, for example), there was also a broadly shared sense of age-appropriate style. If, as Mary Douglas and Baron Isherwood define it, consumption is "a use of material possessions that is beyond commerce and free within the law. . . . Seen under this aspect, consumption decisions become the vital source of the culture of the moment. . . . Consumption is the very arena in which culture is fought over and licked into shape" (Douglas and Isherwood 1996:37), we must ask what was being contested in South Korea in the 1990s.

A variety of meanings can be encoded in goods and in their exchange, sale, acquisition, or possession. To return to the case of automobiles: Cer-

tainly the development of a native car industry and the spread of car ownership are significant markers of societal modernity—with all its attendant
promise and problems—not just in South Korea but in *many* places. (Recall
the phrase, "What's good for General Motors is good for America.") In part
this is because the successful development of an automobile industry demon-
strates significant wealth and know-how. Michael Taussig uses the story of
the ownership and sale of a used Australian-made Holden as an illustration
of the ways goods can help to pass on collective symbolic meanings, in this
case the heroic character of Australian national identity (Taussig 1992).
David Plath explores how collective and individual values were caught in
tension by car ownership in Japan (Plath 1990). In his study of modernism
and consumerism in Trinidad, Daniel Miller provides a long discussion of
the local practices of personalizing cars and puts that practice in the context
of a highly competitive culture. Miller writes,

> In contemporary Trinidad the car is probably the artifact which out-
> weighs even clothing in its ability to incorporate and express the concept
> of the individual. Three elements of the relationship between persons
> and vehicles seem conspicuous: the first is the tendency to use cars as a
> shorthand labeling for persons, the second lies in the antipathy to other
> modes of travel and the third lies in the physical transformation of cars.
>
> (Miller 1994:236)

South Korea shares the first two elements, but not the third.[2] And in preuni-
fication Germany, West Germans saw car ownership as a symbol of the postwar return to prosperity, while East Germans used the trouble-prone car
built in the German Democratic Republic, the Trabant, "as a synecdoche for
Eastern existence" (Borneman 1992). South Korea's native automobile industry and the spread of car ownership echo these experiences, yet the pace
and the complexity of the social relations of production have made automobiles a particularly significant element in the making of the contemporary
cultural, social, and spatial environment in South Korea. And it is worth noting that one of the harbingers of the coming economic troubles was the
bankruptcy of Kia Motors in 1997. The entire South Korean automobile industry, one of the nation's proudest industrial sectors, was vulnerable in part
because of the tremendous excess capacity in South Korean car factories—
production capacity that was often seen as an end in itself. Hyundai Motors,
for example, boasted of the world's largest automobile plant. The scale of

production in South Korea itself was closely tied to the important symbolic (as well as commercial) role the industry played in domestic and international image-making.

## THE 1997 ASIAN CRISIS

A decade ago, David Harvey commented on the social and cultural effects of new global financial markets: "The transition from Fordism to flexible accumulation, such as it has been, ought to imply a transition from our mental maps, political attitudes, and political institutions," he wrote.

> But political thinking does not necessarily undergo such easy transformations, and is in any case subject to contradictory pressures that derive from spatial integration and differentiation. There is an omni-present danger that our mental maps will not match current realities. The serious diminution of the power of individual nation states over fiscal and monetary policies, for example, has not been matched by any parallel shift towards an internationalization of politics. Indeed there are abundant signs that localism and nationalism have become stronger precisely because of the quest for the security that place always offers in the midst of all the shifting that flexible accumulation implies.
>
> (Harvey 1989:305–306)

Until the late 1980s, South Korea was buffered somewhat from some of the most destabilizing influences of foreign investment capital. Direct foreign investment in South Korean companies was strictly limited, and foreigners could hold no more than 12 percent of a South Korean company's stock. The South Korean financial markets were notoriously chilly environments for foreign bankers. Foreign—especially Western—investors were chary of South Korean management practices. The government still retained a great deal of influence over banking practices, and foreign loans were frequently channeled by policy to support targeted export industries. Shifts both in South Korea's ability to direct the financial sector and in the international investment environment, however, opened South Korea up to the crisis of the late 1990s. When South Korea signed the agreement with the International Monetary Fund in late 1997 for $57 billion in rescue loans, the average debt-to-equity ratio of the largest South Korean *chaebŏl* had climbed to nearly 500 percent.

South Korea's own success altered the conditions under which the relationship between the state and the *chaebŏl* was conducted. For one thing, the election of Kim Young-sam in 1992—South Korea's first civilian president since 1961 and, arguably, the inauguration of real democratization of national politics—began with a series of reforms including the implementation of what was known as the "real name system," which required investors to conduct business using their own names, rather than names they had fabricated or borrowed from others. This change eliminated the most common method relatively wealthy people used to avoid high taxes (they divided up their holdings into smaller parts to lower their rates) and to dodge other laws limiting their activities (including limits on real estate holdings). President Kim also directed public officials to reveal their assets in order to discourage the enrichment of public officials through bribes. During this period, former presidents Chun and Roh were prosecuted and convicted of graft. *Chaebŏl* owners as well as much of the general public saw these moves as efforts to limit the influence the *chaebŏl* had over national politics and to assert moral leadership in the issue of the increasing appearance of wealth disparity between the classes. The *chaebŏl* responded by quietly circumventing government regulations to the fullest extent possible.

On the international scene, South Korea's status as one of the world's top fifteen trading countries was recognized through its increasing participation in international economic organizations. South Korea graduated from its status as a World Bank loan recipient and joined the World Trade Organization in 1995, and it became a member of the Organization for Economic Cooperation and Development (OECD) in 1996. Membership was a source of significant pride for South Koreans, but it also entailed specific agreements to liberalize sectors of their economy—including, most important, the financial sector—that had retained protection.

The 1990s were an uneasy decade for South Koreans even before the crisis. Real wages continued to climb, and real estate price increases slowed—in some places real estate prices even fell—alleviating some of the sources of tension around class inequities. But at the same time, rising wages exacerbated the problem of national comparative advantage: South Korean labor costs were high compared to those in Southeast Asia, for example, while South Korean corporations lacked the technological advantages of industrial powerhouses such as Japan and the United States. In fact, both Japan and the United States demonstrated an increasing reluctance to transfer technology to South Korea as South Korean *chaebŏl* gained in sophistication. In the political arena, people grew disillusioned with Kim Young-sam's administration, which seemed increasingly to resemble the administrations that had preceded it. North Korean instability cast a dark shadow: the death of Kim Il Sung in 1994 left the issue of North Korean leadership in question despite the ascension of Kim's son, Kim Jong Il. Tensions around weapons development and repeated incursions into South Korean territorial waters by spy submarines were deeply unsettling. In the summer of 1994 the situation was so tense that Seoulites began stocking up on daily necessities in preparation for a military emergency—there were widespread shortages of ramen and batteries. After the devastating famine that began in 1995 the image of unification, possibly as a helter-skelter process of national collapse, was looming over South Korean prosperity.

When the Southeast Asian nations' economies began to unravel in the summer of 1997, South Korea at first asserted that it would avoid the fate of the junior tigers. Just weeks before requesting IMF assistance, South Korean government officials denied that the economy was in trouble. Yet South Korea could isolate itself neither from the economic effects proper nor from the psychological crisis that accompanied and fed the region's economic distress. South Korean banks were themselves heavily entangled in Southeast Asia. Moreover, South Korean industry watched exchange rates tumble across Southeast Asia, knowing that with each day their exports grew comparatively more expensive in overseas markets. Finally, the structure of South Korean indebtedness to foreign lenders left the nation particularly vulnerable for two reasons. First, a great deal of the money had been invested in industries in which there was significant overcapacity; second, to elude government regulations on loans in foreign denominations, many of the loans were structured as short-term debt (which the government did not regulate closely, assuming such lending was used to fund export-oriented inputs) even if the money was intended for longer term investment purposes. The mismatch between the term and use of the funds was one of the reasons the crisis hit South Korea with such urgency.

The effects of the crisis were immediately visible on the streets and broadcast in the media. Unemployed workers lined up for ineffective employment assistance programs, and Seoul Station (the major train depot) became a de facto hotel for hundreds of homeless men. Many out-of-work men left home every morning according to their old routines but spent the day wandering the city or sitting on park benches, unwilling to tell their families that they had lost their jobs. Husbands abandoned their families out of shame over not being able to support them. There were countless stories of children placed by their parents in orphanages to ensure they would have food and shelter. For those who kept their jobs, wages plummeted: by the fall of 1998, real household income had dropped 20 percent compared to a year earlier. Consumption contracted even more dramatically and was down 22.3 percent. The poorest quintile suffered the greatest loss of income (24.4 percent), compared to the richest quintile's 8 percent decline (*Korea Newsreview*, 28 November 1998).

In the wake of this crisis, South Koreans have been struggling to understand the reasons why their government was driven to seek international assistance to forestall national bankruptcy. Pundits and ordinary people offered their opinions. Initially, the IMF drew much of the blame: "to be IMFed" became a verb meaning to suffer the dislocations of unemployment, underemployment, or reduced income. Seoul National University Professor Cho Dong-sung identified three types of responses to the circumstances: shame, coupled with calls for identifying the culprits responsible (including President Kim Young-sam and his economic aides); theories of a conspiracy on the part of foreign powers to crush and then buy up the South Korean economy;[3] and a sense of individual, popular responsibility for the economic crisis (Cho 1998). In an article in the *Korea Economic Daily*, economics professor Kim Pyung-joo, after describing what he saw as fundamental defects in the South Korean economy (businesses that pushed expansion over profitability, workers who demanded wage hikes in excess of productivity increases, overheated household consumption, and political slush funds), summed up his viewpoint: "If anyone should ask why Korea was hit by a financial crisis in the first place, one could say that a major reason was the international community's rather low regard for Korea" (P. Kim 1998:30). Prescriptions for ameliorative action ranged from economic restructuring to a call for hard work and loyalty to domestic brands (*Chungang Ilbo*, 4 December 1998) to the suggestion that "spiritual renewal is the priority" (*Chungang Ilbo*, 28 February 1997).

This response has drawn on the discourse and outlooks developed in previous decades. Much of the blame is allotted to individuals and to their profligate habits. In the summer of 1999 a familiar-sounding scandal erupted concerning the wives of several high government officials: the accusation was that the officials had received bribes in the form of expensive clothing for their wives. Many of the suggestions for change emphasized a return to frugality, a vow to work harder, and a call for the moral regeneration of the nation. In a newspaper article entitled "The End of *kwasobi* and Vanity," the author implies that suffering is necessary for the development of social responsibility: "The youth who have never experienced hardship and have grown accustomed to our present abundance don't know how to use their things or the things of others sparingly. . . . It is not possible to explain the meaning of enduring troubles to someone who hasn't truly experienced 'the heart of hunger.' . . . Whoever is to blame—the government, the big corporations, the people—all the careless behavior receives as compensation the foreign exchange of the IMF" (*Chungang Ilbo*, 4 December 1998). One of the most picturesque and oddly familiar responses to the crisis was the public collection of gold jewelry to sell on the world markets to generate foreign exchange—in an eerie reproduction of the efforts to forestall Japanese colonial domination in the early years of this century.[4] South Koreans, by and large women, lined up at banks and other public collection points and handed over family heirlooms, school awards, tokens of honor or sentiment, to be melted into gold bars at a moment when the international gold market was notably weak.

Yet clearly the current analysis of what is wrong with the economy has gone beyond the earlier era's focus on individuals. In the current context, the *chaebŏl* have been targeted with sharp criticism, and *chaebŏl* owners have been accused of poor judgment, corruption, and the blind pursuit of individual enrichment at the cost of the nation's solvency. As part of the terms of the IMF's rescue package, the government has been orchestrating a dramatic restructuring of the *chaebŏl* landscape, including the reallocation of businesses among the *chaebŏl*, accompanied by an end to the disastrous cross-financing practices within a single corporate group. Previously, the more profitable businesses within a *chaebŏl* often propped up poor performers with cash infusions or loan guarantees, causing a contagion of financial problems throughout the group. The dismantling of Daewoo was the first shaky victory of this strategy.

In this context, South Koreans appear to be adopting a new stance toward the world. Foreign companies have been invited to bid on bankrupt south Korean businesses; South Korean tourists have visited Mount Kumgang in North Korea, and in October 1998 the government officially ended a half-century ban on the import of Japanese popular culture. Long-time opposition leader Kim Dae Jung was elected president and took office in January 1999. In contrast to the "globalization" (*segyehwa*) rhetoric of Kim Young-sam's administration—a defensive embrace of international institutions in an effort to shore up competitiveness—Kim Dae Jung's approach is less tied to institutions and economic strategies. His attempt to engage North Korea has been called Kim's "Sunshine Policy." Kim, a former political prisoner himself who is a survivor of a death sentence, has also released many long-term political prisoners from South Korean jails, in effect acknowledging the right to differences of opinion. These changes have not pleased everyone. For instance, Kang Man-kil, a well-known professor of history, protested the lifting of the ban on Japanese cultural products: "I don't think that Korea has fully recovered its identity from the brutal oppression of Japanese colonialists" (*Korea Newsreview*, 31 October 1998), but along with the depression and fear, many people are looking to these changes as a basis for national renewal.

The crisis has prompted both an intense examination of internal conflicts and problems as well as calls for a renewal of national unity. Richard Grinker's (1998) study of discourses of Korean unification points to a tendency to assert an ideal of national homogeneity[5] in South Korea. Grinker observes that the image of homogeneity is a fiction Koreans tell themselves—the division of north and south notwithstanding, Korea has a long history of regional, class, gender, and age-based distinctions—and he sees the struggle with imagining reunification as possibly

> open[ing] up an avenue of exploring alternative Korean realities such as diversity or heterogeneity; that is, for exploring the future(s) in plural rather than singular terms. . . . Difference, according to this argument, could be seen as a foundation for new communities that bring together Koreans' separate and yet shared experiences of division in a way that strengthens the nation. Thus, the unification of all Koreans into a single nation may require popular and political views and domestic policies oriented more toward a national organization of difference than a divided organization of imagined similarity.
>
> (Grinker 1998:xiv)

Responding to the social and economic dislocations of the post-IMF period offers a similar opportunity for South Koreans to face the reality of differences within the nation.

In general, the development of a consumer culture works in contradictory ways. On the one hand, "mass consumption promise[s] to overcome class-based political cleavages by advancing the idea that individuals, even entire peoples, could mount a new kind of social claim, that to well-being" (de Grazia 1996b:280). Subway posters show dream homes that could be everyone's fantasy and cotton underwear that could give everyone the confidence of a businessman. All South Koreans can take pride in the modern world they have forged, which they can see and even possess. On the other hand, the demonstration of differences through the possession of goods undermines the story of national unity, creating rifts not just between the wealthy and the poor, but within the comfortable classes themselves as new forms of wealth generate new networks, new practices, new values, and new styles (see Robinson and Goodman 1996), and between generations and genders. As South Koreans respond to their current economic troubles, this remains true. Only a generation or two ago, "the situation in Korea could be described as a relatively equal distribution of poverty" (Mason et al. 1980:26). The particular trajectory of South Korea's economic development has lifted many from poverty but has left a few behind, and in so doing has illuminated differences within the nation that transcend class and income.

## CONSUMPTION TIME

Ultimately, given the continued high rates of savings and the economic importance of the development of a domestic market to the South Korean economy, one might wonder why consumption has attracted—and continues to attract—so much negative attention in South Korea. Much of the ethnographic treatment of consumption in other places takes as its focus the symbolic and social uses made of goods themselves: the social and cultural contexts in which they are acquired, exchanged, or displayed; the transgressive or resistant uses that demarcate and generate communities; the status distinctions made by consumption, and ways those distinctions become resources for hierarchical position; the cultures that arise around types of consumption practices or styles; the place of goods in imagining and enacting identities. We can recognize all these processes as part of the contemporary South Korean cultural practices of consumption; they appear to be the target of *kwasobi* criticism.

There is another aspect to consumption, however, that is often overlooked although it is a critical element in understanding South Korean perspectives on consumption and overconsumption: consumption's temporal dimensions. The practice of an act of "consumption" unfolds over time—

desire, resolve, acquisition, possession, loss. While the steps may not always proceed in precisely that order, the process nevertheless is not instantaneous. Each stage has duration, and the process as a whole has a rhythm. Others have focused on aspects of this tempo: Arjun Appadurai has addressed the role of the desire for objects in the imaginative processes of identity (1986a); Pierre Bourdieu (building on Mauss) has seen strategic possibilities in the rhythms of exchange (1977); Daniel Miller (1987) has written of the act of consumption as a Hegelian process of objectification through externalization and sublation; and Grant McCracken (1988) has considered patina as the process whereby money is turned into status through the aging of owned objects. Generally, though, studies of consumption focus on the moments of acquisition (shopping) and possession (the marking of difference).

The temporal aspects of consumption are most often considered in the context of changes in fashion. Michael Taussig, for example, inspired by the writings of Walter Benjamin and by the Surrealist movement, has written, "Fashion is the realm in which the obsolescent character of the commodity is nourished and ritualized. In its tensed articulation of future and past, fashion heralds birth and death. This is one reason why the commodity is endowed with a spectral quality" (Taussig 1993:233–234). The agonized considerations of postmodernist superficiality and evanescence (e.g., Jameson 1984; Harvey 1989) draw connections between production (and finance) regimes, postmodern culture, and the fleeting moment of fashion. In the South Korean context, Laurel Kendall (1996) has analyzed the changing fashions of wedding expenditures and ceremonies in an increasingly commodified social economy. Fashion is, however, just the extreme of consumption ephemerality, and ephemerality is just one aspect of consumption time.

The *kwasobi ch'ubang* discourse points to yet another aspect of the temporal place of consumption, one that is key to understanding the link between consumption and the political constructions of South Korean national identity: each act of consumption is the end of a period of anticipation. The present-time act of consumption severs the bond of imagination that links the past and present to the future through desire. The period before acquisition is inherently future-oriented. Within the time of desire, the state of not-yet-having-acquired contains a kind of optimism, the potential for a moment when a better object choice or the means to acquire will be realized. It is this state of anticipation, this phase of consumption, that *kwasobi ch'ubang* discourse privileges. Acquisition is a celebration of the present; desire honors the future.

History and memory are central themes in the construction of South Korean national identity, as they have been shown to be elsewhere. Five thousand years of history is a mantra repeated in meditations on the value of "Korean" culture in a noisy globalized context. The Three Kingdoms, Hideyoshi's invasions, Shilhak, the *Tonghak* rebellion, the Enlightenment Club, colonization, resistance, liberation, separation, war, poverty, industrialization, demonstrations, democratization . . . these historical elements and others are the material of what it can mean to be "Korean." But however important the material of the past is for imagining the Korean community, the future is just as critical. The unfulfilled promise of reunification dangles in the future as the reclamation of real nationhood, a unified people, and a coherent polity. Moreover, Korea has had a long history of imagining a future nation: thirty-five years under colonial rule imagining liberation and fifty imagining unification. Add to this the habit of imagining a prosperous future, the future in which the entire nation looks like the Kangnam image of modernity: sleek, wealthy, cosmopolitan. For decades, the South Korean state demanded authority on the basis of these promises, insisting that it not be judged in the present, but rather by the achievements of future dreams. In the era of democracy, this argument became more difficult to sustain.

I am arguing that the *kwasobi ch'ubang* campaign was fundamentally—in addition to all its more prosaic elements—a campaign to ensure that South Koreans identified not with what was, but with what would be. Psychologists (e.g., Kastenbaum 1961; Lens and Moreas 1994) have studied the phenomenon of "future time perspective" and its role in motivation. While they have identified constituent components of time perspective (extension, density, orientation, structure, coherence, directionality) and have analyzed individual variation, clearly the time perspective itself is situated in cultural frameworks (Durkheim 1995; Yamba 1992). Despite the widespread academic interest in the way time as *history* works in constructing national community, few scholars have examined futuristic discourses as elements in the formation of national identity. The idea of the future shares with the idea of the past the potential to join people into an imagined community; the past situates this in experience and authenticity, while the future bonds people in hope and hopeful action. For those who conceive of a linear passage of time, the future is, like the past, on an imaginative temporal continuum extending from "now" to "then." Past and future are the poles of heritage and destiny. The envisioned future, however, authorizes national action in a way history cannot: this is because the future *must be achieved*. State plans and programs evoke images of a collective future and elicit national cooperation in attaining expressed goals. In this way, too, state institutions exercise power and claim authority in defining national identity.

The delay of gratification is bound up in such themes. Enduring present privations or troubles (*kyŏndida* or *ch'amda*) for future rewards is an elaborated ethos in South Korea. Not-consuming is part of investing materially and imaginatively in the national future. This link was explicit in government *kwasobi ch'ubang* materials, and it was picked up in some of the civic discourse as well. "Now is not the time to rest." "Don't pop the champagne cork too soon." "If one person rests, forty million will be late." The choice to celebrate the present was perceived as an abandonment of the future.

It is, in fact, in this context that mothers became one of the last possible defenses against the celebration of the present and therefore became prime targets for *kwasobi ch'ubang* propaganda. Mothers were asked to shoulder the burden of denying the temptations of the present in order to make the future their children would inhabit more prosperous. *Kwasobi ch'ubang* discourse was pervasive in South Korea in the late 1980s and early 1990s, and it was not entirely ineffective. Many people were conscious of the social responsibilities potentially present in each act of consumption. But many of the women I spoke with in Yoido and in Talgoljjagi were beginning in the early 1990s to see the obsolescence of a national program of delay. The present had become reality. Half a decade later, the shattering loss of confidence following the IMF "rescue" of the South Korean economy only heightened the tension between those who saw reality in the present or in the future. In both cases the mismatch between discourse and experience—whether for women regarding *kwasobi* or for the general populace faced with the economic crisis—has the potential to facilitate the formation of new perspectives.

Between 1988 and 1991 pessimism about the possibility for social class mobility grew in South Korea. National polls showed that among city dwellers only 59.1 percent thought it was "easy" to move up in social status from one generation to the next, compared to 65.2 percent earlier. The percentage of those who considered upward mobility within a single generation "easy" fell from 53.1 percent to 42.1 percent, a 21 percent drop in the number of people who believed South Korean society offered opportunities for individual status improvement (National Statistics Office 1991). Of course, one shouldn't overlook fact that an impressive two out of five urban South Koreans still believed social mobility was "easy." After the IMF bailout, one out of three individuals who had identified themselves as members of the middle class believed they had fallen to a lower socioeconomic rung, and 80 percent of those did not believe they would regain their position within three years, according to a survey conducted by the Hyundai Economic Research Institute (*Han'guk Ilbo* Internet, 14 April 1999).

A generational shift in outlook was also taking place: According to a Korea-Gallup poll taken in 1992, all but 2 percent of South Koreans in their forties would wait until they had purchased a home before buying a car, whereas 10 percent of respondents in their thirties and 25 percent of respondents in their twenties said they would buy a car first. An article reporting these poll results in the progressive *Hangyore* newspaper quotes a thirty-year-old man, resident of a rented apartment, who says that he's decided to buy himself a car. "Of course I'll need to buy a house, too. But just because I'm saving to buy a house, I don't want to give up all the rest of life. The youthfulness of right now, isn't that something precious—what is more irreplaceable?" The newspaper commented, "This new 'now' trend, more than anything, can be blamed on the stress of the new generation on buying. . . . However, if one doesn't own one's own house, one is driven to the obvious conclusion that the poignant result is a lifelong lack of Korean-style security, like duckweed that has not rooted in the ground."

These were fundamentally unsettling trends for the South Korean government. For three decades, national development—not individual mobility—had served as the measure of opportunity, and national economic growth—not individual affluence—had been the index of prosperity. This pact depended, however, on a promise of equity and better things to come. In South Korea a national utopian imagination had helped to secure two generations' cooperation in the project of building a nation, but "the future" could not be postponed indefinitely. There were signs that people were beginning to see themselves—and their nation—as existing in the present.

Economic dislocation was not unique to South Korea, and neither was government meddling in the way people experience the morality of economic change. In contemporary post-Mao China, for example, newly wealthy households are made anxious by their conspicuousness. "This anxiety is in part a legacy of the past, when to stand out in this way was foolish if not dangerous, but it is also equally a product of the present. The line between proper and improper pathways to wealth has not remained fixed and continues to be defined in practice" (Anagnost 1989:218). The party takes an interest in "generat[ing] a moral climate in which people feel obligated to share their prosperity with others" (ibid.:223). In Sri Lanka, capitalism is seen as both in the interests of and as a danger to the nation; the national lottery is one means through which the potential dangers of capitalism are harnessed for the good of the imagined and material national community, reincorporating individual self-interest into the shared project. "By blurring the line between a political act and a consumption decision, a lottery ticket puts the nation in the hands of ordinary people" (Kemper 1993:393).

In South Korea political projects have been, from time to time, tied to the mobilization of a nationalistic material desire and the advocating of frugality. Ongoing contradictions between these positions were negotiated through a particularly gendered patriotism, in which women were charged with making choices about how to carry out this program. It was as though the nation's heritage, future, and cultural honor could be defended by women through appropriate consumer decisions. In practice, however, the connections between imagination and material experience, individual and community, are murky. In South Korea many women who had been "positioned" as consumer patriots by virtue of their gender were beginning to reconsider the whole pact of gender, motherhood, family, and nation when inconsistencies in interests became more apparent. As Sally Falk Moore writes in her introduction to *Moralizing States and the Ethnography of the Present*, "Political ideas are not always easy to consecrate, at least not durably. However, moral principle is often invoked in the attempt" (Moore 1993:4).

The story of making consumer nationalism in South Korea indicates the complexity of interrelations between state, nation, and community; between identities and ideologies; between localities and the "globalized, deterritorialized world" (Appadurai 1991:196). In thinking through these complexities, it is useful to bear in mind in how many different ways people in one "locality" can engage a discursive field, even one as pervasive as *kwasobi*. I offer, in parting, one final example:

One hot and humid afternoon in the middle of the summer's rainy weeks, as I walked along the road tracing the spine of Talgoljjagi hill, an old woman sitting in the shade on a raised wooden platform outside her home patted the spot next to her and said, "*Come here. Sit.*" No one else was out in the heat. I thanked her and sat. She asked me the usual questions (where was I from, was I married), and when I told her a little about my research project, she said, "*Ah, kwasobi! People are so wasteful nowadays! Look at this dress.*" She pinched some of the synthetic fabric in her fingers and shook it. "\*I have two others at home. My daughter-in-law bought them for me.\*" She smiled. "\*They are pretty. But why do I need three dresses? When I was young, I had one dress. When it was torn, I had to mend it. Now, when a dress is torn, my daughter-in-law tells me to throw it away and buy a new one. That's true *kwasobi*.\*"

# APPENDIX

## EXCHANGE RATES

In this book I make frequent reference to money. The currency in South Korea is called the *wŏn*. The exchange rate between the dollar and the *wŏn* has been allowed to fluctuate since 1980; before that, between 1974 and 1979 the *wŏn* was pegged to the dollar in international currency transactions at a rate of 484 *wŏn* to the dollar (see table A.1 below.)

TABLE A.1    Exchange Rate, 1981–1992, R.O.K. *wŏn* to U.S. Dollar

| YEAR | ROK *(WŎN)* — U.S. $1 |
|------|------------------------|
| 1981 | 700.5 |
| 1982 | 748.8 |
| 1983 | 795.5 |
| 1984 | 827.4 |
| 1985 | 890.2 |
| 1986 | 861.4 |
| 1987 | 792.3 |
| 1988 | 684.1 |
| 1989 | 679.6 |
| 1990 | 716.4 |
| 1991 | 760.8 |
| 1992 | 788.4 |

Source: The Bank of Korea.

## INFLATION

It is difficult to settle on a good indicator of inflation in South Korea, as the rate of inflation of specific aspects (e.g., consumer prices, wages, housing prices, bank interest rates, curb-market interest rates) of the economy varies widely (see table A.2.)

TABLE A.2    Some Measures of Inflation, 1981–1992

| YEAR | CONSUMER PRICE INDEX | YEAR-ON-YEAR INCREASE IN CONSUMER PRICES | NOMINAL WAGE INCREASE RATE | OFFICIAL INFLATION RATE |
|------|------|------|------|------|
| 1981 | 66.8 |        | 21.5% | 20.6% |
| 1982 | 68.4 | 2.40%  | 15.9% | 7.1%  |
| 1983 | 69.4 | 1.46%  | 11.0% | 3.4%  |
| 1984 | 70.4 | 1.44%  | 8.7%  | 2.3%  |
| 1985 | 73   | 3.69%  | 9.2%  | 2.4%  |
| 1986 | 74.8 | 2.47%  | 8.2%  | 2.7%  |
| 1987 | 77.1 | 3.07%  | 10.1% | 3.0%  |
| 1988 | 85   | 10.25% | 15.5% | 7.1%  |
| 1989 | 90.9 | 6.94%  | 21.1% | 5.7%  |
| 1990 | 100  | 10.01% | 18.8% | 8.6%  |
| 1991 | 112.4| 12.40% | 17.5% | 9.3%  |
| 1992 | 119.3| 6.14%  | 15.5% | 8.3%  |

Sources: Ministry of Trade, Industry, and Energy; National Statistical Office; The Bank of Korea.

# NOTES

## PREFACE

1. Kamala Visweswaran similarly has discussed betrayal "as allegory for the practice of feminist ethnography" in the context of relations of power that are not erased by some "feminist innocence" (Visweswaran 1994:40). Like the women in Visweswaran's narrative, the women I spoke with in Seoul often demonstrated impressive canniness in their selective revelation of private matters; nevertheless, differences between my perspective and theirs still make me uneasy.

2. E. E. Evans-Pritchard, an eminent British anthropologist working in colonial Africa, in the introduction to his canonical ethnography, *The Nuer*, writes of the difficulties he had in getting people to tell him what he wanted to know. He innocently quotes the following interchange:

> I: ... What is the name of your lineage?
> CUOL: Do you want to know the name of my lineage?
> I: Yes.
> CUOL: What will you do with it if I tell you? Will you take it to your country?
> I: I don't want to do anything with it. I just want to know it since I am living at your camp.
> CUOL: Oh well, we are Lou.
> I: I did not ask you the name of your tribe. I know that. I am asking you the name of your lineage.
> CUOL: Why do you want to know the name of my lineage?
> I: I don't want to know it.
> CUOL: Then why do you ask me for it? Give me some tobacco.

Evans-Pritchard then comments, "I defy the most patient ethnologist to make headway against this kind of opposition. One is just driven crazy by it" (Evans-

Pritchard 1969:13). Evans-Pritchard barely mentions the conditions of hostility and mistrust in which he, a citizen of an empire that had just defeated the Nuer in battle, presses them for answers, nor does he seem aware of the disingenuousness of his own statements.

3. There is, of course, a large and well-known body of thought on issues of representation and voice. I acknowledge that representation is an act fraught with the tensions of unequal position. Although not all acts of representation are equivalent, I *have* considered the political effects of this strategy. In the end, I chose to create voices as true to the tone and substance of the utterances themselves as I could achieve. I hope that drawing attention here to my process of construction can also serve as a flag for the artifice behind *all* ethnographic quotation. For an elegant and artistic discussion of comparable issues in the reenactment of translated interviews in Trinh T. Minh-ha's film, *Surname Viet, Given Name Nam*, see Trinh 1992. Gillian Feeley-Harnik provides another example of a similar strategy: she used double pairs of quotation marks to distinguish constructed from verbatim quotes (Feeley-Harnik 1991).

4. Yoido is such a recognizable, distinctive, and large neighborhood in Seoul that I have not attempted to disguise it. Rather, I have relied on the fact that there are many apartment complexes with thousands of households on the island, so that the particular complex in which I did much of my fieldwork will not be obvious. Talgoljjagi, on the other hand, is a pseudonym I have created for a hillside neighborhood in north-central Seoul.

## 1. CONSUMER NATIONALISM

1. Throughout this book I use the informal term "South Korea" (and its adjectival form, "South Korean"), rather than the more formal "Republic of Korea" (R.O.K.). It is, however, common practice in South Korea, the United States, and elsewhere to use the word "Korea" (and "Korean") to refer to the R.O.K., linguistically erasing North Korea (the Democratic People's Republic of Korea, or DPRK) from the sphere of thought. As I deal in this text in part with the problem of South Korean national identities in the context of Korean peninsular division, I believe it is important to preserve, in writing, a reminder of the sibling nation to the north. At the same time, I will attempt to recognize the discursive power of the assertion of a unitary "Korea" by using the unmodified term "Korea" (or "Korean") in those contexts where that single word (or its equivalent in the language of South Korea, *Han'guk*) was employed. I also use "Korea" to refer to the pre-1945 nation. Occasionally, I will insert an editorial "South" in parentheses to clarify or to indicate a complex relation between the ideas of "Korean" and "South Korean."

2. I don't recall a single instance in which anyone in Talgoljjagi, the low-in-

come neighborhood where I also conducted research, asked me about the clip-board. On the other hand, compared to women in Yoido, women in Talgoljjagi expressed much more interest in and admiration of handmade things of mine, such as clothing, hats, and some pottery I brought as gifts.

3. A fourth manufacturer, Ssangyong, built light trucks and vans. In 1992, after years of maneuvering, Samsung obtained government permission to enter the automotive industry. See chapter 3 for more information on the evolution and structure of the South Korean automobile industry.

4. The popular 1993 movie *Sŏp'yŏnje*, which focused on a small group of itin-erant musicians who performed *p'ansori* (a form of solo narrative song) during key transitional decades of the twentieth century, sparked a faddish nationwide ro-mance with *p'ansori*. For an analysis of the film as a reflection of androcentric na-tionalism and an "internalized colonial male gaze," see Chungmoo Choi 1998.

5. Nonwage income (rental income, income from investments, gifts, etc.) was a significant factor in urban household income.

6. For readers interested in a good, basic introduction to Korean history, see *Korea Old and New: A History*, by Carter J. Eckert et al. (1990). Written by one of the foremost authorities in the field, Bruce Cumings's *Korea's Place in the Sun: A Modern History* (1997) provides an account of modern Korean history and the role of the U.S. in it and is intended for the general reader. Cumings's generous per-sonal interjections and editorial observations enliven this volume.

7. Many others have noted also the importance of the Taft-Katsura Memo-randum of 1905, in which the United States agreed to respect Japan's rights over Korea in exchange for the same courtesy being extended to the United States with regard to the Philippines. Martin Hart-Landsberg provides a concise overview of the role of foreign nations and expansionist rivalries in the shaping of the Korean political economy from the middle of the nineteenth century on in *Korea: Division, Reunification, and U.S. Foreign Policy* (1998).

8. For a thorough and fascinating study of the development of a Korean class of capitalists, see Carter J. Eckert's *Offspring of Empire: The Koch'ang Kims and the Colonial Origins of Korean Capitalism, 1876–1945* (1991).

9. The decision to divide Korea into two occupied zones was first entertained two years before the end of the war, as an enticement to draw the Soviets into the Pacific fighting and to forestall a fully Soviet-aligned postwar Korea. The exact dividing line was determined in a half-hour-long midnight meeting of two young American colonels a few days before Japan announced its surrender. The best dis-cussion of the Korea's fate at the end of the Second World War and the years fol-lowing the end of Japanese rule is still Bruce Cumings's *The Origins of the Korean War*, two volumes (published in 1981 and 1990) of closely argued and densely documented international history.

10. The DPRK suffered perhaps even greater destruction, particularly from

the saturation bombing strategy of the U.S.-U.N. forces. Cumings writes that "By 1952 just about everything in northern and central Korea was completely leveled. What was left of the population survived in caves, the North Koreans creating an entire life underground, in complexes of dwellings, schools, hospitals, and factories" (1997:296). A total of approximately two million North Koreans are estimated to have died in the war.

11. According to Woo, the South Korean state sought American (and Japanese) loans in preference to lower-rate European financing in order to bond the nations together "so that they may rise and fall, sink and swim together" (Woo 1991:159). In this way, the South Korean state attempted to, paradoxically, leverage national autonomy through enmeshment in American interests.

12. George Ogle (1990) provides an English-language account of labor struggles and repressive policies in his book, *South Korea: Dissent Within the Economic Miracle.*

13. The history of foreign invasion cut two ways. On the one hand, it was a history of vulnerability; on the other, Korean resistance to the invaders (especially the story of the defeat of Hideyoshi in 1598) is a great source of national pride and reinforces a sense of national unity.

14. During this period South Korea was occasionally pressured to change its industrial and trade practices. The first episode, in 1971, involved objections the Nixon administration had to South Korean textile exports; at that time, textiles were still South Korea's principal manufacturing sector and accounted for 30 percent of its exports. The United States wrested from the South Korean government an agreement to limit the rate of growth of exports of synthetic fiber and other textiles. This was followed by five other trade disputes (focused on textiles and footwear) during the 1970s between South Korea and the United States (Woo 1991:127). But these conflicts were minor compared to those of the 1980s.

15. In 1980 the southwestern city of Kwangju rebelled against the new national government that had seized power in a coup several months earlier. The South Korean government sent special troops to the city to quell the uprising; hundreds of civilians were killed in the incident. The failure of the United States to stop or protest the brutal actions of the South Korean paratroopers (and the widespread belief that the U.S. must have granted the South Korean military permission to move the troops to Kwangju) inflamed anti-American rage across the country (see Clark 1988).

16. Others have also noted that the Park administration was largely composed of men trained in the Japanese philosophy of politics and economy, whereas the Chun administration was staffed by a large number of American-trained economists and political scientists who advocated a more "free-market" approach to economic development (Woo 1991:191).

## FIRST VIGNETTE: 1992

1. In the center of town and in several other places, a network of subterranean walkways provide pedestrians with an alternative to battling weather and traffic crossings. Most of these passages are lined with small shops and are crowded with pedestrians.

## 2.  "SEOUL TO THE WORLD, THE WORLD TO SEOUL"

1. The administrative territory of Seoul had grown by a mere 10 square kilometers in that period.

2. Very recently, *hanok* (Korean) style buildings have come back in style, as part of the current fashion of rediscovering "traditional" culture.

3. These quotes are taken from a book produced by the Seoul Metropolitan Government for the XVIIth Milano Triennale Exhibition, "World Cities and the Future of the Metropoles."

4. Between 1960 and 1990, the average annual rate of population increase in Seoul was 5 percent, one of the world's fastest and most sustained urban growth rates. In 1990 Seoul was by far the dominant city in South Korea, as it had been throughout the century. The population of the next four largest cities put together did not equal that of Seoul. In the 1960s and 1970s, when Seoul was growing quickly, all domestic immigrants came from much less cosmopolitan places.

5. For example, the *P'yŏnghwa Sijang*, or "Peace Market," was established in an area of town heavily settled by refugees from the North.

6. In part because of rising real estate prices and the opening of new satellite cities around Seoul, for the first time since the 1950–1953 war, in 1990 more people moved *out* of Seoul than moved *in*. The population continued to grow, however, thanks to a greater number of births than deaths. For the first time since that war, the city registered a net population loss in 1993, and even that has been attributed to the movement of people to Seoul's own outskirts—expanding the city, rather than abandoning it.

7. Until 1983 the population of Seoul was under a nightly security curfew. Between the hours of midnight and 4 A.M., citizens were required to stay off the streets. Periodic citywide drills (monthly, generally in the afternoon, as well as less frequent nighttime blackout exercises) reinforced the sense of vulnerability to attack.

8. "*Pundang is close to Kangnam [the wealthy and stylish southern half of the capital city],*" one of Pundang's new homeowners told me when I asked why she had chosen Pundang over Ilsan for her move from Yoido, "*but also Ilsan is too close to North Korea. I know it wouldn't make much difference, but I would not want to have to cross the Han River to escape if the North Korean

Army came down. The traffic would be worse than on *chusŏk*—we'd never get across.*" *Chusŏk*, the Korean autumn harvest moon festival, has since the mid-1980s been the occasion for nightmarish traffic jams across the nation but particularly near Seoul, as families head to their patrilineal homes of origin. One friend of mine told me her family gave up on a scheduled *chusŏk* drive to Pusan in 1993 because, after three hours in backed-up traffic, they still had not reached the highway, just five kilometers from her apartment. The woman interviewed above may also have been thinking of the disastrous exodus from Seoul during the first days of the war in 1950, which was made even more hazardous by the premature strategic destruction of one of the only bridges south across the Han River—stranding thousands of Seoul residents in the path of the advancing North Korean army.

9. In the 1960s and 1970s this was a question economists and urban planners around the world were debating. Is "primacy," the dominance of one city in a nation, beneficial or detrimental to economic development and efficiency (e.g., Gilbert 1976; Richardson 1976)?

10. The strong axis of development (established by the Japanese as part of their main transportation line from Japan up the Korean peninsula and into Manchuria) running between the south-eastern city of Pusan and Seoul was reinforced in several projects led by the South Korean state in the 1960s and 1970s (the Seoul-Pusan Expressway, improvements in rail transportation, the establishment of industrial estates in the southeastern Kyŏngsan provinces) to the exclusion of the Chŏlla provinces in the southwest. The appearance (and fact) of preferential policies not only gave the lie to the stated philosophy of equitable national development. For example, according to the 1982–1986 five-year plan, one of the principal goals of new infrastructure development projects was to bring new opportunities to underserviced regions. Given the Kyŏngsan origins of many high-ranking government officials (and the Chŏlla origins of opposition leaders), uneven development fed the impression of regional favoritism and exacerbated the problem of regionally based political affiliation.

11. By the late 1960s it was apparent that the Park administration was significantly less popular in Seoul than in the countryside, and that even in the countryside declining incomes relative to urban household earnings were threatening Park's position. The *Saemaŭl Undong* (New Village Movement) rural development policy (launched in the winter of 1971–1972) can been seen, at least in part, as an attempt to resecure rural approval for Park (Moore 1984).

12. Land "readjustment," adapted from Japanese colonial redevelopment techniques, involves the assembly of land parcels from private owners and replotting property lines to reflect planned uses. After providing the necessary infrastructure, the KLDC returns approximately half the area to the original owners (in proportion to their initial property). The half remaining is divided into a part for

public use, a part is sold below cost to the Korea National Housing Corporation to provide public housing, and a part is sold for profit to pay for the development of infrastructure and to cross-subsidize housing. For more on land readjustment, see Menzenes 1988, or Kitay 1985.

13. A few earlier neighborhood development projects were undertaken in the 1960s.

14. The U.S. occupying forces used the Japanese governing offices for their own administration of southern Korea during the period after World War II; the South Korean government continued this practice. After the National Assembly was moved to Yoido, the old building was used as the National Museum, but it has continued to provoke criticism and was demolished in 1996.

15. Although all these nodes lie on the southern banks of the Han River (the island of Yoido is separated from the Yŏngdŭngp'o shore by a narrow muddy channel, while to Yoido's north the Han is a broad, flowing river), it is the south-*eastern* half of the southern district that has come to be called "Kangnam."

16. As late as 1983, the population had just reached 651,700, while by 1988 there were 1,326,000 people living in those neighborhoods. Note, however, that these population figures do not correspond to precisely the same area; the jurisdictions have shifted over time. The 1983 figure applies to the area then known as Kangnam-gu, which was later subdivided.

17. The practice of "land readjustment" (see note 11, above) constrains somewhat the windfall profits of many original landowners in development areas (Menzenes 1988; Kitay 1985).

18. In chapter 5 I discuss the relationship between women, consumption, and crime stories.

19. Again, this is not unlike the experience in the United States. Not surprisingly, many South Korean urban planners were trained in the U.S. or in Japan.

20. Area in Korea is typically measured in *p'yŏng*. One *p'yŏng* is approximately 3.3 square meters or about 36 square feet. To help you picture a *p'yŏng*, imagine a typical, small academic office of approximately 8 feet by 10 feet: that is a little more than 2 *p'yŏng*.

21. Note in contrast, however, that during the late 1980s the price of property in the greenbelt encircling Seoul (property on which significant new development had been forbidden by law) was one of the fastest appreciating ones in South Korea. Speculation that development restrictions would be lifted from the greenbelt circulated widely in this period.

22. Official statistics on "wages and salaries" consider only those who are officially employed and ignore the self-employed and day laborers, who typically have lower average incomes.

23. The remainder made alternative arrangements, such as residing in free housing provided by their employers or finding shelter in true squatter enclaves.

24. The percentage tended to vary with the expense—and prestige—of the unit itself. More expensive homes generally commanded higher percentage deposits.

25. Even the monthly rental system in Seoul was distinctive. Some households deposited the equivalent of ten to twelve months' rent with the landlord and then paid an additional monthly rent, while other households deposited a similar amount and their rent was deducted from the deposit each month. These monthly rental agreements (called *wŏlse*) tended to be with small-scale landlords. The state also began to provide long-term monthly rental housing specifically for low-income households in the late 1980s. Almost all the monthly rental units (private *and* public), however, were at the very low end of the housing market. Generally, only those households incapable of gathering together enough money for the most modest *chŏnse* unit would resort to monthly rental.

26. In South Korea, people often referred to one another by their social position or roles. First names were rarely used between women in Seoul and generally only by older women addressing younger ones. Women with children were often called "So-and-so's Mother," a practice known in anthropology as "teknonomy." Most of the women I spoke with preferred that I refer to them in this way, or that I call them "Older Sister" *(ŏnni)*, although a few of those with more international exposure invited me to call them by their personal names. I have used their chosen forms of address, although I have altered the names themselves.

27. Wages rose 15.5 percent in 1988, 21.1 percent in 1989, but they fell in the first quarter of 1990 (National Bureau of Statistics 1990).

28. For an economist's explanation of the workings of the *kye*, see Campbell and Ahn 1962.

29. Throughout this entire period (and into the 1990s) government planning policy came into conflict with different segments of the South Korean population around the issue of real estate. The continual changes in the approach to the "housing problem" chart not only lessons learned but also different conditions and balances struck between different constituencies. Those urban planners who themselves advocated a policy of housing investment were outvoted by the majority of economists and policymakers, who (in the words of World Bank housing analyst Bertrand Renaud) "kept arguing that housing and urban policies were secondary issues that could wait until macroeconomic balance had been achieved, i.e., 'until later'" (Renaud 1993:326). The housing and urban policies that *were* implemented have all tended to exacerbate disparities between wealthier and less wealthy households. Thus, the "housing problem" has become one of the major causes of wealth disparity in contemporary South Korea.

30. In 1990 the loan ceiling was 20 million *wŏn* per household, with an average loan of 12 million *wŏn*. Dwelling units could be no larger than 25.7 *p'yŏng* and could not be more than five years old.

31. There were laws governing the ownership of multiple homes, and taxes

were high. Few people were willing to tell me how much real estate they really owned.

32. In the mid-1980s officials estimated that more than half of all residents of Seoul were immigrants to the capital (United Nations 1986). As this estimate included children (who represented a higher proportion of native-born Seoulites), the proportion of adult immigrants would have been much higher.

33. Namsan, literally "South Mountain" because it was south of the city walls, is a high hill that, after Seoul's expansion, now lies well within the central area. Most of the housing on Namsan was relatively inexpensive and of low prestige. The Japanese garrison was located on the southern side of Namsan; the U.S. army took over the base after "liberation." The foreign soldiers and their attendant sex and entertainment industries appear to have depressed the value one might expect of an area with such natural charm and convenience. It is, however, a neighborhood favored by foreigners and some small number of the most wealthy and cosmopolitan South Koreans.

34. Part of my interest in the travel journals stemmed from the extreme traffic congestion that characterized Seoul from the late 1980s through the early 1990s. Construction on several new subway lines tore holes in streets all over the city, and the tremendous increase in the number of private automobiles was straining the capacity of the road network. Under these conditions, driving a car (or riding in a taxi), while frustrating, was immeasurably more comfortable and tended to be much faster than swinging from a strap on a jerking bus.

35. Kevin Lynch (1960) elicited mental maps in Jersey City in his originative research on urban experience.

36. The map was conceptual to an extreme: the bounds of the city were drawn as a rough circle, and the only orienting feature was the swaying slash of the Han River. Nearly everyone needed some help in finding their bearings on the map. I soon regretted that I had chosen to use an abstract map (rather than a photocopy of a more familiar, official city map); my original intention was to provide as few prompts as possible to elicit a personal response from each individual. After collecting a half dozen responses, however, I learned that the abstract figure was confusing, but it was too late to change my research tool.

37. All but one of the maps were marked by women; I have not used the one map marked by a man in this analysis. The wealthier women lived in many different neighborhoods in Seoul, although the majority lived in Yoido or Map'o; all of the lower income women who completed this exercise lived in Talgoljjagi.

38. I expected the working-class women to show places where they worked, where their families lived, where they shopped, and perhaps childhood homes, whereas I expected wealthier women to show where their parents-in-law lived, where their children studied (in particular, the after-school institutions), and places they went for relaxation and entertainment.

39. If I add together the women who identified their parents' home and those who identified a previous home (counting only once those who identified both), assuming for the moment that the parents still lived in the home where the respondent grew up, more than half of the women identified a former home as significant. Of course, not only might some of the parents have moved, but also, even if they had not, the perspective the individual had toward that home may have changed so that it was of present, rather than nostalgic, significance.

40. Note that my observations are not based on any scientific sample or on an analysis of statistical rigor: the twenty-five women who participated in the map exercise represent no random sample. The maps do, however, add to the pool of information I gathered on these women's lives.

41. When I began my research in Seoul, I was inspired in part by sociologist Michel de Certeau's vision of the everyday tactics enacted in people's daily practices and in particular in their use of space: "Dwelling, moving about, speaking, reading, shopping, and cooking are activities that seem to correspond to the characteristics of tactical ruses and surprises; clever tricks of the 'weak' within the order established by the 'strong,' an art of putting one over on the adversary on his own turf, hunter's tricks, maneuverable, polymorph mobilities, poetic, and warlike discoveries" (de Certeau 1984:40). Certainly I did not find that the women in Talgoljjagi had recourse to this kind of resistant mobility, although in a sense the command of space demonstrated by the wealthier women was a demonstration of mastery denied them in many other social contexts.

42. The women in Talgoljjagi were not the only ones who lacked a workable cognitive map of Seoul. One day I stopped by a tiny, one-room real estate office in Talgoljjagi to chat with the proprietor (and a visiting friend of his) about local housing prices. We got into a conversation about housing price differences in different neighborhoods of Seoul. He pointed to a large city map on the wall and explained that in Sŏngbuk-gu (the borough where Talgoljjagi is located) the prices are higher than in Unp'ŏng-gu, the neighboring borough to the north and west. In giving this explanation, however, he rested his finger not on Sŏng*buk*-gu, but on Sŏng*dong*-gu, a borough south and east of Talgoljjagi. Curious, I asked him to show me where we were. He searched for a few minutes in the wrong spot, and then concluded that Talgoljjagi was too small to be mentioned on the map. His friend quietly nodded.

43. At the time, the Sŏch'o flower market was being torn down to make room for new construction.

44. "Scene" *is* Pred's chosen word (not, as several readers have asked, "seen").

## 3. PRODUCING NEW CONSUMPTION

1. During this period, South Korean agricultural programs also shifted further from a rural support orientation: government support of grain prices was cur-

tailed, and many protections on the domestic market were lifted. Protests against these changes are discussed in chapter 4.

2. This particular change is also implicated in changes in socio-temporal geography, as members of a household stayed away from home (by choice or forced by the development of vastly separated urban spaces) during mealtimes.

3. Most of the Talgoljjagi women I met worked part of the year at home on piecework and part of the year in small factories dotting the neighborhood.

4. One day, five women were sitting around the small table in the *kongbubang* discussing their aspirations. Suni said she had been planning to open a small cosmetics store until she gave up the idea a few months earlier. I asked her why. "*Nowadays there are so many chain stores, and shops all have to look a certain way—it's very expensive. It's not as easy just to start to sell something anymore.*" Jaewŏn's Mother agreed and said her sister-in-law's *kage* was facing stiff competition from a new 7-Eleven. "*The kids all want to go to the new stores. Now even small businesses have foreign competition.*" Since among Talgoljjagi residents ownership of a small business was one of the principal sources of hope for increased income, the chain stores posed a specific threat to the hopes of low-income Seoulites.

5. Many middle-income women did go to the markets to shop for clothing.

6. As recently as 1989, the black market for American goods smuggled from the military PX was thriving. The goods were generally purchased from the PX and then sold on the black market to South Koreans, violating South Korean import laws in the process. The popularity of Chivas Regal Scotch was demonstrated by the fact that about fifty times the amount of that brand of scotch was sold per capita in South Korean PXs as in European PXs. More than three sets of Corning Visionware dishware were sold per family, and approximately two irons for every three persons were sold per year (United States Senate 1990).

7. In the mid-1990s South Korean manufacturers introduced refrigerator models designed for South Korean food habits. In particular, these models (dubbed "kimchi refrigerators") had odor-locking compartments to ensure that the garlicky smell of kimchi did not permeate the rest of the food and provided multiple shelves to store the many small containers of side dishes that characterize Korean meals.

8. Until the 1980s, most upper-income families and many middle-income families had live-in or daily housekeeping assistance. The women who performed this work were either young women from the countryside or older women, often with children of their own; some were distant relatives of the householders themselves, and their hiring was in part seen as a family responsibility. Rising pay rates in the 1980s and expanded formal service employment opportunities had taken a toll on the market for paid housekeepers. Although most of the Yoido families I interviewed had hired housekeeping help, few of the women hired came more than twice a week, and none of the maids lived in.

9. The *turebang* was another local community-service group that (among other activities) organized neighborhood men into work groups and sought construction work on good terms, using the political leverage of a nationally recognized minister who lived and worked in the neighborhood. The *turebang* was a few doors down from the *kongbubang*, and the members of both organizations were on very friendly terms.

10. Kia was again given permission to produce passenger cars in 1987.

11. At the time, Daewoo was a 50 percent owner in a joint venture with GM, under the name of Saehan Motors. The name was changed to Daewoo Motor Company in 1982.

12. Andrew Green identified four elements of direct government intervention in the shaping of the South Korean automobile industry in the 1980s: import restrictions, strict controls on foreign equity investment, limits on the number of firms allowed to produce, and government commitment to forcing South Korean manufacturers to meet international quality standards. He writes, "In order to achieve its economic ambitions, the South Korean government has subordinated many political and social goals to the enhancement of auto industry competitiveness. . . . Rather than rely on Adam Smith's invisible hand, the government has nurtured, prodded, and sometimes bulldozed South Korean industry in order to make it efficient and competitive" (Green 1992:421). Green also notes the contribution of other aspects of the South Korean economic structure and in particular that of the dominance of the *chaebŏl* in the successful development of the South Korean automobile industry: the *chaebŏl*s' size and diversity mean that they have both the productive and financial capacity to develop large-scale industry and that within a single *chaebŏl*, automobile materials, production, shipping, and insurance are handled in separate affiliates: "Within this structure, prices can be adjusted so that profitable subsidiaries can be used to subsidize the losses of others" (Green 1992:423).

13. Note that these statistics refer to passenger cars owned by the government and commercial entities as well as those owned by private individuals.

14. Similarly, according to a survey of Seoulites undertaken in 1989, 27 percent owned a car, 11 percent planned to purchase a car within a year, and 62 percent had no plans to buy a car (Han'guk Yut'ong Chosa Yŏn'guso 1991).

15. On the other hand, at the same time, the tax authorities continued to set high taxes on automobile ownership, undercutting the efforts to promote car buying.

16. There are striking linguistic echoes between these statements and those of South Korea's modernizing reformers in the late nineteenth and early twentieth centuries, who advocated such changes as women's education and the emancipation of slaves as methods of joining the community of modern nations (see, for example, Choi 1986.)

17. In an interview I had with Dr. Suh, he told me almost the same story, but edited out the pronouncement that South Korea would surpass the United States.

18. In South Korea the price of cars is set by the government (and is not subject to negotiation at the dealer's) on the basis of liter capacity (for example, the 3,000 cc super luxury class, the 2,000 cc luxury class, etc.). Cars of similar sizes therefore do not compete in terms of price, but on other factors (styling, safety, gas economy, resale value, reputation, and so on.)

19. This kind of direct questioning is, in fact, often used as a means of drawing critical attention to mildly transgressive or individualized behavior.

## THIRD VIGNETTE: 1991

1. My host family in Yoido was wonderfully welcoming; I'm merely referring here to an opportunity I gave up to learn about the lifestyles of the truly rich nouveaux riches.

2. Both the flight attendant and Mrs. Lee herself used this English form of address, a recognition of my foreign difference and an invocation of international positioning.

3. Adults use a familiar form of speech, known as *panmal*, with children. My *panmal* ability was very clumsy, so our conversation was particularly awkward.

## 4. *KWASOBI CH'UBANG*: MEASURING EXCESS

1. The term *kwasobi* seems to be a new word and is not an entry in most dictionaries (for example, it is absent from both the 1982 *Kukŏ Taesajŏn* [Minjung Sŏrim 1982] and the 1992 *Urimal K'ŭnsajŏn* [Han'guk Hakhoe 1992]; it *does*, however, appear in a 1992 pronunciation dictionary, *Urimal Parŭm Sajŏn* [I Unchŏng 1992]), although the word *kwasosobi*, meaning *under*consumption, occurs in dictionaries. For most of the history of Korea, meager consumption (starvation, extreme poverty) has been a more common problem than unrestrained indulgence.

2. *Yangban* were expected to be moral exemplars.

> The scholar-official fulfilled a prominent role as a morally superior man (*hyŏn*) who was called upon to lead the ignorant masses. . . . Governing was essentially an educative and regulatory process by which the unruly nature of the people was subjected to state control and brought into harmony with the universe. It was a matter of "renovating the people" (*sinmin*) by invigorating society's basic relationships (*kanggi*), which were expressed in its customs (*p'ungsok*).
>
> (Deuchler 1992:110)

3. It was also true, on the other hand, that those families that were enriched during the colonial period were vulnerable to criticism as collaborators.

4. This was during the period between the 1905 Protectorate Treaty allotting to Japan the authority to run Korea's foreign relations and the formal Treaty of Annexation in 1910.

5. Changes in the strategies and policies of Japanese colonial rule and the various Korean nationalist movements are discussed in Eckert et. al (1990); Michael Robinson's *Cultural Nationalism in Colonial Korea, 1920—1925* (1988) provides a thorough examination of competing approaches to nationalist resistance during that critical period.

6. The Chinese characters used were *chajak chagŭp*.

7. Wells (1985) outlines some of the reasons for the brevity of the movement's popularity: the Japanese government continued to maintain practices that limited the ability of many Korean industrialists to succeed in establishing new companies or expanding their production, and the colonial government suppressed some of the more inflammatory aspects of the movement. In addition, internal debates within the wider nationalist movement are evident in the criticism socialist nationalists lobbed at the Society for the Promotion of Korean Products, which was vulnerable to charges of elitism and of supporting the bourgeoisie rather than workers.

8. They were released after a bargain had been struck to ensure cooperation of state and industry (Hart-Landsberg 1993:165).

9. Of course, Park's speeches were also one means of asserting government authority over the potentially competing interests of business leaders.

10. Other activities the women recalled included capturing rats and mice and planting trees.

11. This invocation of a dream of economic independence echoes the self-sufficiency vocabulary of the 1920s and parallels the "*chuje*" (often spelled *juche*) self-reliance philosophy of Kim Il Sung in North Korea. Note that the conception of an "independent" economy rarely criticizes the importance of *exports* to the South Korean economy. Rather, import-substitution, export success, and agricultural self-reliance are the key elements of national economic independence in this construction of a healthy economy.

12. This concern echoed the attempt to forestall Japanese annexation in the first decade of the twentieth century by repaying the national debt to Japan, as described above. The South Korean leeriness of foreign debt stemmed in part from this experience. It is true that the South Korean national foreign debt was among the world's highest in the mid-1980s, at the time of the Latin American debt crisis. This debt differs from the debt crisis in South Korea in late 1997 in that most of the 1986 debt was long-term debt generally funneled through government channels, whereas the crisis in 1997 was in part a problem of the influx of foreign capital lent on a short-term basis in the changed financial environment of the 1990s.

13. In room salons, friends can gather together in small, private rooms to drink and be served and entertained by women attendants; stand bars have a more typical public-bar layout, and many barber shops offer massage and sexual services along with a haircut and a shave.

14. In this last category they noted transfers between relatives as well as illegal bribes received and money simply received from someone else (Seoul YMCA 1990a:12).

15. The largest government-sponsored rural assistance program, *Saemaŭl Undong*, did not ensure the profitability of the farming life. Many analysts see in government agricultural policies an attempt to, on the one hand, maintain the rural peace and the political loyalty of farmer-voters and, on the other hand, to secure a steady supply of cheap workers for new factories (see, for example, Moore 1984; Hamilton 1986; Hart-Landsberg 1993).

16. The *minjung* movement is a crucial and important force in contemporary South Korean history. For more information in English on the movement and its underlying ideas, see especially Abelmann (1993 and 1995), Kim (1995), and Wells (1995a and b).

17. Farmers' activism also received coverage in the print and broadcast media.

18. Pamphlet dated May 1992, acquired in the underground Ulchiro walkway.

19. During the 1960s, 1970s, and 1980s, South Korean agriculture had changed significantly. Increasing use of chemical fertilizers, mechanical farm equipment, and other industrial farming techniques allowed farmers to increase their yields and experiment with higher-value crops. At the beginning of the Park era, three-fourths of the typical farm income came from grains; by the mid-1970s, this had been cut to just over half, while cash crops and livestock gained in importance (Mason et al. 1980:210). Fields covered in what appeared to be black plastic garbage bags were common roadside views as vinyl greenhouses, coddling fresh vegetables, sprouted across the country.

20. Many meals are accompanied by several side dishes and condiments. It was common for restaurant owners to collect the unused dishes after a patron had left, and prepare the same food for presentation at another table.

21. This is, of course, what Hong Kong is famous for among tourists from many countries.

22. This particular fable appeared commonly in Aesop collections published in the United States in the nineteenth century but had been dropped from most later anthologies by the early twentieth century. The version I offer here is a retelling of the story as it was (repeatedly) told to me in Seoul.

23. This is consistent with the moral drawn in early U.S. versions. One particularly colorful anthology provided this instruction: "How many vain people, of moderate easy circumstances, by entertaining the silly ambition of vying with their superiors in station and fortune, get into the direct road to ruin. . . . [Such]

conduct . . ., it is to be feared, will continue to fill our gaols with debtors, and Bed-
lam with lunatics" (Bewick 1975: 18).

24. Of course, very few South Koreans were accumulating personal, household debt at the rate of $14,000 per year.

25. This fable and the interpretation resonate nicely with a common Korean
aphorism: "Like a frog in a well," which refers to someone with no experience or
knowledge of the larger world, a country bumpkin. A frog who lives its life within
the confines of a well cannot imagine the cosmopolitan world beyond. I have on occasion heard South Koreans speak critically of the South Korean nation as "like a
frog in a well," ignorant and unprepared to compete with larger, more powerful nations more experienced at negotiating and manipulating international terms of trade.
South Koreans viewing this poster might interpret the foolishness of the mother frog
not just as an example of laughable vanity but also as fatal provincialism.

26. For clarification: in the North, Korea is known as *Chosŏn*. Both *Chosŏn* and
*Han'guk*, like the word "Korea," refer to an undivided nation.

27. School textbooks are used uniformly across South Korea in the public
schools.

28. Girls and young women are taught that keeping complete records of the
family expenditures is an important part of proper housekeeping. Very few of the
women I interviewed, however, actually kept records in such detail.

29. AmCham speculated that the government phoned the directive in to
avoid a paper trail.

## 5. ENDANGERING THE NATION, CONSUMING THE FUTURE

1. *Newsweek* publishes various editions for different markets. This story appeared in the Pacific International edition.

2. In this particular example, unlike in the cited cases of women's fashion purchases, *Newsweek* neglected to provide an equivalent in dollars.

3. A related article, on South Korea's foreign aid program, included a photograph of a female South Korean nurse in Nepal with four young Nepalese boys in
a box on two pages within the "Too Rich" article.

4. The other photographs showed the following scenes: a woman ("clad in
fur despite balmy weather" according to the caption) looks at a display of Nina
Ricci handbags along with a female sales assistant; another female sales assistant
stands at attention in a department store (apparently the Lotte); two young
women in casual clothes stand by a tree (this photo was paired with the one of the
bride and shared the caption, "$23,000 shopping sprees and $600 panties: Young
girls on a fashionable Seoul shopping street, a bride in a European-style gown";
and a woman with a very young daughter standing in a spacious and well-
equipped kitchen.

5. For example, the same month the *Newsweek* article appeared, the daily newspaper *Chung'ang Ilbo* wrote, "Excessive consumption is, nowadays, becoming even more of a social problem. There are many too many ultraluxurious commodities laid in stock without restraint, and the tendency to waste is becoming diffused throughout society" (*Chung'ang Ilbo*, *"TV kwanggowa kwasobi"* [TV advertisements and overconsumption]).

6. Ewha Woman's University takes its name from *ihwa*, plum blossoms. While the school and its students have been criticized as elitist, Ewha is understood to play an important role in educating women of influence and position in South Korean society. Ewha students and faculty are also famous for their contributions to anticolonial resistance and to contemporary social critique.

7. Munhwa Broadcasting Center (MBC), along with KBS1, KBS2, and SBS, is one of South Korea's four major broadcast networks.

8. The fact that "Too Rich, Too Soon" appeared only in the *Newsweek* editions sold in Asia escaped notice; most readers assumed that the article could be found in *Newsweek* magazines around the world.

9. Note that in neither the "West" nor in South Korea was the position of "housewife" a role with deep historical roots. One interesting discussion of the development of housewives that places this phenomenon in a global context is presented by Maria Mies (1986). In South Korea, nuclear family households are increasingly common in the 1980s and 1990s, and households that can afford it often allocate to the adult woman the role of "housewife." For a look at the evolution of South Korean nuclear families and housewives, see for example Kim (1993), Cho (1995), Chung (1986:145–148), Choi (1998).

10. It should not go without notice that in "Too Rich, Too Soon" the specific items women were reported to have purchased were goods for female adornment (lingerie, boutique clothing, bridal gown), or the women were shown in gender-specific roles (wives of generals, unmarried women looking for a high-class husband, mothers arranging for their children's education).

11. One can read the two children's stories from the previous chapter as reflecting this perspective. In "Mina's Pledge," the records Mina's mother has kept show Mina that she has spent much more than her brother, and she vows to save more from now on. In "Shoeleather Grandfather," Suyŏng was at first embarrassed that his Grandfather was considered a tightwad, but once his grandfather explains to him the honor of their parsimonious lifestyle, Suyŏng pledges to uphold the family code. While these two stories are, on the surface, quite similar, the treatment of the two children's capacity for (consumer) responsibility differs in important ways. Mina, but not Suyŏng, is shown to have been wasteful in the past. In fact, Mina's *brother* is depicted as economical in contrast to his sister. Suyŏng is shown to be concerned with defending the family honor, both in his initial pugilism and in his conversion to the ethics of frugality, while Mina's motivation

to try to save money is not so clearly stated: Is she embarrassed, or is she concerned about the family? Of course, a comparison such as this, drawn ad hoc from a pair of children's textbooks, must be taken for what it is: not convincing evidence, but a telling glimpse of trends, tendencies, and assumptions.

12. Aihwa Ong describes a similar dynamic in the moral criticisms of young working women's consumer pleasures in Malaysia (Ong 1987).

13. The personal indulgences of wealthy men received much milder media attention. Men were rarely associated with the purchase of things; rather, men's consumption was perceived as almost restricted to services. As noted in chapter 4, the "pleasure culture industry" was targeted early on by the YMCA as immoral and a drain of financial resources, but it ceased to be the central topic as the trade balance turned negative. In addition, most other treatments of the topic focused narrowly on issues of political corruption and bribery. Moreover, because men often partook of these services in circumstances that could be construed as work-related (with colleagues, while negotiating deals, in an effort to gain the favor of someone in a position of power), personal indulgences were often excused as productive activities. One woman in Yoido told me that she often had to wait for her husband to come home late from a night at a room salon with customers of his trading company. "*I don't think he enjoys it,*" she told me. "*He has to go, for business.*" Anne Allison has written an ethnography of male consumption of sexually charged services in Japan and found men and women similarly excused men's use of hostess bars as a necessary part of work (Allison 1994).

14. Despite government studies showing that the crime rate was stable, in the 1990s several shocking, violent crimes received disproportionate publicity, with particular emphasis on the perpetrators' reported motivation: revenge on the rich. Most people treated this as a new and disturbing phenomenon. The more notorious crimes included a man who drove his car into a crowd of families in Yoido Plaza, a public recreation spot, killing more than a dozen people; several attacks on rich women in the parking lots of shopping centers; a series of brutal murders of wealthy families carried out by a gang espousing a politics of equity; and a parricide committed by a young man studying in the United States who wanted more money from his parents. There were also many reports of young women who were kidnapped, raped, and then forced to work in the sex industry.

15. The sense of class/gender vulnerability may have reinforced the trend of class segregation in space, as many of the affluent women thought of the *sijang* as dangerous and rarely went there.

16. This division of responsibility was reflected in traditional Korean architecture. To the extent feasible (varying to a certain extent by class), women were isolated in women's quarters far from the entrance to the home and from the view of visitors in the *anbang*, or inside room.

17. The complaint that young people no longer were willing to work at "dirty,

difficult, or dangerous" jobs (and instead took jobs in the service sector) was often linked to this criticism of the new generation's egoism and indulgent lifestyles.

18. Even the issue of class presidency had become entangled in the public discussions of *kwasobi* and of corruption. The mothers of a class president and vice president were expected to contribute financially and materially to the class, and often their extra contact with the teacher made them feel pressure to contribute more envelopes of money, a common form of petty bribery—or, alternatively, a means of expressing gratitude for the teachers' efforts on behalf of one's child.

19. The dreams women said they had for their children were remarkably homogeneous: most daughters were to be teachers or housewives, while sons might work for the government, work in a corporation, or become teachers, professors, or doctors. The rough outlines of the dreams varied little with income between Talgoljjagi and Yoido. The wealthier mothers, however, had more specific ideas and plans for achieving their visions, perhaps reflecting more solid belief in the possibility of attaining their goals. A few women in both Yoido and Talgoljjagi answered that they just wanted their children to do whatever would make them happy.

20. Many of the women in their twenties and thirties had stayed in school only through elementary grades and had then started to work in factories.

21. During the time of my fieldwork, the Seoul city government was erecting a social services center at the crest of Talgoljjagi hill, which would ultimately offer study rooms for students. Since many families lived in just one room, children who were inclined to study had a hard time finding any place to concentrate on their homework. There were a few commercial study rooms at the bottom of the hill, where students could pay a fee to study in a quiet place, but even these were too expensive for many of the Talgoljjagi families.

22. *Han'gul* is the Korean language syllabary; although Chinese characters are also often used in Korean writing, *han'gul* is the basic writing system.

23. On the other hand, Talgoljjagi women generally did feel torn between buying cheap vegetables imported from China or buying more expensive produce grown by South Korean farmers. Because many Talgoljjagi families still kept in touch with relatives in the countryside, the patriotic imperative around food purchases presented a poignant dilemma.

24. It was common to say that many of the rich people who indulge in *kwasobi* were nouveau-riche upstarts, former farmers who were able to sell their land for a high price. They were to be distinguished from the "more respectable" middle class and upper class, who were assumed to have inherited their status and wealth, or who had attained it through the rewards of educational achievements.

25. This is somewhat different from the sense of frustration around economic inequity that Joungwon A. Kim noted in the 1970s before the development of the domestic car industry: "Most troublesome was the conspicuous consumption of the new elite, who began building luxurious homes and riding

through Seoul in expensive imported Cadillacs and Mercedes-Benzes" (quoted in Hart-Landsberg 1993:184).

26. In 1993 the Sable was the most popular imported car in South Korea. Still, only 826 Sables were sold that year, accounting for 45 percent of all foreign car sales. Imported cars made up less than one-tenth of 1 percent of the car market in South Korea.

27. In the 1960s and 1970s, low savings rates prompted one economist to write an article to try to explain, "Why do Koreans Save So Little?" (Williamson 1979).

28. One of the participants at a symposium sponsored by the Association of Consumer Protection Agencies commented: "Let's look closely at our consumer lifestyle up to now: We have thrown around the money earned without effort. Because it is money earned without sweating, we don't know how to be thankful and it is used wastefully. Because it is not money earned by working diligently, we don't know how to use it sparingly, and it is used extravagantly" (Sobija pohodanch'e hyŏpŭi hwe [Association of Consumer Protection Agencies] 1989).

29. See chapter 4.

30. If the trip was a visit to relatives living abroad, often the husband/father would stay behind to work, leaving the wife/mother to travel alone with their children.

31. Not entirely coincidentally, English is one of the test subjects for college admission evaluations, and so the pursuit of English skills (as defined by the tests, as opposed to communication competency) takes up a great deal of energy in college-bound households.

32. International travel was, in fact, another expensive supplement to many Yoido children's school education. One twelve-year-old boy went to Japan for a week during the spring vacation to "Space Camp" (a camp focused on space exploration and astronomy), at a cost of nearly $1,000.

33. Kim Hyun Mee examines the transformation, over time, of the portrait of women engaged in a labor protest against a U.S.-owned corporation, from illegal strikers and troublemakers to victims and finally to patriotic *ajumma* worker heroes (Kim 1998).

## FIFTH VIGNETTE: 1991

1. Literally "aunties," a term commonly used to refer to middle-aged women, particularly those who do not appear to belong to the middle or upper classes.

## CODA

1. Fine and Leopold take pains not to paint all members of each discipline

with the same brush; they are careful to acknowledge exceptions within each particular disciplinary framework. They themselves construct a theory of consumption focused on the "vertical" interrelations between pieces (production, distribution, marketing, and consumption) of various "systems of provision" and in doing so they illuminate weaknesses in scholarship that focuses on one element and sees it as the cause of the others. For example, several historians (e.g., McKendrick et al. 1982) have produced studies supporting the argument that demand has been the driving force behind supply, even though at times that demand is engineered by entrepreneurs' leadership in the shaping of taste and fashion. Fine and Leopold dismiss such studies as misleadingly one-sided.

2. Although car ownership itself marked distinctions between haves and have-nots (between comfortable, independent, self-directed car drivers and cramped, passive bus riders, for example), and car *models* marked class and age distinctions among owners, owners did not make much of an effort to play with these distinctions. Few cars in Seoul were marked with stickers or personalized in other ways on the exterior. Even commercial small trucks and vans generally rode incognito through the streets. Cars as pure products were left to speak for themselves to outside observers. A few car owners applied stickers to their cars that emulated the markings of expensive models, and the practice of attaching false car-phone antennae was so widespread in the early 1990s that the National Assembly passed a law prohibiting them, on the theory that this only exacerbated envy of the rich: these seemingly subversive practices in fact *acknowledged* and *reinforced* the legitimacy of the automobile hierarchy. In other words, these were not attempts to stake out an alternative style. The *interior* space, however, was the site that owners chose to make their own: the driver's seats of many cars were covered with a woven grid of wooden-balls that were said to massage a tired back; lace doilies and ruffled tissue box covers graced many dashboards and backseat ledges; pastel, floral-patterned cushions offered comfort to the passengers. Even inside, however, variety and individual expression was subdued: a dainty domesticity was far and away the most common theme, spanning women's personal cars and business sedans, all the way to rattling pick-up trucks.

3. Nationalism and national identity in South Korea have a specific valence vis-à-vis key foreign countries. Japan has cast a shadow as both oppressor *and* exemplar; the United States has stood as big brother *and* big bully, and North Korea has been a lost twin *and* a bitter enemy. Political legitimacy has been asserted through a complicated discourse of resistance, differentiation, cosmopolitanism, uniqueness, history, and hope. In the post-IMF context, South Koreans continue use these same elements to construct a vision of their nation as victim and hero.

4. One of the anonymous reviewers of this manuscript also pointed out that Koreans were forced by the Japanese to give up their gold for the empire during the late colonial period.

5. Brackette Williams looks at state interests in defining the national mainstream and the marginal in the process of generating a sense of unity in a process she terms "homogenizing heterogeneity" (Williams 1989).

# REFERENCES

Abelmann, Nancy and John Lie. 1995. *Blue Dreams: Korean Americans and the Los Angeles Riots.* Cambridge: Harvard University Press.

Abelmann, Nancy. 1996. *Echoes of the Past, Epics of Dissent.* Berkeley: University of California Press.

Abelmann, Nancy. 1995. "Minjung Movements and the Minjung: Organizers and Farmers in a 1980s Farmers' Movement." In Kenneth M. Wells, ed., *South Korea's Minjung Movement: The Culture and Politics of Dissidence*, 119–153. Honolulu: University of Hawaii Press.

Abelmann, Nancy. 1993. "*Minjung* Theory and Practice." In Harumi Befu, ed., *Cultural Nationalism in East Asia: Representation and Identity*, 139–165. Berkeley: Institute of East Asian Studies.

Abu-Lughod, Lila. 1991. "Writing Against Culture." In Richard G. Fox, ed., *Recapturing Anthropology: Working in the Present*, 137–162. Santa Fe: School of American Research Press.

Adam, Barbara. 1990. *Time and Social Theory.* Philadelphia: Temple University Press.

Allison, Anne. 1994. *Nightwork: Sexuality, Pleasure, and Corporate Masculinity in a Tokyo Hostess Club.* Chicago: University of Chicago Press.

American Chamber of Commerce in Korea. 1993 (March). "US-Korea Trade Issues." Seoul.

American Chamber of Commerce in Korea. 1990. *Pillars of Protectionism in Korea.* Seoul: American Chamber of Commerce.

Amsden, Alice H. 1989. *Asia's Next Giant: South Korea and Late Industrialization.* New York: Oxford University Press.

Anagnost, Ann. 1989. "Prosperity and Counterprosperity: The Moral Discourse on Wealth in Post-Mao China." In Arif Dirlik, ed., *Marxism and the Chinese Experience*, 210–234. Armonk, NY: Sharpe.

Anderson, Benedict. 1983. *Imagined Communities: Reflections on the Origins and Spread of Nationalism.* London: Verso.

Appadurai, Arjun. 1993. "Patriotism and Its Futures." *Public Culture* 5 (3): 411–430.

Appadurai, Arjun. 1991. "Global Ethnoscapes: Notes and Queries for a Transnational Anthropology." In Richard G. Fox, ed., *Recapturing Anthropology: Working in the Present*, 191–210. Santa Fe: School of American Research Press.

Appadurai, Arjun. 1990. "Disjuncture and Difference in the Global Economy." *Public Culture* 2 (2): 1–24.

Appadurai, Arjun. 1988. "Putting Hierarchy in its Place." *Cultural Anthropology* 3 (1): 36–49.

Appadurai, Arjun. 1986a. "Introduction: Commodities and the Politics of Value." In Arjun Appadurai, ed., *The Social Life of Things: Commodities in Cultural Perspective*, 3–63. Cambridge: Cambridge University Press.

Appadurai, Arjun. 1986b. *The Social Life of Things: Commodities in Cultural Perspective*. Cambridge: Cambridge University Press.

Auslander, Leora. 1996. "The Gendering of Consumer Practices in Nineteenth-Century France." In Victoria de Grazia, ed., with Ellen Furlough, *The Sex of Things: Gender and Consumption in Historical Perspective*, 79–112. Berkeley: University of California Press.

Baek, Uk-in. 1993. "*Taejung'ŭi samgwa han'guk sahoe pyŏnŭi yoch'e*" (The secret of mass culture and Korean society). In Kim Ch'ŏl-mi, ed., *Han'guk sahoeundongŭi hyŏksinŭl wihayŏ* (On the reform of Korean social movements). Seoul: Paeksan Sŏdang. (In Korean.)

Baudrillard, Jean. 1975. *The Mirror of Production*. Translated by Mark Poster. St. Louis: Telos Press.

Befu, Harumi, ed. 1993. *Cultural Nationalism in East Asia: Representation and Identity*. Berkeley: Institute of East Asian Studies.

Bello, Walden and Stephanie Rosenfeld. 1990. *Dragons in Distress: Asia's Miracle Economies in Crisis*. San Francisco: The Institute for Food and Development.

Benjamin, Walter. 1969. *Illuminations*. New York: Schocken.

Bewick, Thomas. 1975 [1818]. *The Fables of Aesop with designs on wood by Thomas Bewick*. Reprint. New York: Paddington Press.

Bhabha, Homi K. 1990. "DissemiNation: Time, narrative, and the margins of the modern nation." In Homi K. Bhabha, ed., *Nation and Narration*, 291–322. London: Routledge.

Borneman, John. 1992. "State, Territory, and Identity Formation in the Postwar Berlins, 1945–1989." *Cultural Anthropology* 7 (1): 45–62.

Bourdieu, Pierre. 1984. *Distinction: A Social Critique of the Judgement of Taste*. Translated by Richard Nice. Cambridge: Harvard University Press.

Bourdieu, Pierre. 1977. *Outline of a Theory of Practice*. Cambridge: Cambridge University Press.

Boyarin, Jonathan, ed. 1994. *Remapping Memory: The Politics of Time Space*. Minneapolis: University of Minnesota Press.

Brandt, Vincent S. R. 1971. *A Korean Village Between Farm and Sea*. Cambridge: Harvard University Press.

Butler, Judith. 1990. *Gender Trouble: Feminism and the Subversion of Identity*. New York: Routledge.

Campbell, Colin D. and Chang Shick Ahn. 1962 (October). "Kyes and Mujins: Financial Intermediaries in South Korea." *Economic Development and Cultural Change* 11 (1): 55–68.

Chang, Yun-shik. 1991. "The Personalist Ethic and the Market in Korea." *Society for Comparative Study of Society and History* 33:106–129.

Chatterjee, Partha. 1993. *The Nation and Its Fragments: Colonial and Postcolonial Histories*. Princeton: Princeton University Press.

Chatterjee, Partha. 1990. "A Response to Taylor's 'Modes of Civil Society.'" *Public Culture* 3 (1): 119–132.

Cho, Dong-sung. 1998 (January-February). "Korea's Economic Crisis: Causes, Significance and Agenda for Recovery." *Korea Focus* 6 (1): 15–26.

Cho, Haejoang (Cho, Hyejŏng). 1995. "Living with Conflicting Femininity of Mother, Motherly Wife, and Sexy Woman: A Transition from Colonial-modern to Post-modern." Paper presented at the Workshop on Gender and Social Change in Late Twentieth-Century Korea. Photocopy.

Cho, Hyejŏng. 1992. "Apkujŏngdong 'Kongkan'ŭi sisŏndŭl: Munhwa chŏngch'ijŏk silch'ŏnŭl wihayŏ" (Perspectives on the space of Apkujŏngdong: A practice of political culture). In Kim Jin-Song et al., *Apkujŏngdong: Yut'op'ia / Tist'op'ia*, 32–59. Seoul: Hyŏngsil munhwa yŏngu. (In Korean.)

Cho, Haejoang (Cho, Hyejŏng). 1986. "Male Dominance and Mother Power: The Two Sides of Confucian Patriarchy in Korea." In Walter H. Slote, ed., *The Psycho-Cultural Dynamics of the Confucian Family: Past and Present*. Seoul: International Cultural Society.

Cho, Joo-Hyun. 1989. "A Theory of Housing Price and Demand under Credit Constraints: The Case of Korea." *The Journal of Korea Planners Association* 24 (1): 103–130.

Choi, Chungmoo. 1998. "Nationalism and the Construction of Gender in Korea." In Elaine H. Kim and Chungmoo Choi, eds., *Dangerous Women: Gender and Korean Nationalism*, 9–31. New York: Routledge.

Choi, Chungmoo. 1995. "The Minjung Culture Movement and the Construction of Popular Culture in Korea." In Kenneth M. Wells, ed., *South Korea's Minjung Movement: The Culture and Politics of Dissidence*, 105–118. Honolulu: University of Hawaii Press.

Choi, Chungmoo. 1993 (Spring). "The Discourse of Decolonization and Popular Memory: South Korea." *Positions: East Asia Cultures Critique* 1 (1).

Ch'oi, Chong-uk. 1991 (November). "Kwasobiwa 90 nyŏndaep'an ojŏk" (Excessive consumption and the five thieves of the 90s). *Mal.* (In Korean.)

Choi, Jang Jip. 1993. "Political Cleavages in South Korea." In Hagen Koo, ed., *State and Society in Contemporary Korea*, 13–50. Ithaca: Cornell University Press.

Ch'oi, Jin-sŏp. 1992 (September). "Chungganch'ŭng undong apjangsŏn kyŏngsillyŭnŭi samnyŏn" (Three years of the Citizen's Coalition for Economic Justice: The leading edge of the middle class movement). *Mal.* (In Korean.)

Choi, Sook-kyung. 1986. "Formation of Women's Movements in Korea: From the Enlightenment Period to 1910." In Chung Sei-wha, ed., *Challenges for Women: Women's Studies in Korea*, 103–126. Translated by Shin Chang-hyun, et al. Seoul: Ewha Womans University Press.

Chŏng, Chae-ryŏng, ed. 1990. *Sinsedae: Kŭdŭrŭn nuguinga?* (The new generation: Who are they?) Seoul: Han'guk Ilbo. (In Korean.)

Chŏng, Kwŏn-sŏp. 1981. "A Study of Korean Land Law." In Pyŏng-ho Pak, et al., eds., *Modernization and Its Impact on Korean Law*, 39–63. Berkeley: Institute of East Asian Studies, University of California.

Chung, Dai-hyun. 1986. "Women's Liberation and the Korean Ordinary Language. " In Sei-wha Chung, ed., *Challenges for Women: Women's Studies in Korea*, 127–149. Translated by Shin Chang-hyun et al. Seoul: Ewha Womans University Press.

Clark, Donald N., ed. 1988. *The Kwangju Uprising: Shadows Over the Regime in South Korea.* Boulder: Westview Press.

Clifford, James. 1986. "Introduction: Partial Truths." In James Clifford and George E. Marcus, eds., *Writing Culture: The Poetics and Politics of Ethnography*, 1–26. Berkeley: University of California Press.

Clifford, Mark L. 1994. *Troubled Tiger: Businessmen, Bureaucrats, and Generals in South Korea.* Armonk, NY: Sharpe.

Collins, Susan. 1994. "Saving, Investment, and External Balance in South Korea." In Stephen Haggard et al., eds., *Macroeconomic Policy and Adjustment in Korea, 1970–1990*, 239–259. Cambridge: Harvard Institute for International Development and Korea Development Institute.

Cotton, James and Kim Hyung-a van Leest. 1996. "The new Rich and the new Middle Class in South Korea: The Rise and Fall of the 'Golf Republic.'" In Richard Robison and David S. G. Goodman, eds., *The New Rich in Asia: Mobile Phones, McDonald's, and Middle-Class Revolution*, 185–204. New York: Routledge.

Creighton, Millie R. 1992. "The Depato: Merchandising the West While Selling Japaneseness." In Joseph J. Tobin, ed., *Remade in Japan: Everyday Life and Consumer Taste in a Changing Society.* New Haven: Yale University Press.

Creighton, Millie R. 1991. "Maintaining Cultural Boundaries in Retailing: How Japanese Department Stores Domesticate 'Things Foreign.'" *Modern Asian Studies* 25 (4): 675–709.

Cumings, Bruce. 1997. *Korea's Place in the Sun: A Modern History*. New York: Norton.

Cumings, Bruce. 1981. *Origins of the Korean War*. Vol. 1: *Liberation and the Emergence of Separate Regimes, 1945–1947*. Princeton: Princeton University Press.

Cumings, Bruce. 1990. *Origins of the Korean War*. Vol. 2: *The Roaring of the Cataract, 1947–1950*. Princeton: Princeton University Press.

Davis, Belinda. 1996. "Food Scarcity and the Empowerment of the Female Consumer in World War I Berlin." In Victoria de Grazia, ed., with Ellen Furlough, *The Sex of Things: Gender and Consumption in Historical Perspective*, 287–310. Berkeley: University of California Press.

de Certeau, Michel. 1984. *The Practice of Everyday Life*. Translated by Steven Rendall. Berkeley: University of California Press.

de Grazia, Victoria, ed., with Ellen Furlough. 1996a. *The Sex of Things: Gender and Consumption in Historical Perspective*. Berkeley: University of California Press.

de Grazia, Victoria. 1996b. "Nationalizing Women: The Competition between Fascist and Commercial Cultural Models in Mussolini's Italy." In Victoria de Grazia, ed., with Ellen Furlough, *The Sex of Things: Gender and Consumption in Historical Perspective*, 337–358. Berkeley: University of California Press.

Deuchler, Martina. 1992. *The Confucian Transformation of Korea: A Study of Society and Ideology*. Cambridge: Council on East Asian Studies, Harvard University.

Dirks, Nicholas B. 1990. "History as a Sign of the Modern." *Public Culture* 2 (2): 25–31.

Douglas, Mary and Baron Isherwood. [1979] 1996. *The World of Goods*. New York: Routledge.

Douglas, Mary. 1966. *Purity and Danger: An Analysis of the Concepts of Pollution and Taboo*. London: ARK Paperbacks.

Durkheim, Emile. 1995 (1912). *The Elementary Forms of Religious Life*. Translated by Karen E. Fields. New York: Free Press.

Eatwell, John, Murray Milgate, and Peter Newman. 1987. *The New Palgrave: A Dictionary of Economics*. London: Macmillan Press.

Ebron, Paulla and Anna Lowenhaupt Tsing. 1995. "In Dialogue? Reading Across Minority Discourses." In Ruth Behar and Deborah A. Gordon, eds., *Women Writing Culture*, 390–411. Berkeley: University of California Press.

Eckert, Carter J. 1993. "The South Korean Bourgeoisie: A Class In Search of Hegemony." In Hagen Koo, ed., *State and Society in Contemporary Korea*, 95–130. Ithaca: Cornell University Press.

Eckert, Carter J. 1991. *Offspring of Empire: The Koch'ang Kims and the Colonial Origins of Korean Capitalism, 1876–1945.* Seattle: University of Washington Press.

Eckert, Carter J. et al., eds. 1990. *Korea Old and New: A History.* Seoul: Ilchokak, for the Korea Institute, Harvard University.

Economic Planning Board. Various Years. *Population and Housing Census of Korea.* Seoul: Economic Planning Board.

Emerson, Tony with Bradley Martin. 1991 (11 November). "Too Rich, Too Soon." *Newsweek,* 12–16. (Pacific International Edition.)

Evans-Pritchard, Edward E. [1940] 1969. *The Nuer: A Description of the Modes of Livelihood and Political Institutions of a Nilotic People.* New York: Oxford University Press.

Ewen, Stuart. 1990. "Marketing Dreams: The Political Elements of Style." In Alan Tomlinson, ed., *Consumption, Identity, and Style,* 41–56. London: Routledge.

Fabian, Johannes. 1983. *Time and the Other: How Anthropology Makes Its Object.* New York: Columbia University Press.

Featherstone, Mike. 1990. "Introduction." In Mike Featherstone, ed., *Global Culture: Nationalism, Globalization, and Modernity.* Newbury Park: Sage.

Feeley-Harnik, Gillian. 1991. *A Green Estate: Restoring Independence in Madagascar.* Washington, D.C.: The Smithsonian Institution Press.

Ferguson, James and Akhil Gupta. 1992. "Beyond 'Culture': Space, Identity, and the Politics of Difference." *Cultural Anthropology* 7 (1): 6–22.

Fine, Ben. 1995. "From Political Economy to Consumption." In Daniel Miller, ed., *Acknowledging Consumption: A Review of New Studies,* 127–165. New York: Routledge.

Fine, Ben and Ellen Leopold. 1993. *The World of Consumption.* New York: Routledge.

Fischer, Michael. 1986. "Ethnicity and the Post-Modern Arts of Memory." In James Clifford and George Marcus, eds., *Writing Culture: The Poetics and Politics of Ethnography,* 194–233. Berkeley: University of California Press.

Follain, James R., Gill-Chin Lim, and Bertrand Renaud. 1982. *Housing Crowding in Developing Countries and Willingness to Pay for Additional Space: The Case of Korea.* Syracuse: Maxwell School of Citizenship and Public Affairs, Metropolitan Studies Program. Occasional Paper No. 55.

Foster, Robert J. 1991. "Making National Cultures in the Global Ecumene." *Annual Review of Anthropology* 20:235–260.

Fraser, Nancy. 1991. *Unruly Practices: Power, Discourse, and Gender in Contemporary Social Theory.* Minneapolis: University of Minnesota Press.

Frow, John. 1997. *Time and Commodity Culture: Essays in Cultural Theory and Postmodernity.* Oxford: Clarendon Press.

General Agreement on Tariffs and Trade. 1989. *Republic of Korea: Restrictions on*

*Imports of Beef: Complaint by the United States*. Report of the Panel adopted on 7 November.

Giddens, Anthony. 1987. *Social Theory and Modern Sociology*. Cambridge: Polity Press.

Gilbert, Alan. 1976. "The Arguments for Very Large Cities Reconsidered." *Urban Studies* 13:27–34.

Gilroy, Paul. 1987. *'There Ain't No Black in the Union Jack': The Cultural Politics of Race and Nation*. London: Hutchinson.

Glennie, Paul. 1995. "Consumption Within Historical Studies." In Daniel Miller, ed., *Acknowledging Consumption: A Review of New Studies*, 164–302. New York: Routledge.

Green, Andrew E. 1992. "South Korea's Automobile Industry: Development and Prospects." *Asian Survey* 32 (5): 411–428.

Grinker, Roy Richard. 1998. *Korea and Its Futures: Unification and the Unfinished War*. New York: St. Martin's Press.

Ha, Seong-kyu. 1987. "Korea." In S. K. Ha, ed., *Housing Policy and Practice in Asia*, 80–116. New York: Croom Helm.

Haggard, Stephen et al. 1994. *Macroeconomic Policy and Adjustment in Korea, 1970–1990*. Cambridge: Harvard Institute for International Development and Korea Development Institute.

Haggard, Stephen, Chung-in Moon, and David Kang. 1997 (January). "Japanese Colonialism and Korean Development." *World Development* 25 (1).

Hall, Catherine. 1992. *White, Male, and Middle-Class: Explorations in Feminism and History*. New York: Routledge.

Hall, Stuart and Martin Jacques. 1990. "Introduction." In Stuart Hall and Martin Jacques, ed., *New Times: The Changing Face of Politics in the 1990s*, 11–20. New York: Verso.

Hall, Stuart. 1991. "Brave New World." *Socialist Review* 21 (1): 57–64.

Hamilton, Clive. 1986. *Capitalist Industrialization in Korea*. Boulder: Westview Press.

Han, Kyung Koo. 1994. "Some Foods are Good to Think: Kimchi and the Epitomization of National Character." Paper presented at the Annual Meeting of the Association for Asian Studies, Boston.

Han'guk Hakhoe. 1992. *Urimal K'ŭnsajŏn* (Large dictionary of our language). Seoul: Omungak. (In Korean.)

Han'guk Yut'ong Chosa Yŏn'guso (Korea Institute of Retail Analysis). 1991. *Sŏul chumin syop'ing haengt'ae chosa pogosŏ* (Report on a survey of Seoul residents' shopping behavior, results of '89 and '90 survey). Seoul: Han'guk Yut'ong Chosa Yŏn'guso. (In Korean.)

Hart-Landsberg, Martin. 1998. *Korea: Division, Reunification, and U.S. Foreign Policy*. New York: Monthly Review Press.

Hart-Landsberg, Martin. 1993. *The Rush to Development: Economic Change and Political Struggle in South Korea.* New York: Monthly Review Press.

Harvey, David. 1989. *The Condition of Postmodernity: An Enquiry into the Origins of Cultural Change.* Oxford: Blackwell.

Hebdige, Dick. 1979. *Subculture: The Meaning of Style.* London/New York: Methuen.

Heng, Geraldine and Janadas Devan. 1992. "State Fatherhood: The Politics of Nationalism, Sexuality, and Race in Singapore." In Andrew Parker et al., eds., *Nationalisms & Sexualities,* 343–364. New York: Routledge.

Hobsbawm, Eric and T. Ranger, eds. 1983. *The Invention of Tradition.* Cambridge: Cambridge University Press.

Hong, Doo-Seung. 1992 (July). "Spatial Distribution of the Middle Classes in Seoul, 1975–1985." *Korea Journal of Population and Development* 21 (1).

I, Chŏng-hŭi. 1992. "Sŏul Kangnamjiyŏk namja kogyosaeng 70%-ga kwaoe suŏp patgo'itda" (70% of male high-school students in Seoul's Kangnam area are receiving extracurricular instruction). *Shisa Journal,* 26 July, pp. 72–73.

I, Chun-hŭi. 1992. *"Han'gukŭi palhyo sikp'um iyonghan matkkalsŭrŏn sosŭ mandŭnŭn pŏp"* (Method to make Korea's fermented food a useful delectable sauce). *Chug'an Yŏsŏng* (Weekly women). 18 October. (In Korean.)

I, Hŭi-kyŏng. 1990 (May). "Anjŏng doen chipesŏ salgo sip'da" (I want to live in a secure home). *Kyŏngje Chŏngŭi,* pp. 72–73.

I, Kang-su. 1980. *"Maesŭ k'omyunik'eisyŏngwa munhwa pyŏndong"* (Mass communication and cultural change). In Kim Kyŏng-dong et al., eds., *Han'guk Sahoe 70 Nyŏndae: Pyŏndonggwa Chŏnmang* (Korean society of the 1970s: Change and future prospects), 343–364. Seoul: Han'guk Sahwoehakhwoe P'yŏn. (In Korean.)

I, Un-chŏng. 1992. *Urimal Parŭm Sajŏn* (A pronunciation dictionary of our language). Seoul: Paeksan Ch'ulp'ansa. (In Korean.)

Ikels, Charlotte. 1996. *The Return of the God of Wealth: The Transition to a Market Economy in Urban China.* Stanford: Stanford University Press.

Irwan, Alexander. 1987. "Real Wages and Class Struggle in South Korea." *Journal of Contemporary Asia* 17 (4): 385–408.

Jameson, Frederic. 1994. *The Seeds of Time.* New York: Columbia University Press.

Jameson, Frederic. 1984. "Postmodernism, or The Cultural Logic of Late Capitalism." *New Left Review* 146:53–92.

Janelli, Roger L. with Dawnhee Yim. 1993. *Making Capitalism: The Social and Cultural Construction of a South Korean Conglomerate.* Stanford: Stanford University Press.

Janelli, Roger L. and Dawnhee Yim Janelli. 1982. *Ancestor Worship and Korean Society.* Stanford: Stanford University Press.

Jayawardena, Kumari. 1986. *Feminism and Nationalism in the Third World*. London: Zed Press.

Jones, Jennifer. 1996. "Coquettes and Grisettes: Women Buying and Selling in Ancien-Régime Paris." In Victoria de Grazia, ed., with Ellen Furlough, *The Sex of Things: Gender and Consumption in Historical Perspective*, 25–53. Berkeley: University of California Press.

Kang, Nae-hŭi. 1992. "Apkujŏngdongŭi 'Munjesŏljŏng': Han'guk Chabonchuŭiŭi Yongmang kujo" (The generation of the "problem" of Apkujŏngdong: The structure of the desire of Korean capitalism). In Kim Jin-Song et al., eds., *Apkujŏngdong: Yut'op'ia / Tist'op'ia*. Seoul: Hyŏngsil munhwa yŏn'guso. (In Korean.)

Kastenbaum, Robert. 1961. "The Dimensions of Future Time Perspective: An Experimental Analysis." *Journal of General Psychology* 65:203–218.

Kemper, Steven. 1993. "The Nation Consumed: Buying and Believing in Sri Lanka." *Public Culture* 5 (3): 377–394.

Kendall, Laurel. 1996. *Getting Married in Korea: Of Gender, Morality, and Modernity*. Berkeley: University of California Press.

Kendall, Laurel. 1994. "A Rite of Modernization and Its Postmodern Discontents: Of Weddings, Bureaucrats, and Morality in the Republic of Korea." In Charles F. Keyes et al., eds., *Asian Visions of Authority: Religion and the Modern States of East and Southeast Asia*. Honolulu: University of Hawaii Press.

Kendall, Laurel. 1988. *The Life and Times of a Korean Shaman: Of Tales and the Telling of Tales*. Honolulu: University of Hawaii Press.

Kim, Elaine H. 1998. "Men's Talk: A Korean-American View of South Korean Constructions of Women, Gender, and Masculinity." In Elaine H. Kim and Chungmoo Choi, eds., *Dangerous Women: Gender and Korean Nationalism*, 67–117. New York: Routledge.

Kim, Elaine H. and Chungmoo Choi, eds. 1998. *Dangerous Women: Gender and Korean Nationalism*. New York: Routledge.

Kim, Hong-mok et al., eds. 1991. *Han'gukin Chindan: Chagi Sŏngch'arŭl T'onghaebon Uriŭi Chahwasan*. (Koreans' Diagnosis: Our self-portrait seen through introspection). Seoul: Tong-a Ilbosa. (In Korean.)

Kim, Hyŏng-kuk. 1989. *Tosi Sidaeŭi Han'guk Munhwa* (Korean culture of the urban era). Seoul: Na Nam. (In Korean.)

Kim, Hyung-A. 1995. "Minjung Socioeconomic Responses to State-led Industrialization." In Kenneth M. Wells, ed., *South Korea's Minjung Movement: The Culture and Politics of Dissidence*, 39–59. Honolulu: University of Hawaii Press.

Kim, Hyun Mee. 1998. "Power and Representation: The Case of South Korean Women Workers." *Asian Journal of Women's Studies* 4 (3): 61–108.

Kim, Jeong-Ho and Gill-Chin Lim. 1988. "Development Strategies for Low-Income Housing in Developing Countries." *Proceedings of Regional Seminar: Workshop on Shelter for the Homeless*. Seoul: Korea Planners Association.

Kim, Jeong-Ho. 1990 (July). "Housing Study" [Manuscript]. Seoul: Korea Research Institute on Human Settlements. Photocopy. (In Korean.)

Kim, John T. and Yong Ju Hwang. 1979. "A new Capital City for South Korea." *Ekistics* 22:262–267.

Kim, Kyong-dong. 1976. "Political Factors In the Formation of the Entrepreneurial Elite in South Korea." *Asian Survey* 16:465–471.

Kim, Kyung-Hwan. 1987. "An Analysis of the Inefficiency of Urban Housing Market Investment: The Case of Seoul, Korea." Ph.D. diss., Princeton University.

Kim, Linsu. 1993. "National System of Industrial Innovation: Dynamics of Capability Building in Korea." In Richard R. Nelson, ed., *National Innovation Systems: A Comparative Analysis*, 357–383. New York: Oxford University Press.

Kim, Myung-hye. 1993. "Transformation of Family Ideology in Upper-Middle-Class Families in Urban South Korea." *Ethnology* 32:69–83.

Kim, Pyung-joo. 1998. (November-December). "Time to Focus on Economic Growth over Distribution." *Korea Focus* 6 (6): 25–30.

Kim, Young-Hwa. 1992. "*Hakbumoui Kyoyungyŏl: Sahoe kyech'ŭnggan Pigyorŭl Chungshimŭro*" (Social class and parents' demand for children's education). *Journal of Educational Research* (Seoul) 30 (4). (In Korean.)

Kim, Yung-chung. 1986. "Women's Movement in Modern Korea." In Chung Sei-wha, ed. *Challenges for Women: Women's Studies in Korea*, 75–102. Seoul: Ewha Womans University Press.

Kitay, Michael G. 1985. *Land Acquisition in Developing Countries: Policies and Procedures of the Public Sector*. Boston: Lincoln Institute of Land Policy/ Oelgeschlager, Gunn and Hain.

Kohli, Atul. 1994 (September). "Where do High-Growth Economies Come From?" *World Development* 22 (9): 1269–1293.

Koo, Hagen. 1990. "From Farm to Factory: Proletarianization in Korea." *American Sociological Review* 55:669–681.

Korea Housing Bank. Various issues. *Chut'aek Kŭmyung: Monthly Economic Review* (Housing finance). (In Korean.)

Korea National Housing Corporation. 1989. "Seoul, A Metropolis in the Making: Excavating a Layered Reality." Seoul Exhibition, "World Cities and the Future of the Metropoles." The XVIIth Milano Triennale Exhibition. Seoul: Seoul Metropolitan Government.

Korean Statistical Association. 1992. *Annual Report on the Family Income and Expenditure Survey*. Seoul: The Korean Statistical Association.

Krause, Lawrence B. and Fun-koo Park. 1993. *Social Issues in Korea: Korean and American Perspectives*. Seoul: Korea Development Institute Press.

Kukŭn Kyŏngje Yŏn'guso (Research Institute for the National Economy). 1993. *Han'gukinŭi Sobisaenghwal* (The consumer lifestyle of the Korean people). Seoul. (In Korean.)

Kuchta, David. 1996. "The Making of the Self-Made Man: Class, Clothing, and English Masculinity, 1688–1832." In Victoria de Grazia, ed., with Ellen Furlough, *The Sex of Things: Gender and Consumption in Historical Perspective*. Berkeley: University of California Press.

Kweon, Sug-in. 1993 (November). "Shintobuli (Body-Earth-Not-Separate): Imported Agricultural Products and Nationalism in Korea and Japan." Paper presented at the annual meeting of the American Anthropological Association, Washington, D.C.

Laermans, Rudi. 1993. "Learning to Consume: Early Department Stores and the Shaping of Modern Consumer Culture, 1860–1914." *Theory, Culture, and Society* 10 (4): 79–102.

Lawrence, Denise L. and Setha M. Low. 1990. "The Built Environment and Spatial Form." *Annual Review of Anthropology* 19:453–505.

Leach, William. 1984. "Transformations in a Culture of Consumption: Women and Department Stores, 1890–1925." *Journal of American History* 71:319–342.

Lee, Chung H. 1995. *The Economic Transformation of South Korea: Lessons for the Transition Economies*. Paris: OECD.

Lee, Joohee. 1997. "Class Structure and Class Consciousness in South Korea." *Journal of Contemporary Asia* 27 (2): 135–155.

Lee, June J. H. 1996. "Health Food as Gendered Commodity: Body, Health, and Sexuality Among Middle-Class Korean Men." *International Journal of Politics, Culture, and Society* 10 (1): 73–94.

Lee, Ki-baek. 1984. *A New History of Korea*. Translated by Edward W. Wagner. Cambridge: Harvard University Press.

Lee, Kyubang. 1990. "Policy Directions for Housing Finance and Real Estate Taxation." Seoul: Korea Research Institute on Housing Settlements. Manuscript, photocopy.

Lee, O-young. 1967. *In this Earth* and *In that Wind: This is Korea*. Translated by David I. Steinberg. Royal Asiatic Society, Korea Branch, Handbook Series. Seoul: Seoul Computer Press.

Lefebvre, Henri. 1996. *Writings on Cities*. Translated and edited by Eleonore Kofman and Elizabeth Lebas. Oxford: Blackwell.

Leipziger, Danny M. et al. 1992. *The Distribution of Income and Wealth in Korea*. Washington, D.C.: Economic Development Institute of the World Bank.

Lens, Willy and Marie-Anne Moreas. 1994. "Future Time Perspective: An Individual and a Societal Approach." In Zbigniew Zaleski, ed., *Psychology of Future Orientation*, 23–38. Lublin (Poland): Society of the Catholic University of Lublin.

Lett, Denise Potrzeba. 1998. *In Pursuit of Status: The Making of South Korea's "New" Urban Middle Class*. Cambridge: Harvard University Asia Center.

Lie, John. 1992. "The Political Economy of South Korean Development." *International Sociology* 7 (3): 285–300.

Lie, John. 1998. *Han Unbound: The Political Economy of South Korea*. Stanford: Stanford University Press.

Lowry, Tom. 1987. *The South Korean Motor Industry: A Rerun of Japan?* Automotive Special Report No. 9. London: The Economist Publications.

Luedde-Neurath, Richard. 1986. *Import Controls and Export-Oriented Development: A Reassessment of the South Korean Case*. Boulder: Westview Press.

Lynch, Kevin. 1960. *The Image of the City*. Cambridge: MIT Press.

Maher, Vanessa. 1987. "Sewing the Seams of Society: Dressmakers and Seamstresses in Turin Between the Wars." In Jane Fishburne Collier and Sylvia Junko Yanagisako, eds., *Gender and Kinship: Essays Toward a Unified Analysis*. Stanford: Stanford University Press.

Malkki, Liisa. 1990. "Context and Consciousness: Local Conditions for the Production of Historical and National Thought among Hutu Refugees in Tanzania." In Richard G. Fox, ed., *Nationalist Ideologies and the Production of National Cultures*. Washington: American Anthropological Association.

Mason, Edward S. et al. 1980. *The Economic and Social Modernization of the Republic of Korea*. Cambridge: Harvard University Press.

Massumi, Brian. 1993. "Everywhere You Want to Be: Introduction to Fear." In Brian Massumi, ed., *The Politics of Everyday Fear*. Minneapolis: University of Minnesota Press.

Mauss, Marcel. [1925] 1967. *The Gift: Forms and Functions of Exchange in Archaic Societies*. New York: Norton.

McCracken, Grant. 1988. *Culture and Consumption: New Approaches to the Symbolic Character of Goods and Activities*. Bloomington: Indiana University Press.

McKendrick, Niel, John Brewer, and J. H. Plumb. 1982. *The Birth of Consumer Society: The Commercialization of Eighteenth-Century England*. London: Hutchinson.

McKendrick, Niel. 1974. "Home Demand and Economic Growth: A New View of the Role of Women and Children in the Industrial Revolution." In N. McKendrick, ed., *Historical Perspectives: Studies in English Thought and Society in Honour of J. H. Plumb*, 152–210. London: Hutchinson.

Meier Richard L. 1979. "Socio-technical Considerations in Planning a new Capital City for South Korea." *Ekistics* 22:258–262.

Menzenes, L. M. 1988. "Urban Land Policy Trends in Asia: An Overview." *Land Use Policy* 5:291–300.

Michell, Tony. 1986. "Generational Change and Confucianism: Organization and Interaction in Korea." *Transactions* (Royal Asian Society, Korea Branch) vol. 61.

Mies, Maria. 1986. *Patriarchy and Accumulation on a World Scale: Women in the International Division of Labour*. London: Zed Press.

Miller, Daniel. 1997. *Capitalism: An Ethnographic Approach*. Oxford: Berg Publishers.

Miller, Daniel, ed. 1995a. *Acknowledging Consumption: A Review of New Studies*. London: Routledge.

Miller, Daniel. 1995b. "Consumption as the Vanguard of History: A Polemic by Way of an Introduction." In Daniel Miller, ed., *Acknowledging Consumption: A Review of New Studies*, 1–57. London: Routledge.

Miller, Daniel. 1994. *Modernity—An Ethnographic Approach: Dualism and Mass Consumption in Trinidad*. Oxford: Berg Publishers.

Miller, Daniel. 1987. *Material Culture and Mass Consumption*. Oxford: Blackwell.

Mills, Edwin S. and Byung-Nak Song. 1979. *Urbanization and Urban Problems*. Cambridge: Harvard University Press.

Minjung Minjok Undong Yŏn'guso. 1990. *Chut'aek munjeŭi insikgwa taean* (An understanding of the housing problem and a proposal). Seoul: Nonjang. (In Korean.)

Minjung Sŏrim. 1982. *Kukŏ Taesajŏn* (Great dictionary of the language). Seoul: Minjung Sŏrim. (In Korean.)

Mintz, Sidney W. 1985. *Sweetness and Power: The Place of Sugar in Modern History*. New York: Penguin Books.

Mitchell, Wesley C. 1912 (June). "The Backward Art of Spending Money." *American Economic Review* 2 (2): 269–281.

Moon, Katharine. 1997. *Sex Among Allies: Military Prostitution in U.S.-Korea Relations*. New York: Columbia University Press.

Moon, Seungsook. 1994. "Economic Development and Gender Politics in South Korea, 1963–1992." Ph.D. diss., Brandeis University.

Moore, Mick. 1984. "Mobilization and Disillusion in Rural Korea: The Saemaul Movement in Retrospect." *Pacific Affairs* 57 (4): 577–598.

Moore, Sally Falk, ed. 1993. *Moralizing States and the Ethnography of the Present*. American Ethnological Society Monograph Series, Number 5. Arlington, VA: American Anthropological Association.

Mukerjee, Dilip. 1986. *Lessons from Korea's Industrial Experience*. Kuala Lumpur: Institute of Strategic and International Studies, Malaysia.

Mukerji, Chandra. 1983. *From Graven Images: Patterns of Modern Materialism*. New York: Columbia University Press.

Müller, Georg P. 1989. *Comparative World Data: A Statistical Handbook for Social Science*. Baltimore: Johns Hopkins University Press.

National Bureau of Statistics. 1988. *Korea Statistical Yearbook*. Seoul: Economic Planning Board.

National Bureau of Statistics. 1990. *Korean Economic Indicators 1990*. Vol. 2 no. 4. Seoul: Economic Planning Board.

National Statistics Office. 1991. *Social Indicators in Korea*. Seoul: National Statistics Office.

Needham, Joseph. 1981. "Time and Knowledge in China and the West." In Julius T. Fraser, ed., *The Voices of Time*, 92–135. Amherst: University of Massachusetts Press.

Nelson, Laura. 1990. "The Korean *Chonsei* System of Housing Rental: Creative Housing Finance With Hidden Costs for Renters." Master's thesis, University of California, Berkeley.

Ogle, George E. 1990. *South Korea: Dissent Within the Economic Miracle*. London: Zed Books.

Ong, Aihwa. 1987. *Spirits of Resistance and Capitalistic Discipline: Factory Women in Malaysia*. Albany: State University of New York Press.

Pak, Wan-sŏ. [1980] 1991. "Mother's Stake 1" (Ommaŭi malttuk). Translated by Yŏng-nan Yu. In Yŏng-nan Yu, ed., *Pŏnyŏkiran Muŏsin'ga?* Seoul: Taehaksa.

Palais, James B. 1975. *Politics and Policy in Traditional Korea*. Cambridge: Harvard University Press.

Park, Choon Bae. 1984. "Housing and Housing Finance in the Republic of Korea." *Federal Home Loan Bank Board Journal* 17 (1): 15–21 and (2): 24–31.

Park, Chung Hee (Pak, Chŏng-hŭi). 1970. *Major Speeches by Korea's Park Chung Hee*. Compiled by Shin Bum Shik. Seoul: Hollym Publishers.

Park, Yang-Woo. 1988. "Rental Housing Development Experiences: The Case of Saekyung Rental Housing." *Proceedings of Regional Seminar: Workshop on Shelter for the Homeless*. Seoul: Korea Planners Association.

Parker, Andrew, Mary Russo, Doris Sommer, and Patricia Yaeger, eds. 1992. *Nationalisms and Sexualities*. New York: Routledge, Chapman and Hall.

Plath, David W. 1990. "My-Car-isma: Motorizing the Showa Self." *Daedalus* 119 (3): 229–244.

Pratt, Mary Louise. 1986. "Fieldwork in Common Places." In James Clifford and George E. Marcus, eds., *Writing Culture: The Poetics and Politics of Ethnography*, 27–50. Berkeley: University of California Press.

Pred, Allan. 1985. "The Social Becomes the Spatial, the Spatial Becomes the Social: Enclosures, Social Change, and the Becoming of Places in Skane." In Derek Gregory and John Urry, eds., *Social Relations and Spatial Structures*. London: MacMillan.

Ra, Sang-Soo. 1986. "The Planning and Development of New Towns in Korea." *The Appraisal Journal* 54 (2): 282–293.

Rabinow, Paul. 1989. *French Modern: Norms and Forms of the Social Environment.* Cambridge, MA: MIT Press.

Renaud, Bertrand. 1993. "Confronting a Distorted Housing Market: Can Korean Policies Break with the Past?" In Lawrence B. Krause and Fun-koo Park, eds., *Social Issues in Korea,* 291–331. Seoul: Korea Development Institute Press.

Renaud, Bertrand. 1989. "Understanding the Collateral Qualities of Housing for Financial Development: The Korean 'chŏnse' as Effective Response to Financial Sector Shortcomings." World Bank Policy Planning and Research Staff Discussion Paper, Infrastructure and Urban Development Department. Photocopy.

Renaud, Bertrand. 1988. "Compounding Financial Repression with Rigid Urban Regulations: Lessons of the Korean Housing Market." World Bank Policy Planning and Research Staff Discussion Paper, Infrastructure and Urban Development Department. Photocopy.

Renaud, Bertrand. 1987. "Financing Shelter." In Lloyd Rodwin, ed., *Shelter, Settlement, and Development,* 179–203. Boston: Allen & Unwin.

Richardson, Harry W. 1976. "The Argument for very Large Cities Reconsidered: A Comment." *Urban Studies* 13:307–310.

Robison, Richard and David S. G. Goodman, eds. 1996. *The New Rich in Asia: Mobile Phones, McDonald's, and Middle-Class Revolution.* New York: Routledge.

Robinson, Michael. 1988. *Cultural Nationalism in Colonial Korea, 1920–1925.* Seattle: University of Washington Press.

Rotenberg, Robert and Gary McDonogh, eds. 1993. *The Cultural Meaning of Urban Space.* Westport, CT: Bergin & Garvey.

Sahlins, Marshall. 1976. *Culture and Practical Reason.* Chicago: University of Chicago Press.

Said, Edward W. 1985. "Orientalism Reconsidered." *Cultural Critique* 1:87–107.

Schields, Rob. 1992. "Spaces for the Subject of Consumption." In Rob Schields, ed., *Lifestyle Shopping: The Subject of Consumption,* 1–20. London: Routledge.

Scitovsky, Tibor. 1992. *The Joyless Economy: The Psychology of Human Satisfaction.* Revised Edition. New York: Oxford University Press.

Seoul Metropolitan Government. 1992. *Seoul: Her History and Culture.* Seoul: Seoul Metropolitan Government.

Seoul Metropolitan Government. 1989. *Seoul, a Metropolis in the Making: Excavating a Layered Reality.* The XCII Milano Triennale Seoul Exhibition. Seoul: Korea National Housing Corporation.

Seoul Metropolitan Administration. 1982. *Seoul.* Seoul: Metropolitan Administration.

Seoul Metropolitan Government. 1979. *The Construction of Seoul.* Seoul: Seoul Metropolitan Government.

Seoul Metropolitan Government. 1964. *Welcome to Seoul*. Seoul: Seoul Metropolitan Government, Tourist Section.

Seoul Special City. 1985. *Dong myŏng yŏnhyŏkko* (The history and origin of borough names). Seoul: Sŏul t'ŭkbyŏlsisa P'yŏn wŏnhoe. (In Korean.)

Seoul YMCA. 1991. "Choŭn urisangp'um changt'ŏ ch'amgasangp'um annae" (Information about market places [to buy] goods participating in good native products). Photocopied manuscript. (In Korean.)

Seoul YMCA. 1990a. "Hyangnak munhwa ch'ubang simin undong pogosŏ" (Report of the citizen's movement to eradicate the pleasure culture). Photocopied manuscript. (In Korean.)

Seoul YMCA. 1990b. "Olparŭn ch'usŏkmunhwaŭi chŏngripŭl wihayŏ" (On a thesis of proper *ch'usŏk* culture). Photocopied manuscript. (In Korean.)

Seoul YMCA. 1990c. "Sobijanŭn nongminŭi saenghwarŭl! Nongminŭn sobijaŭi saengmyŏng'ŭl!" (Consumers are the livelihood of farmers! Farmers are the life of consumers!). Photocopied manuscript. (In Korean.)

Seoul YMCA. 1990d. "Uri kyŏngjeŭi hyŏnjaewa kwasobihyŏnsang" (The present [state of] our economy and the *kwasobi* phenomenon). Photocopied manuscript. (In Korean.)

Seoul YMCA. 1989 (July). "Hyangnak sanŏpgwa kwasobi" (The pleasure industry and *kwasobi*). Photocopied manuscript. (In Korean.)

Seoul YMCA. 1986 (3 March). "*Kŏnjŏn sobi saenghwal ŭisik hamyang'ŭl wihan sahoe tanch'e taet'oronhoe*" (Social forum for the cultivation of the consciousness of a wholesome consumer lifestyle). Photocopied manuscript. (In Korean.)

Seoul YMCA. N.d. "Oeguk sangp'yo pŏmnamgwa kisuldoip" (The flood of foreign brands and techniques). Photocopied manuscript. (In Korean.)

Simmons, Alan B. 1979. "Slowing Metropolitan City Growth in Asia: Policies, Programs, and Results." *Population and Development Review* 5 (1): 87–104.

Smith, Carol A. 1996. "Race/Class/Gender Ideology in Guatemala: Modern and Anti-Modern Forms." In Brackette F. Williams, ed., *Women Out of Place: The Gender of Agency and the Race of Nationality*, 50–78. New York: Routledge.

Sobija pohodanch'e hyŏpŭi hwe (Association of Consumer Protection Agencies). 1989 (December). "Kyŏngje chŏngŭiwa kwasobi" (Righteous economics and overconsumption). Paper presented at the Kŏnjŏnsobisaenghwal Simp'ojium (Wholesome consumer lifestyle symposium). Seoul.

*Sobija Sidae* (The Age of the Consumer). 1992. "Nongsusanmul: Suipsan & kuk'-naesan irŏke kubyŏlhanda" (Agricultural and fisheries products: This is how to distinguish imported goods and domestic goods). (In Korean.)

Soja, Edward W. 1989. *Postmodern Geographies: The Reassertion of Space in Critical Social Theory*. New York: Verso.

Spivak, Gayatri. 1988. "Subaltern Studies: Deconstructing Historiography." In Ranajit Guha and Gayatri Spivak, eds., *Selected Subaltern Studies*. New York: Oxford University Press.

Stoler, Ann. 1991. "Carnal Knowledge and Imperial Power." In Micaela di Leonardo, ed., *Gender at the Crossroads of Knowledge*, 51–101. Berkeley: University of California Press.

Taussig, Michael. 1992. *The Nervous System*. New York: Routledge.

Taussig, Michael. 1993. *Mimesis and Alterity: A Particular History of the Senses*. New York: Routledge.

Taylor, Charles. 1990. "Modes of Civil Society." *Public Culture* 3 (1): 95–118.

Tobin, Joseph J. 1992b. "Domesticating the West." In Joseph J. Tobin, ed., *Remade in Japan: Everyday Life and Consumer Taste in a Changing Society*. New Haven: Yale University Press.

Tobin, Joseph J., ed. 1992a. *Remade in Japan: Everyday Life and Consumer Taste in a Changing Society*. New Haven: Yale University Press.

Tomlinson, Alan. 1990. "Introduction: Consumer Culture and the Aura of the Commodity." In Alan Tomlinson, ed., *Consumption, Identity, and Style: Marketing, Meanings, and the Packaging of Pleasure*, 1–38. New York: Routledge.

Trinh, T. Minh-ha. 1992. *Framer Framed*. New York: Routledge.

United Nations, Department of Economic and Social Affairs. 1962. "Industrialization for Economic Development in the Under-Developed Countries." *World Economic Survey 1961*. New York: United Nations.

United Nations. 1986. "Population Growth and Policies in Mega-Cities: Seoul." Department of International Economic and Social Affairs Population Policy Paper No. 4. Photocopy. New York: United Nations.

United States Army Forces in Korea. 1948 (January). "South Korean Interim Government Activities." Seoul: National Economic Board, No. 28.

United States Department of State. 1994. *A Report to Congress on Competitiveness: Country Reports on Economic Policy and Trade Practices*. Washington, D.C.

United States Senate, Committee on Governmental Affairs. 1990. *Black Market and South Korean Trade Practices*. Hearing. Washington: U.S. Government Printing Office.

Veblen, Thorstein. [1899] 1994. *The Theory of the Leisure Class*. Mineola, NY: Dover Publications.

Visweswaran, Kamala. 1994. *Fictions of Feminist Ethnography*. Minneapolis: University of Minnesota Press.

Wells, Kenneth M., ed. 1995a. *South Korea's Minjung Movement: The Culture and Politics of Dissidence*. Honolulu: University of Hawaii Press.

Wells, Kenneth M. 1995b. "The Cultural Construction of Korean History." In

Kenneth M. Wells, ed., *South Korea's Minjung Movement: The Culture and Politics of Dissidence*, 11–29. Honolulu: University of Hawaii Press.

Wells, Kenneth M. 1990. *New God, New Nation: Protestants and Self-Reconstruction Nationalism in Korea, 1896–1937*. Honolulu: University of Hawaii Press.

Wells, K[enneth] M. 1985. "The Rationale of Korean Economic Nationalism Under Japanese Colonial Rule, 1922–1932: The Case of Cho Man-sik's Products Promotion Society." *Modern Asian Studies* 19 (4): 823–859.

Williams, Brackette. 1996. "Introduction: Mannish Women and Gender After the Act." In Brackette F. Williams, ed., *Women Out of Place: The Gender of Agency and the Race of Nationality*, 1–33. New York: Routledge.

Williams, Brackette. 1990. "Nationalism, Traditionalism, and the Problem of Cultural Inauthenticity." In Richard G. Fox, ed., *Nationalist Ideologies and the Production of National Cultures*, 112–139. Washington: American Anthropological Association.

Williams, Brackette. 1989. "A Class Act: Anthropology and the Race to Nation Across Ethnic Terrain." *Annual Review of Anthropology* 18:401–444.

Williams, Rosalind H. 1982. *Dream Worlds: Mass Consumption in Late Nineteenth Century France*. Berkeley: University of California Press.

Williamson, Jeffrey G. 1979. "Why do Koreans Save 'So Little'?" *Journal of Development Economics* 6:343–362.

Williamson, Judith. 1986. *Consuming Passions: The Dynamics of Popular Culture*. New York: Marion Boyars.

Woo, Jung-en (Meredith). 1991. *Race to the Swift: State and Finance in Korean Industrialization*. New York: Columbia University Press.

Yamba, C. Bawa. 1992. "Going There and Getting There: The Future as a Legitimating Charter for Life in the Present." In Sandra Wallman, ed., *Contemporary Futures: Perspectives from Social Anthropology*. New York: Routledge.

Yang, Yun-chae (Yang, Yoon Jae). 1991. *Chŏsodŭkch'ŭng'ŭi Chugŏji Hyŏngt'ae Yŏn'gu: Kŏdaedosi Sŏurŭi Ttodarŭn Samt'ŏ* (Forms of low-income family housing: Another living place in Seoul). Seoul: Yŏlhwadang. (In Korean.)

Yi, Eunhee Kim. 1990. "'The Home is a Place to Rest:' The Construction of the Concepts of Work, Family, and Gender Domains Among Middle-Class Urban Koreans." Paper presented at the 89th annual meeting of the American Anthropological Association, 27 November–1 December 1990. (Typescript.)

Yoo, Jae-Hyun (Yu, Chae-hyŏn). 1988. "Characteristics of Multifamily Housing and Its Prospects." *Proceedings of Regional Seminar: Workshop on Shelter for the Homeless*. Seoul: Korea Planners Association.

Yoo, Jae-Hyun (Yu, Chae-hyŏn). 1988. "The Logic of the Rental Housing Market." *Chutaek* no. 49. Seoul: Korea National Housing Corporation. (In Korean.)

Yu, Tae-jong and Young-nan Yu (Yu Yŏng-nan). 1993. *Korean Foods*. Seoul: The Korean Cultural Research Center, Korea University.

Yu, Won-dong. 1978. "Korean Markets and Peddlers." In International Cultural Foundation, ed., *Economic Life in Korea*. Seoul: Si-sa-yong-o-sa Publishers.

Yu, Yŏng-nan. 1991. *Pŏnyŏkiran Muŏsin'ga?* ("What is Translation?") Seoul: T'aehaksa. (In Korean and English.)

# INDEX